FTCE

English 6
Teacher Certification Exam

By Sharon Wynne, M.S.
Southern Connecticut State University

"And, while there's no reason yet to panic, I think it's only prudent that we make preparations to panic."

XAMonline, Inc.
Boston

XAMonline, Inc.
21 Orient Ave.
Melrose, MA 02176
Toll Free 1-800-509-4128
Email: info@xamonline.com
Web www.xamonline.com
Fax: 1-781-662-9268

Library of Congress Cataloging-in-Publication Data
Wynne, Sharon A.
    English 6-12: Teacher Certification / Sharon A. Wynne. -2nd ed. ISBN 1-58197-292-4
 1. English 6-12. 2. Study Guides. 3. FTCE 4. Teachers' Certification & Licensure.
 5. Careers

Managing Editor   Dr. Harte Weiner, Ph. D.
Copy Editor   Patricia Cuchens
Assistant Editor   Kerrie Forbes, B.A.

Disclaimer:

The opinions expressed in this publication are the sole works of XAMonline and were created independently from the National Education Association, Educational Testing Service, or any State Department of Education, National Evaluation Systems or other testing affiliates.

Between the time of publication and printing, state specific standards as well as testing formats and website information may change that is not included in part or in whole within this product. Sample test questions are developed by XAMonline and reflect similar content as on real tests; however, they are not former tests. XAMonline assembles content that aligns with state standards but makes no claims nor guarantees teacher candidates a passing score. Numerical scores are determined by testing companies such as NES or ETS and then are compared with individual state standards. A passing score varies from state to state.

Printed in the United States of America   œ-1
FTCE: English 6-12
ISBN: 978-1-58197-292-4

Certificate Types and Requirements

Florida offers two types of Educator Certificates: the Temporary Certificate and the Professional Certificate.

The Professional Certificate

Valid for five school years

Renewable

Florida's highest Educator Certificate

Requirements:

Complete all application process requirements

Hold at least a bachelor's degree

Demonstrate Mastery of Subject Area Knowledge for a requested subject

Demonstrate Mastery of General Knowledge

Demonstrate Mastery of Professional Preparation and Education Competence

The Florida Professional Certificate is issued after the individual's fingerprints have been cleared. The individual seeking employment in Florida will be assisted in completing the fingerprint process by his/her employer. The individual who is not seeking employment in Florida or has an immediate need for issuance of the Professional Certificate can contact the Bureau of Educator Certification for assistance. The fingerprint-processing fee is $53.00.

The Temporary Certificate

Valid for three school years

Nonrenewable

Provides time to complete all requirements for a Professional Certificate while teaching full-time

Requirements:

Complete all application process requirements

Hold at least a bachelor's degree

Demonstrate Mastery of Subject Area Knowledge or meet Subject Specialization with a 2.5 GPA for a requested subject

The Florida Temporary Certificate is issued after the individual is employed in a Florida school and his/her fingerprints have been cleared.

Specialization Requirements for Certification in English (Grades 6-12)

(1) Plan One. A bachelor's or higher degree with an undergraduate or graduate major in English

or

(2) Plan Two. A bachelor's or higher degree with thirty semester hours in English to include the areas specified below:

(a) Credit in English composition and grammar beyond freshman English,

(b) Credit in speech or oral interpretation, and

(c) Fifteen (15) semester hours in literature.

About the FTCE Examination in English

The English exam is usually administered in the morning. It consists of mostly multiple-choice questions.

Table of Contents

Great Study and Testing Tips!

What to study in order to prepare for the subject assessments is the focus of this study guide but equally important is *how* you study.

You can increase your chances of truly mastering the information by taking some simple but effective steps.

Study Tips:

1. <u>Some foods aid the learning process</u>. Foods such as milk, nuts, seeds, rice, and oats help your study efforts by releasing natural memory enhancers called CCKs (*cholecystokinin*) composed of *tryptophan*, *choline*, and *phenylalanine*. All of these chemicals enhance the neurotransmitters associated with memory. Before studying, try a light, protein-rich meal of eggs, turkey, and fish. All of these foods release the memory-enhancing chemicals. The better the connections, the more you comprehend.

Likewise, before you take a test, stick to a light snack of energy boosting and relaxing foods. A glass of milk, a piece of fruit, or some peanuts all release various memory-boosting chemicals and help you to relax and focus on the subject at hand.

2. <u>Learn to take great notes</u>. A by-product of our modern culture is that we have grown accustomed to getting our information in short doses (i.e. TV news sound bites or *USA Today*-style newspaper articles.)

Consequently, we've subconsciously trained ourselves to assimilate information better in <u>neat little packages</u>. If you scrawl notes all over the paper, you fragment the flow of the information. Strive for clarity. Newspapers use a standard format to achieve clarity. Your notes can be much clearer through use of proper formatting. A very effective format is called the Cornell Method.

Take a sheet of loose-leaf lined notebook paper and draw a line all the way down the paper about 1-2" from the left-hand edge.

Draw another line across the width of the paper about 1-2" up from the bottom. Repeat this process on the reverse side of the page.

Look at the highly effective result. You have ample room for notes, a left-hand margin for special emphasis items or inserting supplementary data from the textbook, a large area at the bottom for a brief summary, and a little rectangular space for just about anything you want.

3. Get the concept, and then the details. Too often we focus on the details and don't gather an understanding of the concept. However, if you simply memorize only dates, places, or names, you may well miss the whole point of the subject.

A key way to understand things is to put them in your own words. If you are working from a textbook, automatically summarize each paragraph in your mind. If you are outlining text, don't simply copy the author's words.

Rephrase them in your own words. You remember your own thoughts and words much better than someone else's, and you subconsciously tend to associate the important details to the core concepts.

4. Ask Why. Pull apart written material paragraph by paragraph and don't forget the captions under the illustrations.

Example: If the heading is "Stream Erosion," flip it around to read "Why do streams erode?" Then answer the questions.

If you train your mind to think in a series of questions and answers, not only will you learn more but you will also lessen the test anxiety because you are used to answering questions.

5. Read for reinforcement and future needs. Even if you only have 10 minutes, put your notes or a book in your hand. Your mind is similar to a computer; you have to input data in order to have it processed. *By reading, you are creating the neural connections for future retrieval.* The more times you read something, the more you reinforce the learning of ideas.

Even if you don't fully understand something on the first pass, *your mind stores much of the material for later recall.*

6. Relax to learn so go into exile. Our bodies respond to an inner clock called biorhythms. Burning the midnight oil works well for some people, but not everyone.

If possible, set aside a particular place to study that is free of distractions. Shut off the television, cell phone, and pager and exile your friends and family during your study period.

If you really are bothered by silence, try background music. Light classical music at a low volume has been shown to aid in concentration.

Music that evokes pleasant emotions without lyrics are highly suggested. Try just about anything by Mozart. It relaxes you.

7. <u>Use arrows, not highlighters</u>. At best, it's difficult to read a page full of yellow, pink, blue, and green streaks.

Try staring at a neon sign for a while and you'll soon see my point; the horde of colors obscures the message.

A quick note: a brief dash of color, an underline, and an arrow pointing to a particular passage are much clearer than a horde of highlighted words.

8. <u>Budget your study time</u>. Although you shouldn't ignore any of the material, *allocate your available study time in the same ratio that topics may appear on the test.*

Testing Tips:

1. Get smart, play dumb. Don't read anything into the question. Don't assume that the test writer is looking for something other than what is asked. Stick to the question as written and don't read extra things into it.

2. Read the question and all the choices *twice* before answering the question. You may miss something by not carefully reading and then rereading both the question and the answers.

If you really don't have a clue as to the right answer, leave it blank on the first time through. Go on to the other questions as they may provide a clue on how to answer the skipped questions.

If later on, you still can't answer the skipped ones . . . ***Guess.***
The only penalty for guessing is that you *might* get it wrong. Only one thing is certain; if you don't put anything down, you will get it wrong!

3. Turn the question into a statement. Look at the way the questions are worded. The syntax of the question usually provides a clue. Does it seem more familiar as a statement rather than as a question? Does it sound strange?

By turning a question into a statement, you may be able to spot if an answer sounds right, and it may also trigger memories of material you have read.

4. Look for hidden clues. It's actually very difficult to compose multiple-foil (choice) questions without giving away part of the answer in the options presented.

In most multiple-choice questions you can often readily eliminate one or two of the potential answers. This leaves you with only two real possibilities and automatically your odds go to fifty-fifty for very little work.

5. Trust your instincts. For every fact that you have read, you subconsciously retain something of that knowledge. On questions that you aren't certain about, go with your basic instincts. **Your first impression on how to answer a question is usually correct.**

6. Mark your answers directly on the test booklet. Don't bother trying to fill in the optical scan sheet on the first pass through the test.

Just be very careful not to mismark your answers when you eventually transcribe them to the scan sheet.

7. <u>Watch the clock</u>! You have a set amount of time to answer the questions. Don't get bogged down trying to answer a single question at the expense of 10 questions you can more readily answer.

THIS PAGE BLANK

COMPETENCY 1.0 KNOWLEDGE OF THE ENGLISH LANGUAGE AND METHODS FOR EFFECTIVE TEACHING

Skill 1.1 Identify influences on language (e.g., social, cultural, ethnic, religious, historical, regional, and gender).

Language, though an innate human ability, must be learned. Individuals are influenced by the acquisition as well as use of language. Linguists agree that language is first a vocal system of word symbols, enabling humans to communicate their feelings, thoughts, and desires to other human beings. Language was instrumental in the development of all cultures and continues to be influenced by the changes taking place in societies today.

Historical Influences

English is an Indo-European language that evolved through several periods. The origin of English dates to the settlement of the British Isles in the fifth and sixth

> Learn more about the
> **History of the English Language**
> http://ebbs.english.vt.edu/hel/hel.html

centuries by Germanic tribes called the Angles, Saxons, and Jutes. The original Britons spoke a Celtic tongue while the Angles spoke a Germanic dialect. Modern English derives from the speech of the Anglo-Saxons who imposed not only their language but also their social customs and laws on their new land. From the fifth to the tenth century, Britain's language was the tongue we now refer to as Old English. During the next four centuries, the many French attempts at English conquest introduced many French words to English. However, the grammar and syntax of the language remained Germanic.

Middle English, most evident in the writings of Geoffrey Chaucer, dates loosely from 1066 to 1509. William Caxton brought the printing press to England in 1474 and increased literacy. Old English words required numerous inflections to indicate noun cases and plurals as well as verb conjugations. Middle English continued the use of many inflections and pronunciations that treated these inflections as separately pronounced syllables. English in 1300 would have been written "Olde Anglishe" with the "e's" at the ends of the words pronounced as our short "a" vowel. Even adjectives had plural inflections: "long dai" became "longe daies" pronounced "long-a day-as." Spelling was phonetic; thus every vowel had multiple pronunciations, a fact that continues to affect the language.

Modern English dates from the introduction of The Great Vowels Shift because it created guidelines for spelling and pronunciation. Before the printing press, books were copied laboriously by hand; the language was subject to the individual interpretation of the scribes. Printers and subsequently lexicographers like Samuel Johnson and America's Noah Webster influenced the guidelines. As reading matter was mass produced, the reading public was forced to adopt the speech and writing habits developed by those who wrote and printed books.

Despite many students' insistence to the contrary, Shakespeare's writings are in Modern English. Teachers should stress to students that language, like customs, morals, and other social factors, is constantly subject to change. Immigration, inventions, and cataclysmic events change language as much as any other facet of life is affected by these changes.

The domination of one race or nation over others can change a language significantly. Beginning with the colonization of the New World by England and Spain, English and Spanish became dominant languages in the Western hemisphere.

American English today is somewhat different in pronunciation and sometimes vocabulary from British English. The British call a truck a "lorry," baby carriages a "pram," short for "perambulator," and an elevator a "lift." The two languages have very few syntactical differences, and even the tonal qualities that were once so clearly different are converging.

Though Modern English is less complex than Middle English, having lost many unnecessary inflections, it is still considered difficult to learn because of its many exceptions to the rules. It has, however, become the world's dominant language by reason of the great political, military, and social power of England from the fifteenth to the nineteenth century and of America in the twentieth century.

Modern inventions—the telephone, phonograph, radio, television, and motion pictures—have especially affected English pronunciation. Regional dialects, once a hindrance to clear understanding, have fewer distinct characteristics. The speakers from different parts of the United States of America can be identified by their accents, but more and more as educators and media personalities stress uniform pronunciations and proper grammar, the differences are diminishing.

The English language has a more extensive vocabulary than any other language. Ours is a language of synonyms, words borrowed from other languages, and coined words—many of them introduced by the rapid expansion of technology.

Students should understand that language is in constant flux. They can demonstrate this when they use language for specific purposes and audiences. Negative criticism of a student's errors in word choice or sentence structures will inhibit creativity. Positive criticism that suggests ways to enhance communication skills will encourage exploration. Using the *Oxford English Dictionary* is one way students can study the origins of words. By learning the etymology of words, they can understand how language develops.

Geographical Influences

Dialect differences are basically in pronunciation. Bostoners say "pahty" for "party" and Southerners blend words like "you all" into "y'all." Besides the dialect differences already mentioned, the biggest geographical factors in American English stem from minor word choice variances. Depending on the region where you live, when you order a carbonated, syrupy beverage generically called a soft drink, you might ask for a "soda" in the South, or a "pop" in the Midwest. If you order a soda in New York, then you will get a scoop of ice cream in your soft drink, while in other areas you would have to ask for a "float."

Social Influences

Social influences are mostly those imposed by family, peer groups, and mass media. The economic and educational levels of families determine language use. Exposure to adults who encourage and assist children to speak well enhances readiness for other areas of learning and contributes to their ability to communicate their needs. Historically, children learned language, speech patterns, and grammar from members of the extended family just as they learned the rules of conduct within their family unit and community. In modern times, the mother in a nuclear family became the dominant force in influencing children's development. With increasing social changes, many children are not receiving the proper guidance in all areas of development, especially language.

Those who are fortunate to be in educational-day-care programs like Head Start or in certified preschools develop better language skills than those whose care is entrusted to untrained care providers. Once children enter elementary school, they are also greatly influenced by peer language. This peer influence becomes significant in adolescence as the use of teen jargon gives teenagers a sense of identity within their chosen group(s) and independence from the influence of adults. In some lower socio-economic groups, children use Standard English in school and street language outside the school. Some children of immigrant families become bilingual by necessity if no English is spoken in the home.

Research has shown a strong correlation between socio-economic characteristics and all areas of intellectual development. Traditional measurement instruments rely on verbal ability to establish intelligence. Research findings and test scores reflect that children reared in nuclear families providing cultural experiences and individual attention become more language proficient than those who are denied that security and stimulation.

Personal Influences

The rate of physical development and identifiable language disabilities also influence language development. Nutritional deficiencies, poor eyesight, and conditions such as stuttering or dyslexia can inhibit children's ability to master language. Unless diagnosed early, they can hamper communication into adulthood. These conditions also stymie the development of self-confidence and, therefore, the willingness to learn or to overcome the handicap. Children should receive proper diagnosis and positive corrective instruction.

In adolescence, children's choice of role models and decisions about their future determine the growth of identity. Rapid physical and emotional changes and the stress of coping with the pressure of sexual awareness make concentration on any educational pursuits difficult. The easier the transition from childhood to adulthood, the better the competence will be in all learning areas.

Middle school and junior high school teachers are confronted by a student body ranging from fifth graders who are still childish to eighth or ninth graders who, if not in fact at least in their minds, are young adults. Teachers must approach language instruction as a social development tool with more emphasis on vocabulary acquisition, reading improvement, and speaking/writing skills. High school teachers can deal with the more formalized instruction of grammar, usage, and literature meant for older adolescents whose social development allows them to pay more attention to studies that will improve their chances for a better adult life.

As a tool, language must have relevance to students' real environment. Many high schools have developed practical English classes for business/vocational students whose specific needs are determined by their desire to enter the workforce upon graduation. More emphasis is placed upon accuracy of mechanics and understanding verbal and written directions because these are skills desired by employers. Writing résumés, completing forms, reading policy and operations manuals, and generating reports are some of the desired skills. Emphasis is placed on higher-level thinking skills, including inferential thinking and literary interpretation, in literature classes for college-bound students.

Skill 1.2   Identify and apply various approaches to the study of language, usage, grammar, and style.

Language Development

The way language skills are developed depends on many factors: some internal (the age of the child), some external (immigration). Teachers can use a variety of approaches to accommodate individual differences.

Learning Approach

Early theories of language development were formulated from learning theory research. The assumption was that language development evolved from learning the rules of language structures and applying them through imitation and reinforcement. This approach also assumed that language, cognition, and social developments were independent of each other.

Thus, children were expected to learn language from patterning after adults who spoke and wrote Standard English. No allowance was made for communication through child jargon, idiomatic expressions, or grammatical and mechanical errors resulting from too strict adherence to the rules of inflection ("child's" instead of "children") or conjugation ("runned" instead of "ran"). No association was made between physical and operational development and language mastery.

Linguistic Approach

Studies spearheaded by Noam Chomsky in the 1950s formulated the theory that language ability is innate and develops through natural human maturation as environmental stimuli trigger acquisition of syntactical structures appropriate to each exposure level. The assumption of a hierarchy of syntax downplayed the significance of semantics. Because of the complexity of syntax and the relative speed with which children acquire language, linguists attributed language development to biological rather than cognitive or social influences.

Cognitive Approach

Researchers in the 1970s proposed that language knowledge derives from both syntactic and semantic structures. Drawing on the studies of Piaget and other cognitive learning theorists, supporters of the cognitive approach maintained that children acquire knowledge of linguistic structures after they have acquired the cognitive structures necessary to process language. For example, joining words for specific meaning necessitates sensory motor intelligence.

Children must be able to coordinate movement and recognize objects before they can identify words to name the objects or word groups to describe the actions performed with those objects.

Adolescents must have developed the mental abilities for organizing concepts as well as concrete operations, predicting outcomes, and theorizing before they can assimilate and verbalize complex sentence structures, choose vocabulary for particular nuances of meaning, and examine semantic structures for tone and manipulative effect.

Sociocognitive Approach

Other theorists in the 1970s proposed that language development results from sociolinguistic competence. Language, cognition, and social knowledge are interactive elements of total human development. Emphasis on verbal communication as the medium for language expression resulted in the inclusion of speech activities in most language arts curricula.

Unlike previous approaches, the sociocognitive approach allowed that determining the appropriateness of language in given situations for specific listeners is as important as understanding semantic and syntactic structures.

By engaging in conversation, children at all stages of development have opportunities to test their language skills, receive feedback, and make modifications. As a social activity, conversation is as structured by social order as grammar is structured by the rules of syntax. Conversation satisfies the learner's need to be heard and understood and to influence others. Thus, the choices of vocabulary, tone, and content are dictated by the learner's ability to assess the language knowledge of listeners. The speaker is constantly applying his cognitive skills to using language in a social interaction. If the capacity to acquire language is inborn, without an environment in which to practice language, children would not pass beyond grunts and gestures, as did primitive man.

Of course, the varying degrees of environmental stimuli to which children are exposed at all age levels create a slower or faster development of language. Some children are prepared to articulate concepts and recognize symbolism by the time they enter fifth grade because they have been exposed to challenging reading and conversations with well-spoken adults at home or in their social groups. Others are still trying to master the sight recognition skills and are not yet ready to combine words in complex patterns.

Concerns for the Teacher

Because teachers must, by virtue of tradition and the dictates of the curriculum, teach grammar, usage, and writing as well as reading and later literature, the problem becomes when to teach what to whom.

The profusion of approaches to teaching grammar alone are mind-boggling. In the universities, we learn about transformational grammar, stratification grammar, sectoral grammar, and more. But in practice, most teachers, supported by presentations in textbooks and by the methods they learned themselves, keep coming back to the same traditional prescriptive approach—read and imitate—or structural approach: learn the parts of speech, the parts of sentence, punctuation rules, sentence patterns. After enough of the terminology and rules are stored in the brain, then we learn to write and speak. For some educators, the best solution is the worse—don't teach grammar at all.

The same problems occur in teaching usage. How much can we demand students communicate in only Standard English? Different schools of thought suggest that a study of dialect and idiom and recognition of various jargons are a vital part of language development. Social pressures, especially on students in middle and junior high schools, to be accepted within their peer groups and to speak the non-standard language spoken outside the school make adolescents resistant to the corrective, remedial approach. In many communities where the immigrant populations are high, new words are entering English from other languages even as words and expressions that were common when we were children have become rare or obsolete.

Regardless of differences of opinion concerning language development, language arts teachers will be most effective using the styles and approaches with which they are is most comfortable. And, if they subscribe to a student-centered approach, they may find that the students have a lot to teach the teachers and each other. Moffett and Wagner in the Fourth Edition of *Student-centered Language Arts K-12* stress the three I's: individualization, interaction, and integration. Essentially, they are supporting the socio-cognitive approach to language development. By providing an opportunity for students to select their own activities and resources, their instruction is individualized. By centering on and teaching each other, students are interactive. Finally, by allowing students to synthesize a variety of knowledge structures, they integrate them. The teacher's role becomes that of a facilitator.

> Learn more about
> **Student Centered Learning**
> http://www.wcer.wisc.edu/step/ep301/
> Fall2000/Tochonites/stu cen.html

Benefits of the Sociocognitive Approach

This approach has tended to guide the whole language movement currently in fashion. Most basal readers use an integrated, cross-curricular approach to successful grammar, language, and usage. Reinforcement becomes an intradepartmental responsibility. Language incorporates diction and terminology across the curriculum. Standard usage is encouraged and supported by both the core classroom textbooks and current software for technology. Teachers need to acquaint themselves with the computer capabilities in their school district and at their individual school sites. Advances in new technologies require teachers to familiarize themselves with programs that would serve their students' needs. Students respond enthusiastically to technology.

Several highly effective programs are available in various formats to assist students with initial instruction or remediation. Grammar texts, such as the Warriner's series, employ various methods to reach individual learning styles. The school library media center should become a focal point for individual exploration.

Syntax

A common approach to the study of language is examining its syntax, the patterns and rules that form the foundation.

Sentence Completeness

Avoid fragments and run-on sentences. Recognize the sentence elements necessary to make a complete thought and use independent and dependent clauses properly (see *Correct use of coordination and subordination*). Proper punctuation will correct such errors.

Sentence Structure

Recognize simple, compound, complex, and compound-complex sentences. Use dependent (subordinate) and independent clauses correctly to create these sentence structures.

Simple	Joyce wrote a letter.
Compound	Joyce wrote a letter, and Dot drew a picture.
Complex	While Joyce wrote a letter, Dot drew a picture.
Compound/Complex	When Mother asked the girls to demonstrate their new-found skills, Joyce wrote a letter, and Dot drew a picture.

Note: Do **not** confuse compound sentence elements with compound sentences.

Simple sentence with compound subject
<u>Joyce</u> and <u>Dot</u> wrote letters.
The <u>girl</u> in row three and the <u>boy</u> next to her were passing notes across the aisle.

Simple sentence with compound predicate
Joyce <u>wrote</u> letters and <u>drew</u> pictures.
The captain of the high school debate team <u>graduated</u> with honors and <u>studied</u> broadcast journalism in college.

Simple sentence with compound object of preposition
Coleen graded the students' essays for <u>style</u> and <u>mechanical accuracy</u>.

Parallelism

Recognize parallel structures using phrases (prepositional, gerund, participial, and infinitive) and omissions from sentences that create the lack of parallelism. Parallelism provides balance to the grammar and the ideas.

> Learn more about
> **Parallel Structure vs.**
> **Faulty Parallelism**
> http://jerz.setonhill.edu/writing/
> grammar/parallel.html

Prepositional phrase/single modifier
Incorrect: Coleen ate the ice cream with enthusiasm and hurriedly.
Correct: Coleen ate the ice cream with enthusiasm and in a hurry.
Correct: Coleen ate the ice cream enthusiastically and hurriedly.

Participial phrase/infinitive phrase
Incorrect: After hiking for hours and to sweat profusely, Joe sat down to rest and drinking water.

Correct: After hiking for hours and sweating profusely, Joe sat down to rest and drink water.

Misplaced and Dangling Modifiers

Particular phrases that are not placed near the one word they modify often result in misplaced modifiers. Particular phrases that do not relate to the subject being modified result in dangling modifiers.

Error: Weighing the options carefully, a decision was made regarding the punishment of the convicted murderer.

Problem: Who is weighing the options? No one capable of weighing is named in the sentence; thus, the participle phrase "weighing the options carefully" dangles. This problem can be corrected by adding a subject of the sentence capable of doing the action.

Correction: Weighing the options carefully, the judge made a decision regarding the punishment of the convicted murderer.

Error: Returning to my favorite watering hole brought back many fond memories.

Problem: The person who returned is never indicated, and the participle phrase dangles. This problem can be corrected by creating a dependent clause from the modifying phrase.

Correction: When I returned to my favorite watering hole, many fond memories came back to me.

Error: One damaged house stood only to remind townspeople of the hurricane.

Problem: The placement of the misplaced modifier "only" suggests that the sole reason the house remained was to serve as a reminder. The faulty modifier creates ambiguity.

Correction: Only one damaged house stood, reminding townspeople of the hurricane.

Recognition of Syntactical Redundancy or Omission

These errors occur when superfluous words have been added to a sentence or key words have been omitted from a sentence.

Redundancy
Incorrect: Joyce made sure that when her plane arrived that she retrieved all of her luggage.
Correct: Joyce made sure that when her plane arrived she retrieved all of her luggage.

Incorrect: He was a mere skeleton of his former self.
Correct: He was a skeleton of his former self.

Omission
Incorrect: Dot opened her book, recited her textbook, and answered the teacher's subsequent question.
Correct: Dot opened her book, recited from the textbook, and answered the teacher's subsequent question.

Avoidance of Double Negatives

This error occurs from positioning two negatives that, in fact, cancel each other in meaning.

Incorrect: Harold couldn't care less whether he passes this class.
Correct: Harold could care less whether he passes this class.

Incorrect: Dot didn't have no double negatives in her paper.
Correct: Dot didn't have any double negatives in her paper.

Semantic Connotations

To teach language effectively, we need to understand that as human beings acquire language they realize that words have **denotative** and **connotative** meanings. Generally, denotative words point to things and connotative words deal with mental suggestions that the words convey. The word *skunk* has a denotative meaning if the speaker can point to the actual animal as he speaks the word and intends the word to identify the animal. **Skunk** has connotative meaning depending upon the tone of delivery, the socially acceptable attitudes about the animal, and the speaker's personal feelings about the animal.

Informative Connotations

Informative connotations are definitions agreed upon by the society in which the learner operates. A *skunk* is "a black and white mammal of the weasel family with a pair of perineal glands which secrete a pungent odor." The *Merriam Webster Collegiate Dictionary* adds "...and offensive" odor. Identification of the color, species, and glandular characteristics are informative. The interpretation of the odor as *offensive* is affective.

Affective Connotations

Affective connotations are the personal feelings a word arouses. A child who has no personal experience with a skunk and its odor or has had a pet skunk will feel

> Learn more about **Connotation and Denotation in "Elements of Poetry"**
> http://bcs.bedfordstmartins.com/ Virtualit/poetry/denotate_def.html

differently about the word *skunk* than a child who has smelled the spray or been conditioned vicariously to associate offensiveness with the animal denoted *skunk*.

The very fact that our society views a skunk as an animal to be avoided will affect the child's interpretation of the word. In fact, you don't actually have to have seen a skunk (that is, have a denotative understanding) to use the word in either connotative expression. For example, one child might call another child a skunk, connoting an unpleasant reaction (affective use) or, seeing another small black and white animal, call it a skunk based on the definition (informative use).

Using Connotations

In everyday language, we attach affective meanings to words unconsciously; we exercise more conscious control of informative connotations. In the process of language development, the leaner must come not only to grasp the definitions of words but also to become more conscious of the affective connotations and how his listeners process these connotations. Gaining this conscious control over language enables us to use language appropriately in various situations and to evaluate its uses in literature and other forms of communication.

The manipulation of language for a variety of purposes is the goal of language instruction. Advertisers and satirists are especially conscious of the effect word choice has on their audiences. By evoking the proper responses from readers/listeners, we can prompt them to take action.

Choice of the medium through which the message is delivered to the receiver is a significant factor in controlling language. Spoken language relies as much on the gestures, facial expression, and tone of voice of the speaker as on the words that are spoken. Slapstick comics can evoke laughter without speaking a word. Young children use body language overtly and older children more subtly to convey messages. These refinements of body language are paralleled by an ability to recognize and apply the nuances of spoken language. To work strictly with the written work, the writer must use words to imply the body language.

Skill 1.3 Apply knowledge of standard written English.

With its many rules and exceptions, English can be a difficult language to learn. However, to communicate effectively, all speakers and writers must use standard English. Here is a review of a few standards.

Correct Use of Coordination and Subordination

Connect independent clauses with the coordinating conjunctions—*and, but, or, for,* or *nor*—when their content is of equal importance. Use subordinating conjunctions—*although, because, before, if, since, though, until, when, whenever, where*—and relative pronouns—*that, who, whom, which*—introduce clauses that express ideas that are subordinate to main ideas expressed in independent clauses.

Be sure to place the conjunctions so that they express the proper relationship between ideas (cause/effect, condition, time, space).

Incorrect:	Because mother scolded me, I was late.
Correct:	Mother scolded me because I was late.

Incorrect:	The sun rose after the fog lifted.
Correct:	The fog lifted after the sun rose.

Notice that placement of the conjunction can completely change the meaning of the sentence. Main emphasis is shifted by the change.

> Although Jenny was pleased, the teacher was disappointed.
> Although the teacher was disappointed, Jenny was pleased.

> The boys who had written the essay won the contest.
> The boys who won the contest had written the essay.

While not syntactically incorrect, the second sentence makes it appear that the boys won the contest for something else before they wrote the essay.

The longer you teach the more often you will need to review the basic grammar rules. Experienced teachers swear that you will see words misspelled and used incorrectly so often that you'll get confused. So here's a review

> Check out
> **The Tongue Untied**
> http://grammar.uoregon.edu/
> case/possnouns.html

Possessives

Make the possessives of singular nouns by adding an apostrophe followed by the letter *s* (*'s*).

> baby's bottle, father's job, elephant's eye, teacher's desk, sympathizer's protests, week's postponement

Make the possessive of singular nouns ending in *s* by adding either an apostrophe or as (*'s*) depending upon common usage or sound. When making the possessive causes difficulty, use a prepositional phrase instead. Even with the sibilant ending, with a few exceptions, you should use the *'s* construction.

> dress's color, species' characteristics or characteristics of the species, James' hat or James's hat, Delores's shirt

Make the possessive of plural nouns ending in *s* by adding the apostrophe after the *s*.

> horses' coats, jockeys' times, four days' time

Make possessives of plural nouns that do not end in *s* the same as singular nouns by adding *'s*.

> children's shoes, deer's antlers, cattle's horns

Make possessives of compound nouns by adding the inflection at the end of the word or phrase.

> the mayor of Los Angeles' campaign, the mailman's new truck, the mailmen's new trucks, my father-in-law's first wife, the keepsakes' values, several daughters-in-law's husbands

Note: Because a gerund functions as a noun, any noun preceding it and operating as a possessive adjective must reflect the necessary inflection. However, if the gerund following the noun is a participle, no inflection is added.

The general was perturbed by the private's sleeping on duty. (The word *sleeping* is a gerund, the object of the preposition *by*.

but
The general was perturbed to see the private sleeping on duty. (The word *sleeping* is a participle modifying private.)

Use of Pronouns

A pronoun used as a subject of predicate nominative is in nominative case.

<u>She</u> was the drum majorette. The lead trombonists were Joe and <u>he</u>.
The band director accepted <u>whoever</u> could march in step.

A pronoun used as a direct object, indirect object of object of a preposition is in objective case.

The teacher praised <u>him</u>. She gave <u>him</u> an A on the test. Her praise of <u>him</u> was appreciated. The students <u>whom</u> she did not praise will work harder next time.

Common pronoun errors occur from misuse of reflexive pronouns:

Singular: myself, yourself, herself, himself, itself
Plural: ourselves, yourselves, themselves.

Incorrect: Jack cut hisself shaving.
Correct: Jack cut himself shaving.

Incorrect: They backed theirselves into a corner.
Correct: They backed themselves into a corner.

Use of Adjectives

An adjective should agree with its antecedent in number.

> Those apples are rotten. This one is ripe. These peaches are hard.

Comparative adjectives end in -er and superlatives in -est, with some exceptions like worse and worst. More and most precede some adjectives that cannot easily make comparative inflections.

> Mrs. Carmichael is the better of the two basketball coaches.

> That is the hastiest excuse you have ever contrived.

> Candy is the most beautiful baby.

Avoid double superlatives.

> Incorrect: This is the worstest headache I ever had.
> Correct: This is the worst headache I ever had.

When comparing one thing to others in a group, exclude the thing under comparison from the rest of the group.

> Incorrect: Joey is larger than any baby I have ever seen. (Since you have seen him, he cannot be larger than himself.)
> Correct: Joey is larger than any other baby I have ever seen.

Include all necessary words to make a comparison clear in meaning.

> I am as tall as my mother. I am as tall as she (is).
> My cats are better behaved than those of my neighbor.

Subject-Verb Agreement

A verb agrees in number with its subject. Making them agree relies on the ability to identify the subject correctly.

> One of the boys was playing too rough.

> No one in the class, not the teacher nor the students, was listening to the message from the intercom.

> The candidates, including a grandmother and a teenager, are debating some controversial issues.

If two singular subjects are connected by *and,* the verb must be plural.

> A *man* and his *dog* were jogging on the beach.

If two singular subjects are connected by *or,* or *nor*, a singular verb is required.

> Neither <u>Dot</u> nor <u>Joyce</u> <u>has</u> missed a day of school this year.
> Either <u>Fran</u> or <u>Paul</u> <u>is</u> missing.

If one singular subject and one plural subject are connected by *or,* or *nor*, the verb agrees with the subject nearest to the verb.

> Neither the <u>coach</u> nor the <u>players</u> <u>were</u> able to sleep on the bus.

If the subject is a collective noun, its sense of number in the sentence determines the verb: singular if the noun represents a group or unit and plural if the noun represents individuals.

> The <u>House of Representatives</u> <u>has adjourned</u> for the holidays.
> The <u>House of Representatives</u> <u>have failed</u> to reach agreement on the subject of adjournment.

Use of Verbs (Tense)

Present tense is used to express that which is currently happening or is always true.

> Randy is playing the piano.

> Randy plays the piano like a pro.

Past tense is used to express action that occurred in a past time.

> Randy learned to play the piano when he was six years old.

Future tense is used to express action or a condition of future time.

> Randy will probably earn a music scholarship.

Present perfect tense is used to express action or a condition that started in the past and is continued to or completed in the present.

> Randy has practiced piano every day for the last ten years.

> Randy has never been bored with practice.

Past perfect tense expresses action or a condition that occurred as a precedent to some other past action or condition.

> Randy had considered playing clarinet before he discovered the piano.

Future perfect tense expresses action that started in the past or the present and will conclude at some time in the future.

> By the time he goes to college, Randy will have been an accomplished pianist for more than half of his life.

Use of Verbs (Mood)

Indicative mood is used to make unconditional statements; subjunctive mood is used for conditional clauses or wish statements that pose conditions that are untrue. Verbs in subjunctive mood are plural with both singular and plural subjects.

> If I <u>were</u> a bird, I would fly.

> I wish I <u>were</u> as rich as Donald Trump.

Verb Conjugation

The conjugation of verbs follows the patterns used in the discussion of tense above. However, the most frequent problems in verb use stem from the improper formation of past and past participial forms.

> Regular verb: believe, believed, (have) believed

> Irregular verbs: run, ran, run; sit, sat, sat; teach, taught, taught

Other problems stem from the use of verbs that are the same in some tenses but have different forms and different meanings in other tenses.

I lie on the ground. I lay on the ground yesterday. I have lain down. I lay the blanket on the bed. I laid the blanket there yesterday. I have laid the blanket down every night.

The sun rises. The sun rose. The sun has risen.

He raises the flag. He raised the flag. He had raised the flag.

I sit on the porch. I sat on the porch. I have sat in the porch swing.

I set the plate on the table. I set the plate there yesterday. I had set the table before dinner.

Two other verb problems stem from misusing the preposition *of* for the verb auxiliary *have* and misusing the verb *ought* (now rare).

Incorrect: I should of gone to bed.
Correct: I should have gone to bed.

Incorrect: He hadn't ought to get so angry.
Correct: He ought not to get so angry.

Resources

Here is a brief list of basic teaching texts used by teachers and found to be most helpful in teaching structure, grammar, and composition:

English Journal. Urbana, IL: National Council of Teachers of English.

Hixon, Mamie W. *The Essentials of English Language*. Piscataway, New Jersey: Research and Education Association, 1995.

Oshima, Alice and Ann Hogue. *Writing Academic English* (Longman Series) A Writing and Sentence Structure Handbook. Reading, MA: Addison-Wesley Publications Co., 1991.

Warriner's Composition and Grammar. Fourth - First Course and Complete Course, Orlando, FL: Harcourt, Brace, Jovanovich.
Intermediate to advanced college-bound students and international-ESOL students

Teachers will find numerous other published local resources in the school library or district resource centers.

Skill 1.4   Identify how audience and purpose affect language.

Tailoring language for a particular **audience** is an important skill. Writing to be read by a business associate will surely sound different from writing to be read by a younger sibling. Not only are the vocabularies different, but the formality or informality of the discourse will need to be adjusted.

Two characteristics that determine language style are **degree of formality** and **word choice**. The most formal language does not use contractions or slang while the most informal language will probably feature a more casual use of common sayings and anecdotes. Formal language will use longer sentences and will not sound like a conversation. The most informal language will use shorter sentences (not necessarily simple sentences—but shorter constructions) and may sound like a conversation.

In both formal and informal writing, there exists a **tone**, the writer's attitude toward the material and/or readers. Tone may be playful, formal, intimate, angry, serious, ironic, outraged, baffled, tender, serene, depressed, and so on. The overall tone of a piece of writing is dictated by both the subject matter and the audience. Tone is also related to the actual word choice which make up the document, as we attach affective meanings to words, called their **connotations**. Gaining this conscious control over language makes it possible to use language appropriately in various situations and to evaluate its uses in literature and other forms of communication. By evoking the proper responses from readers or listeners, we can prompt them to take action.

Using the following questions is an excellent way to assess the audience and tone of a given piece of writing.

1. Who is your audience (friend, teacher, business person, someone else)?

2. How much does this person know about you and/or your topic?

3. What is your purpose (to prove an argument, to persuade, to amuse, to register a complaint, to ask for a raise)?
4.
4. What emotions do you have about the topic (nervous, happy, confident, angry, sad, no feelings at all)?

5. What emotions do you want to register with your audience (anger, nervousness, happiness, boredom, interest)?

6. What persona do you need to create in order to achieve your purpose?

7. What choice of language is best suited to achieving your purpose with your particular subject (slang, friendly but respectful, formal)?

8. What emotional quality do you want to transmit to achieve your purpose (matter of fact, informative, authoritative, inquisitive, sympathetic, angry), and to what degree do you want to express this tone?

In the past, teachers have assigned reports, paragraphs, and essays that focused on the teacher as the audience with the purpose of explaining information. However, for students to be meaningfully engaged in their writing, they must write for a variety of reasons. Writing for different audiences and aims enables students to be more involved in their writing. If they write for the same audience and purpose, they will continue to see writing as just another assignment. Listed below are suggestions that give students an opportunity to write in more creative and critical ways.

- Write letters to the editor, to a college, to a friend, to another student that would be sent to the intended audience.

- Write stories that would be read aloud to a group (the class, another group of students, to a group of elementary school students) or published in a literary magazine or class anthology.

- Write plays that would be performed.

- Have students discuss the parallels between the different speech styles we use and writing styles for different readers or audiences.

- Allow students to write a particular piece for different audiences.

Make sure students consider the following when analyzing the needs of their audience.

1. Why is the audience reading my writing? Do they expect to be informed, amused or persuaded?

2. What does my audience already know about my topic?

3. What does the audience want or need to know? What will interest them?

4. What type of language suits my readers?

As part of the prewriting exercises, have students identify the audience. Expose students to writing that is on the same topic but with a different audience and have them identify the variations in sentence structure and style.

Remind your students that it is not necessary to identify all the specifics of the audience in the initial stage of the writing process but that at some point they must make some determinations about audience.

Levels of Language

The language level in any form of communication is dependent on the type of audience. While slang and regionalisms may be appropriate in some contexts, they would be inappropriate in others.

Informal and formal language is a distinction made on the basis of the occasion as well as the audience. At a formal occasion, for example, a meeting of executives or of government officials, even conversational exchanges are likely to be more formal. Cocktail parties or golf games are examples where the language is likely to be informal. Formal language uses fewer or no contractions, less slang, longer sentences, and more organization in longer segments.

Speeches delivered to executives, college professors, government officials and other groups like this are likely to be formal. Speeches made to fellow employees are likely to be informal. Sermons tend to be formal; Bible lessons tend to be informal.

Slang comes about for many reasons: Amelioration is an important one that results often in euphemisms. Examples are "passed away" for dying or "senior citizens" for old people. Some usages have become so

> Check out this link:
> **Do You Speak American?**
> http://www.pbs.org/speak/seatosea/st andardamerican/hamlet/

embedded in the language that their sources are long forgotten. For example, "fame" originally meant rumor. Some words originally intended as euphemisms, such as "mentally retarded" and "moron" to avoid using "idiot," have themselves become pejorative.

Slang is lower in prestige than Standard English, tends to appear first in the language of groups with low status, is often taboo, and unlikely to be used by people of high status. It tends to displace conventional terms, either as shorthand or as a defense against perceptions associated with the conventional term.

Jargon is a specialized vocabulary. It may be the vocabulary peculiar to a particular industry such as computers ("firewall") or to field such as religion ("vocation"). It may also be the vocabulary of a social group. Black English is a good example. A Hardee's ad has two young men on the streets of Philadelphia discussing the merits of one of their sandwiches, and captions are required so others may understand what they're saying.

A whole vocabulary that has even developed its own dictionaries is the jargon of bloggers. The speaker must be knowledgeable about and sensitive to the jargon peculiar to the particular audience. That may require some research and some vocabulary development on the speaker's part.

Technical language is a form of jargon. It is usually specific to an industry, profession, or field of study. Sensitivity to the language familiar to the particular audience is important.

Regionalisms are those usages that are peculiar to a particular part of the country. A good example is the second person plural pronoun: you. Because the plural is the same as the singular, various parts of the country have developed their own solutions to be sure that they are understood when they are speaking to more than one "you." In the South, "you-all" or "y'all" is common. In the Northeast, one often hears "youse." In some areas of the Middle West, "you'ns" can be heard.

Vocabulary also varies from region to region. A small stream is a "creek" in some regions but "crick" in some. In Boston, soft drinks are generically called "tonic," but it becomes "soda" in other parts of the northeast. It is "liqueur" in Canada, and "pop" when you get very far west of New York.

Skill 1.5   Identify methods of effectively assessing language skills.

As teachers, you will be called upon to assess the language skills of your students. Here is information that will guide you.

Language Skills to Evaluate

- The ability to talk at length with few pauses and fill time with speech
- The ability to call up appropriate things to say in a wide range of contexts
- The size and range of a student's vocabulary and syntax skills
- The coherence of sentences, the ability to speak in reasoned and semantically dense sentences
- Knowledge of the various forms of interaction and conversation for various situations
- Knowledge of the standard rules of conversation
- The ability to be creative and imaginative with language, and express oneself in original ways
- The ability to invent and entertain, and take risks in linguistic expression

Methods of Evaluation

- Commercially designed language assessment products
- Instructor observation using a rating scale from 1 to 5 (where 1=limited proficiency and 5=native speaker equivalency)
- Informal observation of students' behaviors

> Check out this
> **Oral Presentation Rubric**
> http://www.tcet.unt.edu/START/
> instruct /general/oral.htm

Uses of Language Assessment

- Diagnosis of language strengths and weaknesses
- Detection of patterns of systematic errors
- Appropriate bilingual/ESL program placement if necessary

Common Language Errors

- Applying rules in a student's first language but not in the second
- Using pronunciation that applies to a student's first language but not in the second
- Applying a general rule to all cases even when there are exceptions
- Trying to cut corners by using an incorrect word or syntactic form
- Avoiding use of precise vocabulary or idiomatic expressions
- Using incorrect verb tense

Skill 1.6   Identify methods and strategies for teaching English for speakers of other languages.

Teachers working with English as a Second Language Learners (ESL) should recognize that what works for the English language-speaking student from a primarily English speaking family does not necessarily work for a student coming from a family that speaks another language other than English in the home.

Students who are raised in homes where English is not the first language and/or where standard English is not spoken may have difficulty with hearing the difference between similar sounding words like *send* and *sent*. Any student who is not in an environment where English phonology operates may have difficulty perceiving and demonstrating the differences between English language phonemes. If students can not hear the difference between words that "sound the same" like *grow* and *glow*, they will be confused when these words appear in a print context. This confusion will of course, sadly, impact their comprehension.

Research recommends that ESL students learn to read initially in their first language. Further, a priority for ESL should be learning to speak English before being taught to read English. Research supports oral language development since it lays the foundation for phonological awareness.

Academic literacy, which encompasses ways of knowing particular content and refers to strategies for understanding, discussing, organizing, and producing texts, is key to success in school. To be literate in an academic sense, one should be able to understand and to articulate conceptual relationships within, between, and among disciplines. Academic literacy also encompasses critical literacy, that is, the ability to evaluate the credibility and validity of informational sources. In a practical sense when students are academically literate, they should be able to read and understand interdisciplinary texts, to articulate comprehension through expository written pieces, and to further knowledge through sustained and focused research.

Developing academic literacy is especially difficult for ESL students who are struggling to acquire and improve the language and critical thinking skills they need to become full members of the academic mainstream community. The needs of these students may be met through the creation of a functional language-learning environment that engages them in meaningful and authentic language processing through planned, purposeful, and academically based activities, teaching them how to extract, question, and evaluate the central points and methodology of a range of material. Using the conventions of academic/expository writing, students should be able to construct responses.

Effective academic writing requires that the students be able to choose appropriate patterns of discourse, which in turn involves knowing sociolinguistic conventions relating to audience and purpose. These skills, which are acquired through student attempts to process and produce texts, can be refined over time by having students complete a range of assignments that progress in complexity and are derived from the sustained and focused study of one or more academic disciplines.

Sustained content area study is more effectively carried out when an extensive body of instructional and informational resources, such as those that are found on the Internet, is available. Through its extensive collection of reading materials and numerous contexts for meaningful written communication and analysis of issues, the Internet creates a highly motivating learning environment that encourages ESL students to interact with language in new and varied ways.

Used as a resource for focused disciplined research, the Internet is highly effective in helping all students develop and refine the academic literacy necessary for a successful educational experience.

Used as a tool for sustained content study, the Internet is a powerful resource that offers easier, wider, and more rapid access to interdisciplinary information than do traditional libraries. Using the Internet allows ESL students to control the direction of their reading and research, teaches them to think creatively, and increases motivation for learning as they work individually and collaboratively to gather information.

By allowing easy access to cross-referenced documents and screens, Internet hypertext encourages students to read widely on interdisciplinary topics. This type of reading presents cognitively demanding language and a wide range of linguistic forms; it enables ESL students to build a wider range of schemata and a broader base of knowledge, which may help them grasp future texts. Additionally, hypermedia provides the benefit of immediate visual reinforcement through pictures and/or slideshows, which facilitates comprehension of the often-abstract concepts presented in academic readings.

Academic research skills are often underdeveloped in the ELL student population, making research reports especially frightening and enormously challenging. The research skills students need to complete focused and disciplined projects are the same skills they need to succeed in classes.

Instruction that targets the development of research skills teaches ELL students the rhetorical conventions of term papers, which subsequently leads to better writing and hence improved performance in class. Moreover, research skills acquired through sustained content study, as well as a focused and disciplined research, enables students to manage information more effectively. This practice will serve them throughout their academic years and into the workforce.

COMPETENCY 2.0   KNOWLEDGE OF WRITING AND METHODS FOR EFFECTIVE TEACHING

Skill 2.1   Identify and apply techniques to develop a supportive classroom environment for writing.

Teaching students to write is an extremely important part of an English teacher's life. You will want to instill in your students the confidence to develop their writing skills. Any or all of the activities listed below can be used to promote creative literary response and analysis:

- Have students take a particular passage from a story and retell it from another character's perspective.

- Challenge students to suggest a sequel or a prequel (what happened before) to any given story they have read.

- Ask the students to recast a story in which the key characters are male into one where the key characters are female (or vice versa). Have them explain how these changes alter the narrative, plot, or outcomes.

- Have the students, as the characters of a given story, produce a newspaper that would report the news in their community.

- Transform the story into a ballad poem or a picture book version for younger peers.

An example of an integrated creative writing lesson plan might begin with a discussion about lessons nature can teach us.

- Begin by exploring in a journal a lesson the students have learned from nature. (Writing/pre-reading/prior knowledge)

- Create a brainstorming chart/ cluster on the board from students' responses.

- Students would begin reading selections from "Nature" by Ralph Emerson. (Reading)

- Discuss in class the connections. (Speaking/listening)

- Read aloud models of reflective essays on nature's lessons. Next students would go outside and, using a series of guided questions, observe an object in nature. (Writing/viewing)

- Use observations to allow students to write their own reflective essay on an object in nature. (Writing) Use of peer response and editing would encourage students to share and improve their writing. (Writing/reading/speaking/listening)

- Read final pieces aloud to the class or publish them on a bulletin board.

Skill 2.2   Identify techniques for teaching students to make effective organizational and stylistic choices.

Basic expository writing simply gives information not previously known about a topic or is used to explain or define one. Facts, examples, statistics, cause and effect, direct tone, objective rather than subjective delivery, and non-emotional information are presented in a formal manner.

Descriptive writing centers on person, place, or object, using concrete and sensory words to create a mood or impression and arranging details in a chronological or spatial sequence.

Narrative writing is developed using an incident or anecdote or related series of events. Chronology, the 5 W's, topic sentence, and conclusion are essential ingredients.

Persuasive writing implies the writer's ability to select vocabulary and arrange facts and opinions in such a way as to direct the actions of the listener/reader. Persuasive writing may incorporate exposition and narration as they illustrate the main idea.

Journalistic writing is theoretically free of author bias. It is essential when relaying information about an event, person, or thing that it be factual and objective. Provide students with an opportunity to examine newspapers and create their own. Many newspapers have educational programs that are offered free to schools.

The Writing Process

You can help students by showing them that writing is a process accomplished through a series of steps. Here are some techniques for you to follow and incorporate for your students.

Prior to writing, you will need to prewrite for ideas and details and decide how the essay will be organized. In the hour you have to write you should spend no more than 5-10 minutes prewriting and organizing your ideas. As you prewrite, remember that you should have at least three main points and at least two to three details to support your main ideas. You can practice with several types of graphic organizers as you prepare for the essay portion of the test.

Step 1: Practice

Choose one topic from the chart on the next page and complete the cluster.

Step 2: Prewrite to Explain How or Why

Consider a prompt that asks you to explain how a poet creates tone and mood using imagery and word choice. Then fill out the organizer on the following page that identifies how the poet effectively creates tone and mood. Support with examples from the poem.

NCTE Beliefs about the Teaching of Writing

by the Writing Study Group of the NCTE
Executive Committee
November 2004

1. *Everyone has the capacity to write, writing can be taught, and teachers can help students become better writers.*

2. *People learn to write by writing.*

3. *Writing is a process.*

4. *Writing is a tool for thinking.*

5. *Writing grows out of many different purposes.*

6. *Conventions of finished and edited texts are important to readers and therefore to writers.*

7. *Writing and reading are related.*

8. *Writing has a complex relationship to talk.*

9. *Literate practices are embedded in complicated social relationships.*

10. *Composing occurs in different modalities and technologies.*

11. *Assessment of writing involves complex, informed, human judgment*

VISUAL ORGANIZER: GIVING REASONS

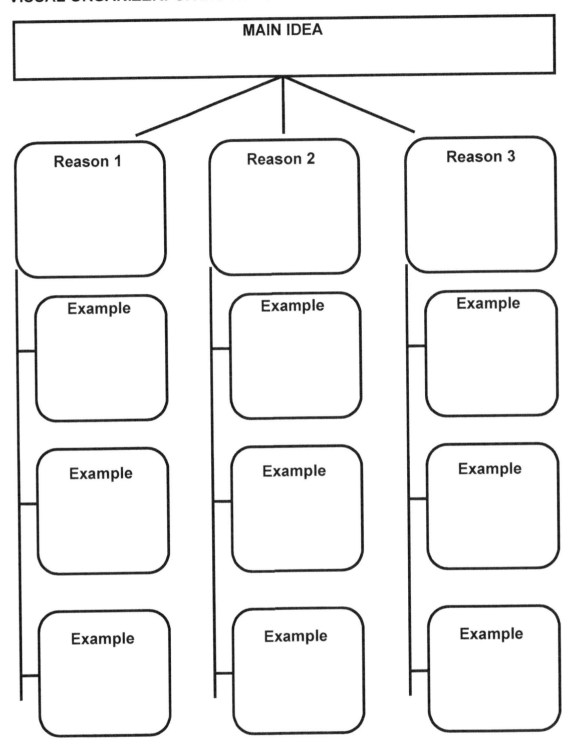

Step 3: Prewrite to Organize Ideas
After you have completed a graphic organizer, you need to decide how you will organize your essay. To organize your essay, you might consider one of the following patterns to structure your essay.

1. Examine individual elements such as **plot, setting, theme, character, point of view, tone, mood, or style**. In this case, consider the single element outline.

   Single Element Outline
   Introduction—main idea statement
   Main point 1 with at least two supporting details
   Main point 2 with at least two supporting details
   Main point 3 with at least two supporting details
   Conclusion (restates main ideas and summary of main points)

2. Compare and contrast two elements. You may develop your ideas point by point or by block.

POINT-BY-POINT	BLOCK
Introduction Statement of main idea about A and B	Introduction Statement of main idea about A and B
Main Point 1 Discussion of A Discussion of B	Discussion of A Main Point 1 Main Point 2 Main point 3
Main Point 2 Discussion of A Discussion of B	Discussion of B Main Point 1 Main Point 2 Main Point 3
Main Point 3 Discussion of A Discussion of B	Conclusion Restate main idea
Conclusion Restatement or summary of main idea	

PRACTICE:
Try using the visual organizer on the next page as part of your prewriting strategy.

VISUAL ORGANIZER: GIVING INFORMATION

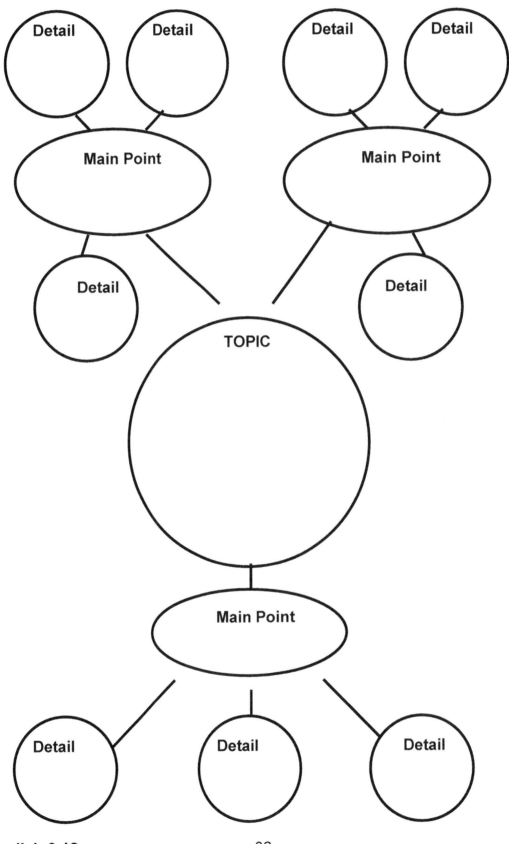

Skill 2.3 **Identify and apply knowledge of the various writing processes (e.g., prewriting, drafting, revising, editing, proofreading, publishing strategies).**

Writing is a recursive process. As students engage in the various stages of writing, they develop and improve not only their writing skills but their thinking skills as well.

Prewriting Strategies

Students gather ideas before writing. Prewriting may include clustering, listing, brainstorming, mapping, free writing, and charting. Providing many ways for students to develop ideas on a topic will increase their chances for success.

Listed below are the most common prewriting strategies students can use to explore, plan, and write on a topic. When teaching these strategies, remember that not all prewriting must eventually produce a finished piece of writing. In fact, in the initial lesson of teaching prewriting strategies, you might have students practice prewriting strategies without the pressure of having to write a finished product.

- Keep an idea book so that they can jot down ideas that come to mind.

- Write in a daily journal.

- Write down whatever comes to mind; this is called **free writing**. Students do not stop to make corrections or interrupt the flow of ideas. A variation of this technique is focused free writing—writing on a specific topic—to prepare for an essay.

- Make a list of all ideas connected with their topic; this is called **brainstorming**. Make sure students know that this technique works best when they let their mind work freely. After completing the list, students should analyze the list to see a pattern or way to group the ideas.

- Ask the questions *who, what, when, where, why and how.* Help the writer approach a topic from several perspectives.

- Create a visual map on paper to gather ideas. Use cluster circles and lines to show connections between ideas. Students should try to identify the relationship that exists between their ideas. If they cannot see the relationships, have them pair up, exchange papers, and have their partners look for some related ideas.

- Observe details of sight, hearing, taste, touch, and taste.

- Visualize by making mental images of something and write down the details in a list.

After they have practiced with each of these prewriting strategies, ask them to pick out the ones they prefer and ask them to discuss how they might use the techniques to help them with future writing assignments. Remind them that they can use more than one prewriting strategy at a time. Also they may find that different writing situations may suggest certain techniques.

Writing

As students compose the first draft, encourage them to write freely. If they get their ideas down first, then they can move to revising. If they have difficulty, have them write as they speak—perhaps have them dictate to another writer or to a recorder.

They might compose their first drafts on computer so they can quickly and easily type out their ideas.

Revising

Students examine their work and make changes in sentences, wording, details and ideas. Revise comes from the Latin word *revidere*, meaning "to see again." This step is often overlooked, unfortunately. Sometimes writers confuse it with proofreading. So students need to understand how important this process is. If they use a computer, they can move and delete without having to rewrite the entire paper. This eliminates some of the frustrations students face with this important but often overlooked step in the writing process.

Editing

Students proofread the draft for punctuation and mechanical errors. If they are using computers, they can run grammar and spell check; however, they should be taught not to rely on these devices.

Publishing

Students may have their work displayed on a bulletin board, read aloud in class, or printed in a literary magazine or school anthology.

These steps are recursive; as students engage in each aspect of the writing process, they may begin with prewriting, write, revise, write, revise, edit, and publish. They do not engage in this process in a lockstep manner; it is more circular.

Teaching the Composing Process

Here is another process you might use with your students.

Prewriting Activities

1. As a class, discuss the topic.

2. Map out ideas, questions, and graphic organizers on the chalkboard.

3. Break into small groups to discuss different ways of approaching the topic and develop an organizational plan and create a thesis statement.

4. Research the topic if necessary.

Drafting/Revising

1. Students write first draft in class or at home.

2. Students engage in peer response and class discussion.

3. Using checklists or a rubric, students critique each other's writing and make suggestions for revising the writing.

4. Students revise the writing.

Editing and Proofreading

1. Students, working in pairs, analyze sentences for variety.

2. Students work in groups to read papers for punctuation and mechanics.

3. Students perform final edit.

Students need to be trained to become effective at proofreading, revising and editing strategies. Begin this process by using both desk-side and scheduled conferences. The following strategies are useful in guiding students through the final stages of the writing process.

- Provide some guide sheets or forms for students to use during peer responses.

- Allow students to work in pairs and limit the agenda.

- Model the use of the guide sheet or form for the entire class.

- Give students a time limit.

- Have the students read their partners' papers and ask at least three who, what, when, why, how questions. The students answer the questions and use them as a place to begin discussing the piece.

- Provide students with a series of questions that will assist them in revising their writing.

  1. Do the details give a clear picture? Add details that appeal to more than just the sense of sight.

  2. How effectively are the details organized? Reorder the details if it is needed.

  3. Are the thoughts and feelings of the writer included? Add personal thoughts and feelings about the subject.

As you discuss revision, begin with discussing the definition of revise. Also, state that all writing must be revised in order to be improved. After students have revised their writing, it is time for the final edit and proofreading. Here are a few key points to remember when helping students learn to edit and proofread their work.

- It is crucial that students are not taught grammar in isolation but in the context of the writing process.

- At this point in the writing process, a mini-lesson that focuses on some of the problems your students are having would be appropriate.

- Ask students to read their writing and check for specific errors like using a subordinate clause as a sentence.

- Provide students with a proofreading checklist to guide them as they edit their work.

Skill 2.4   Select individual, peer, and group activities that support writing processes.

Viewing writing as a process allows teachers and students to see the writing classroom as a cooperative workshop where students and teachers encourage and support each other in each writing endeavor. Listed below are some techniques that help teachers facilitate and create a supportive classroom environment.

> Learn more about
> **Teaching and Managing Peer Review**
> http://www.utexas.edu/cola/progs/wac/
> highschool/hspeerreview/

1. Create peer response/support groups that are working on similar writing assignments. The members help each other in all stages of the writing process—from prewriting, writing, revising, editing, and publishing.

2. Provide several prompts to give students the freedom to write on a topic of their own. Writing should be generated out of personal experience and students should be introduced to in-class journals. One effective way to get into writing is to let them write often and freely about their own lives, without having to worry about grades or evaluation.

3. Respond in the form of a question whenever possible. Teacher/facilitator should respond non-critically and use positive, supportive language.

4. Respond to formal writing acknowledging the student's strengths and focusing on the composition skills demonstrated by the writing. A response should encourage the student by offering praise for what the student has done well. Give the student a focus for revision and demonstrate that the process of revision has applications in other writing situations.

5. Provide students with readers' checklists so that students can write observational critiques of others' drafts. Then they can revise their own papers at home using the checklists as a guide.

6. Pair students so that they can give and receive responses. Pairing students keeps them aware of the role of an audience in the composing process and in evaluating stylistic effects.

7. Focus critical comments on aspects of the writing that can be observed in the writing. Comments like "I noticed you use the word 'is' frequently" will be more helpful than "Your introduction is dull" and will not demoralize the writer.

8. Provide the group with a series of questions to guide them through the group writing sessions.

Skill 2.5   Identify effective responses to student writing.

When assessing and responding to student writing, teachers should follow these guidelines.

Responding to Non-graded Writing (Formative)

- Avoid using a red pen. Whenever possible use a #2 pencil.

- Explain the criteria that will be used for assessment in advance.

- Read the writing once while asking the question, "Is the student's response appropriate for the assignment?"

- Reread and make note at the end whether the student met the objective of the writing task.

- Responses should be non-critical and use supportive and encouraging language.

- Resist writing on or over the student's writing.

- Highlight the ideas you wish to emphasize, question, or verify.

- Encourage your students to take risks.

Responding to and Evaluating Graded Writing (Summative)

- Ask students to submit prewriting and rough-draft materials including all revisions with their final draft.

- For the first reading, use a holistic method, examining the work as a whole.

- When reading the draft for the second time, assess it using the standards previously established.

- Write your responses in the margin and use supportive language.

- Make sure you address the process as well as the product. It is important that students value the learning process as well as the final product.

- After scanning the piece a third time, write final comments at the end of the draft.

You may think this exercise is simply catching errors in spelling or word use, but you should reframe your thinking about revising and editing. This is an extremely important step that often is ignored. Here are some questions you could ask:

- Is the reasoning coherent?

- Is the point established?

- Does the introduction make the reader want to read this discourse?

- What is the thesis? Is it proven?
-
- What is the purpose? Is it clear? Is it useful, valuable, and interesting?

- Is the style of writing so wordy that it exhausts the reader and interferes with engagement?

- Is the writing so spare that it is boring?

- Are the sentences too uniform in structure?

- Are there too many simple sentences?

- Are too many of the complex sentences the same structure?

- Are the compounds truly compounds, or are they unbalanced?

- Are parallel structures truly parallel?

- If there are characters, are they believable?

- If there is dialogue, is it natural or stilted?

- Is the title appropriate?

- Does the writing show creativity, or is it boring?

- Is the language appropriate? Is it too formal? Too informal? If jargon is used, is it appropriate?

Studies have clearly demonstrated that the most fertile area in teaching writing is this one. If students can learn to revise their own work effectively, they are well on their way to becoming effective, mature writers.

Word processing is an important tool for teaching this stage in the writing process. Microsoft Word has tracking features that make the revision exchanges between teachers and students more effective than ever before.

Skill 2.6   Identify a variety of methods to assess student writing.

Nothing defeats a student's writing spirit more than to receive a paper back with red marks all over. Try to vary your assessment methods.

- Have students write a short story, essay or other specified genre of writing.

- Assess their ability to write about a given body of knowledge in a logical and critical way.

-
- Observe their ability to use language resources appropriate for the required task.

- Use a rating system. For example, a scale from 1 to 4 (where 1=unsatisfactory and 4=excellent).

- Monitor their use of source material.

- Evaluate the structure and development of their writing.

- Ensure that their writing style is appropriate for the task assigned.

- Check for grammatical correctness.

- Provide follow-up support for any weaknesses detected.

COMPETENCY 3.0   KNOWLEDGE OF THE USE OF THE READING
                  PROCESS TO CONSTRUCT MEANING FROM A WIDE
                  RANGE OF SELECTIONS

Skill 3.1   Identify techniques for teaching students to understand
             organizational structures of literary and informational material.

Organizational Structures

Authors use a particular organization to present their ideas. Teaching students to recognize organizational structures helps them understand the authors' literary intentions and helps them decide which structure to use in their own writing.

Cause and Effect: When writing about *why* things happen as well as *what* happens, authors commonly use the cause and effect structure. For example, when writing about how he became so successful, a CEO might talk about how he excelled in math in high school, moved to New York after college, and stuck to his goals even after multiple failures. These are all *causes* that lead to the *effect*, or result, of his becoming a wealthy and powerful businessman.

Compare and Contrast: When examining the merits of multiple concepts or products, compare and contrast lends itself easily to the organization of ideas. For example, a person writing about foreign policy in different countries will put the policies against each other to point out differences and similarities, easily highlighting the concepts the author wishes to emphasize.

Problem and Solution: This structure is used in a lot of handbooks and manuals. Anything organized around procedure-oriented tasks, such as a computer repair manual, gravitates toward a problem and solution format because it offers a clear, sequential organization of the text.

An easy and effective way of helping students organize information to be used in a work of nonfiction is by asking specific questions that are geared towards a particular mode of presentation. A sample of these questions follows:

> **What is it?** It is the process of thinking up and writing down a set of questions that you want to answer about the research topic you have selected.

> **Why should I do it?** It will keep you from getting lost or off-track when looking for information. You will try to find the answers to these questions when you do your research.

> **When do I do it?** After you have written your statement of purpose and have a focused topic to ask questions about, begin research.

How do I do it? Make two lists of questions. Label one "factual" questions and one "interpretive" questions. The answers to factual questions will give your reader the basic background information they need to understand your topic. The answers to interpretive questions show your creative thinking in your project and can become the basis for your thesis statement.

Ask factual questions: Assume your readers know nothing about your subject. Make an effort to tell them everything they need to know to understand what you will say in your project.

Make a list of specific questions that ask who, what, when, where, and why.

> **Example**: For a report about President Abraham Lincoln's attitude and policies towards slavery, people will have to know the following: Who was Abraham Lincoln? Where and when was he born? What political party did he belong to? When was he elected president? What were the attitudes and laws about slavery during his lifetime? How did his actions affect slavery?

Asking Interpretive Questions: These kinds of questions are the result of your own original thinking. They can be based on the preliminary research you have done on your chosen topic. Select one or two to answer in your presentation. They can be the basis of forming a thesis statement.

> Learn more about
> **The Art of Asking Good Questions**
> http://www.youthlearn.org/learning/
> teaching/questions.asp

- **Hypothetical**: How would things be different today if something in the past had been different?

  Example: How would our lives be different today if the Confederate (southern) states had won the United States Civil War? What would have happened to the course of World War II if the atomic bomb hadn't been dropped on Hiroshima and Nagasaki?

- **Prediction:** How will something look or be in the future, based on the way it is now?

  Example: What will happen to sea levels if global warming due to ozone layer depletion continues and the polar caps melt significantly? If the population of China continues to grow at the current rate for the next fifty years, how will that impact its role in world politics?

- **Solution:** What solutions can be offered to a problem that exists today?

  Example: How could global warming be stopped? What can be done to stop the spread of sexually transmitted diseases among teenagers?

- **Comparison or Analogy**: Find the similarities and differences between your main subject and a similar subject, or with another subject in the same time period or place.

  Example: In what ways is the Civil War in the former Yugoslavia similar to (or different from) the United States Civil War? What is the difference in performance between a Porsche and a Lamborghini?

- **Judgment:** Based on the information you find, what can you say as your informed opinion about the subject?

  Example: How does tobacco advertising affect teen cigarette smoking? What are the major causes of eating disorders among young women? How does teen parenthood affect the future lives of young women and men?

Skill 3.2   Select effective strategies to analyze text (e.g., word structure, context clues).

For students to understand difficult or complex passages, they must use the skills to define unfamiliar words and infer meaning by surrounding text. By understanding how words are formed to achieve their meaning, student will be better able to analyze challenging vocabulary and phrases.

Phonological Awareness

Phonological awareness means the ability of the reader to recognize the sound of spoken language. This recognition includes how these sounds can be blended together, segmented (divided up), and manipulated (switched around). This awareness then leads to phonics, a method for teaching students to read. It helps them "sound out words."

Check out
A Continuum of Complexity
of Phonological Awareness Activities
http://www.ldonline.org/article/6254

Instructional methods to teach phonological awareness may include any or all of the following: auditory games and drills during which students recognize and manipulate the sounds of words, separate or segment the sounds of words, take out sounds, blend sounds, add in new sounds, or take apart sound to recombine them in new formations. These are good ways to foster phonological awareness.

Identification of Common Morphemes, Prefixes, and Suffixes

This aspect of vocabulary development is to help students look for structural elements within words that they can use independently to help them determine meaning. The terms listed below are generally recognized as the key structural analysis components.

Root Words: A root word is a word from which another word is developed. The second word can be said to have its "root" in the first. This structural component nicely lends itself to the illustration a tree with roots so that students can use a concrete image for an abstract concept.

An example of a root word is "bene" which means "good" or "well." English words from this Latin root include "benefit," "beneficial," "beneficent," and "beneficiary."

Students may also want to construct root words literally by using cardboard trees and/or actual roots from plants to create word family models. This is an effective way to help students own their root words.

Base Words: A base word is a stand-alone linguistic unit which cannot be deconstructed or broken down into smaller words. For example, in the word "re-tell," the base word is "tell."

Contractions: These are shortened forms of two words in which a letter or letters have been deleted. These deleted letters have been replaced by an apostrophe. For example, "hasn't" is the contraction for "has not."

Prefixes: These are beginning units of meaning which can be added (the vocabulary word for this type of structural adding is "affixed") to a base word or root word. They cannot stand alone. They are also sometimes known as "bound morphemes," meaning that they cannot stand alone as a base word. Some examples of prefixes are "pre," "ex," "trans," and "sub."

Suffixes: These are ending units of meaning that can be "affixed" or added on to the ends of root or base words. Suffixes transform the original meanings of base and root words. Like prefixes, they are also known as "bound morphemes," because they cannot stand alone as words. Some examples of suffixes are "ing," "ful," "ness," and "er."

Inflectional endings: These are types of suffixes that impart a new meaning to the base or root word. These endings in particular change the gender, number, tense, or form of the base or root words. Just like other suffixes, these are also termed "bound morphemes." Some examples are "ette," "es," and "ed."

> Learn more about
> **Word Analysis**
> http://www.orangeusd.k12.ca.us/
> yorba/word_analysis.htm

Compound Words: These occur when two or more base words are connected to form a new word. The meaning of the new word is in some way connected with that of the base word. "Bookkeeper," besides being the only English word with three double letters in a row, is an example of a compound word.

The way language skills are developed depends on many factors, some internal (the age of the child), some external (immigration). Teachers can use a variety of approaches to accommodate individual differences.

Context Clues

Context clues help readers determine the meaning of words they are not familiar with. The context of a word is the sentence or sentences that surround the word. Read the following sentences and attempt to determine the meanings of the words in bold print.

> The **luminosity** of the room was so incredible that there was no need for lights.

If there was no need for lights, then one must assume that the word "luminosity" has something to do with giving off light. The definition of "luminosity," therefore, is the emission of light.

> Jamie could not understand Joe's feelings. His mood swings made understanding him somewhat of an **enigma.**

The fact that he could not be understood made him somewhat of a puzzle. The definition of "enigma" is a mystery or puzzle.

Skill 3.3   Identify techniques for teaching students the uses of a wide variety of reference materials.

Whether researching for your own purposes or teaching students to research, the best place to start research is usually at a library. Not only does it have numerous books, videos, and periodicals to use for references, the librarian is always a valuable resource for information and can help retrieve information. In spite of the abundance of online sources, researchers still need librarians.

"Those who declared librarians obsolete when the Internet rage first appeared are now red-faced. We need them more than ever. The Internet is full of 'stuff' but its value and readability is often questionable. 'Stuff' doesn't give you a competitive edge, high-quality related information does."

-Patricia Schroeder,
President of the Association of American Publishers

Keep **content** and **context** in mind when researching. Don't be so wrapped up with how you are going to apply your resources to your project that you miss the author's entire purpose or message. Remember that there are multiple ways to get the information you need. Read an encyclopedia article about your topic to get a general overview, and then focus from there. Note important names of people associated with your subject, time periods, and geographic areas. Make a list of key words and their synonyms to use while searching for information. Finally, don't forget about articles in magazines and newspapers, or even personal interviews with experts related to your field of interest.

- Keep a record of any sources consulted during the research process.

- As you take notes, avoid unintentional plagiarism.

- Summarize and paraphrase in your own words without the source in front of you.

- Cite anything that is not common knowledge. This includes direct quotes as well as ideas or statistics.

To be life-long learners, student should learn to conduct their own research. Thus, they need to know what resources are available to them and how to use them.

Dictionaries are useful for spelling, writing, and reading. Students looking up a word in the dictionary should be an expected behavior, not a punishment or busy work that has no reference to their current reading assignment.

Model the correct way to use the dictionary for some have never been taught proper dictionary skills. As the teacher, you need to demonstrate that as an adult reader and writer, you routinely and happily use the dictionary

Encyclopedias in print or online are the beginning point for many research projects. While these entries may sometimes lack timeliness, they do provide students with general background.

Databases hold billions of records so students should be taught effective search techniques such as using key words and Boolean operators.

Learning that "and" and "or" will increase the number of hits while "not" or "and not" will decrease the number of hits can save researchers time and effort.

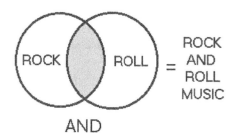

AND

The **Internet** is a multi-faceted goldmine of information, but you must discriminate between reliable and unreliable sources. Use sites that are associated with an academic institution, such as a university or a scholarly organization. Typical domain names will end in "edu" or "org."

Learn more about **Boolean Operators** at http://www.bgsu.edu/colleges/library/info srv/lue/boolean.html

Students (and everyone) should evaluate any piece of information gleaned from the Internet. For example, if you google "etymology" you can find a multitude of sources. Don't trust a single one. The information should be validated by at least three sources. Wikipedia is very useful, but it can be changed by anyone who chooses, so any information on it should be backed up by other sources.

Titles listed in the resource list at the end of this guide are current references with which all language arts teachers should be familiar.

Though the list of literature text publishers is extensive, the following is a tried and true list that meets the needs of students in grades 6-12. Teachers should familiarize themselves with the texts adopted by their own districts and select those resources that best reflect their district's scope and sequence.

- Heritage Edition Series - Harcourt Brace Jovanovich

- Norton Anthologies

- Bedford Introduction to Literature

- *Sound and Sense - Introduction to Poetry,* eds. Laurence Perrine and R. Arp
- *Sound and Sense - Literature Structure*

- *Literary Cavalcade, Read,* and *Scholastic Magazine* - Scholastic supplemental reading

Multimedia Teaching Model

Planning a lesson can involve a variety of methods and media. Here's one model to follow to help you choose and plan more effectively:

Step 1. DIAGNOSE
- Figure out what students need to know.
- Assess what students already know.

Step 2. DESIGN
- Design tests of learning achievement.
- Identify effective instructional strategies.
- Select suitable media.
- Sequence learning activities within program.
- Plan introductory activities.
- Plan follow-up activities.

Step 3. PROCURE
- Secure materials at hand.
- Obtain new materials.

Step 4. PRODUCE
- Modify existing materials.
- Craft new materials.

Step 5. REFINE
- Conduct small-scale test of program.
- Evaluate procedures and achievements.
- Revise program accordingly.
- Conduct classroom test of program.
- Evaluate procedures and achievements.
- Revise in anticipation of next school term.

Tips for using print media and visual aids
- Use pictures over words whenever possible.
- Present one key point per visual.
- Use no more than 3-4 colors per visual to avoid clutter and confusion.
- Use contrasting colors such as dark blue and bright yellow.
- Use a maximum of 25-35 numbers per visual aid.
- Use bullets instead of paragraphs when possible.
- Make sure it is student-centered, not media-centered. Delivery is just as important as the media presented.

Tips for using film and television
- Study programs in advance.
- Obtain supplementary materials such as printed transcripts of the narrative or study guides.
- Provide your students with background information, explain unfamiliar concepts, and anticipate outcomes.
- Assign outside readings based on student viewing.
- Ask cuing questions.
- Watch along with students.
- Observe students' reactions.
- Follow up viewing with discussions and related activities.

Skill 3.4 Select appropriate strategies to develop and enhance reading comprehension.

Reading literature involves a reciprocal interaction between the reader and the text. By understanding the various types of responses, you will be able to improve your students' reading comprehension.

Types of Responses

Emotional: In an emotional response, readers can identify with the characters and situations so as to project themselves into the story. They feel a sense of satisfaction by associating aspects of their own lives with the people, places, and events in the literature. Emotional responses are observed in readers' verbal and non-verbal reactions—laughter, comments on its effects, and retelling or dramatizing the action.

> Learn more about
> **Reading Response Journals**
> http://www.education-
> world.com/a_curr/profdev/profdev085.sh
> tmlreading%20strategies%20index.htm

Interpretive: Interpretive responses result in inferences about character development, setting, or plot; analysis of style elements, such as metaphor, simile, allusion, rhythm, tone; outcomes derivable from information provided in the narrative; and assessment of the author's intent. Interpretive responses are made verbally or in writing.

Critical: Critical responses involve making value judgments about the quality of a piece of literature. Reactions to the effectiveness of the writer's style and language use are observed through discussion and written reactions.

Evaluative: Some reading response theorists add a response that considers the readers' considerations of such factors as how well the piece of literature represents its genre, how well it reflects the social/ethical mores of society, and how well the author has approached the subject for freshness and slant.

Middle school readers will exhibit both emotional and interpretive responses. Naturally, making interpretive responses depends on the degree of knowledge the student has of literary elements. Students show critical reactions on a fundamental level when they are able to say why a particular book was boring or why a particular poem was sad. Adolescents in ninth and tenth grades should begin to make critical responses by addressing the specific language and genre characteristics of literature.

Evaluative responses are harder to detect and are rarely made by any but a few advanced high school students. However, a teacher who knows what to listen for can recognize evaluative responses and incorporate them into discussions.

For example, if a student says, "I don't understand why that character is doing that," she is making an interpretive response to character motivation. However, if she goes on to say, "What good is that action?" she is giving an evaluative response that should be explored in terms of "What good should it do and why isn't that positive action happening?"

At the emotional level, another student might say, "I almost broke into a sweat when the author was describing the heat in the burning house." An interpretive response says, "The author used descriptive adjectives to bring his setting to life." Critically, the student adds, "The author's use of descriptive language contributes to the success of the narrative and maintains reader interest through the whole story." If he goes on to wonder why the author allowed the grandmother in the story to die in the fire, he is making an evaluative response.

Levels of Response

The levels of reader response will depend largely on the reader's level of social, psychological, and intellectual development. Most middle school students have progressed beyond merely involving themselves in the story enough to be able to retell the events in some logical sequence or describe the feeling that the story evoked. They are aware to some degree that the feeling evoked was the result of a careful manipulation of good elements of fiction writing.

They may not explain that awareness as successfully as a high school student, but they are beginning to grasp the concepts and not just the personal reactions. They are beginning to differentiate between responding to the story itself and responding to a literary creation.

**Fostering Self-esteem and Empathy for Others
and the World in Which One Lives**

All-important is the use of literature as bibliotherapy that allows the reader to identify with others and become aware of alternatives while not feeling directly betrayed or threatened. For the high school student the ability to empathize is an evaluative response, a much desired outcome of literature studies. Use of these books either individually or as a thematic unit of study allows for discussion or writing. The titles are grouped by theme, not by reading level.

Abuse
Blair, Maury and Doug Brendel. *Maury, Wednesday's Child*
Dizenzo, Patricia. *Why Me?*
Parrot, Andrea. *Coping with Date Rape and Acquaintance Rape*

Natural World Concerns
Caduto, M. and J. Bruchac. *Keepers of Earth*
Gay, Kathlyn. *Greenhouse Effect*
Johnson, Denis. *Fiskadaro*
Madison, Arnold. *It Can't Happen to Me*

Eating Disorders
Arnold, Caroline. *Too Fat, Too Thin, Do You Have a Choice?*
DeClements, Barthe. *Nothing's Fair in Fifth Grade*
Snyder, Anne. *Goodbye, Paper Doll*

Family
Cormier, Robert. *Tunes for Bears to Dance to*
Danzinger, Paula. *The Divorce Express*
Neufield, John. *Sunday Father*
Okimoto, Jean Davies. *Molly by any Other Name*
Peck, Richard. *Don't Look and It Won't Hurt*
Zindel, Paul. *I Never Loved Your Mind*

Stereotyping
Baklanov, Grigory. (Trans. by Antonina W. Bouis) *Forever Nineteen*
Greene, Betty. *Summer of My German Soldier*
Kerr, M.E. *Gentle Hands*
Reiss, Johanna. *The Upstairs Room*
Taylor, Mildred D. *Roll of Thunder, Hear Me Cry*
Wakatsuki-Houston, Jeanne and James D. Houston. *Farewell to Manzanarr*

Suicide and Death
Blume, Judy. *Tiger Eyes*
Bunting, Eve. *If I Asked You, Would You Stay?*
Gunther, John. *Death Be Not Proud*
Mazer, Harry. *When the Phone Rings*
Peck, Richard. *Remembering the Good Times*
Richter, Elizabeth. *Losing Someone You Love*
Strasser, Todd. *Friends Till the End*

Caution

Teachers should always use caution with reading materials that have a sensitive or controversial nature. You must be aware of the happenings in the school and outside community to spare students undue suffering. A child who has known a recent death in his family or circle of friends may need to distance himself from classroom discussion. Whenever open discussion of a topic brings pain or embarrassment, the child should not be further subjected. Older children and young adults will be able to discuss issues with greater objectivity without making blurted, insensitive comments.

Teachers must be able to gauge the level of emotional development of the students when selecting subject matter and the strategies for studying it. Students or parents may consider some material objectionable. Should a student choose not to read an assigned material, it is the teacher's responsibility to allow the student to select an alternate title. It is always advisable to notify parents if a particularly sensitive piece is to be studied.

In middle and secondary schools, the emphasis of reading instruction spans the range of comprehension skills: literal, inferential, and critical. Most instruction in grades five and six is based on the skills delineated in basal readers adopted for those grade levels. Reading instruction in grades seven through nine is usually part of the general language arts class instead of being a distinct subject in the curriculum, unless the instruction is remedial. Reading in tenth through twelfth grades is part of the literature curriculum—World, American, and British.

Teachers have many techniques to assure that students understand the text but these techniques vary with student age and ability.

Reading Emphasis in Middle School

Reading for comprehension of factual material—content area textbooks, reference books, and newspapers—is closely related to study strategies in the middle/junior high.

Organized study models teach students to locate main ideas and supporting details, to recognize sequential order, to distinguish fact from opinion, and to determine cause/effect relationships. One such model is the SQ3R method, a technique that enables students to learn the content of even large amounts of text (Survey, Question, Read, Recite, and Review Studying),
Strategies

Teacher-guided activities that require students to organize and to summarize information based on the author's explicit intent are pertinent strategies in middle grades. Evaluation techniques include oral and written responses to standardized or teacher-made worksheets.

Through reading fiction, students can develop skills for inferring meaning. Teachers can identify the skills to be studied, choose the appropriate reading resources, and develop activities to guide students' reading for meaning. To monitor the progress of acquiring these comprehension skills, teachers have at their disposal a variety of printed materials as well as individualized computer software programs.

Older middle school students should be given opportunities for more student-centered activities, such as the individual and collaborative selection of reading choices based on student interest, small group discussions of selected works, and greater written expression. Evaluation techniques include teacher monitoring and observation of discussions and written work samples.

Certain students may begin some fundamental critical interpretation, such as recognizing fallacious reasoning in news media, examining the accuracy of news reports and advertising, or explaining their reasons for preferring one author's writing to another's. Development of these skills may require a more learning-centered approach in which the teacher identifies a number of objectives and suggested resources from which the student may choose a course of study. Teachers can stress self-evaluation through a reading diary or they can encourage teacher and peer evaluation of creative projects resulting from such study.

> Learn more about
> **Monitoring Comprehension**
> http://www.indiana.edu/~l517/
> monitoring.html

Teachers should encourage one-on-one tutoring or peer-assisted reading instead of evaluating students as they read aloud before the entire class. However, occasional sharing of favored selections by both teachers and willing students is a good oral interpretation basic.

Reading Emphasis in High School

Students in high school literature classes should focus on interpretive and critical reading. Teachers should guide the study of the elements of inferential (interpretive) reading—drawing conclusions, predicting outcomes, and recognizing examples of specific genre characteristics, for example—and critical reading to judge the quality of the writer's work against recognized standards.

At this level students should understand the skills of language and reading that they are expected to master and be able to evaluate their own progress.

Reading Instruction Strategies

Along with the requisites and prerequisites of most literature courses, teachers need to encourage students to pursue independent study and enrichment reading. Enabling students to be life-long learners is a fundamental goal of teaching.

The teacher becomes more facilitator than instructor. With the teacher's guidance, students should be able to diagnose their individual strengths and weaknesses, keep a record of progress, and interact with other students and the teacher in practicing skills.

Teachers should provide ample opportunities for oral interpretation of literature, special projects in creative dramatics, writing for publication in school literary magazines or newspapers, and speech/debate activities. A student portfolio provides for teacher and peer evaluation.

Skill 3.5   Select appropriate methods of assessing student reading progress to determine strengths and weaknesses.

Skills to Evaluate

- Ability to use syntactic cues when encountering an unknown word. A good reader will expect the word to fit the syntax with which he is familiar. A poor reader may substitute a word that does not fit the syntax, and will not correct himself.

- Ability to use semantic cues to determine the meaning of an unknown word. A good reader will consider the meanings of all the known words in the sentence. A poor reader may read one word at a time with no regard for the other words.

- Ability to use schematic cues to connect words read with prior knowledge. A good reader will incorporate what she knows with what the text says or implies. A poor reader may think only of the word she is reading without associating it with prior knowledge.

- Ability to use phonics cues to improve ease and efficiency in reading. A good reader will apply letter and sound associations almost subconsciously. A poor reader may have one of two kinds of problems. He may have underdeveloped phonics/skills, and use only an initial clue without analyzing vowel patterns before quickly guessing the word. Alternatively, he may use phonics skills in isolation, becoming so absorbed in the word "noises" that he ignores or forgets the message of the text.

- Ability to process information from text. A student should be able to get information from the text as well as store, retrieve, and integrate it for later use.

- Ability to use interpretive thinking to make logical predictions and inferences.

- Ability to use critical thinking to make decisions and insights about the text.

- Ability to use appreciative thinking to respond to the text, whether emotionally, mentally, or ideologically

Methods of Evaluation

- Assess students at the beginning of each year to determine grouping for instruction.

- Judge whether a student recognizes when a word does not make sense.

- Monitor whether the student corrects herself, if she knows to ignore and read on or when to reread a sentence.

- Look for skill such as recognizing cause and effect, finding main ideas, and using comparison and contrast techniques.

- Keep dated records to follow individual progress. Focus on a few students each day. Grade them on a scale of 1-5 according to how well they perform certain reading abilities (e.g. Logically predicts coming events). Also include informal observations, such as "Ed was able to determine the meaning of the word 'immigrant' by examining the other words in the sentence."

- Remember that evaluation is important, but enjoyment of reading is the most important thing to emphasize. Keep reading as a pressure-free, fun activity so students do not become intimidated by reading. Even if the students are not meeting excellent standards, if they continue wanting to read each day that is a success!

COMPETENCY 4.0   KNOWLEDGE OF LITERATURE AND METHODS FOR EFFECTIVE TEACHING

Skill 4.1   Identify various literary devices in both fiction and nonfiction.

Figurative Language

Figurative language allows for the statement of truths that more literal language cannot. Skillfully used, a figure of speech will help the reader see more clearly and focus upon particulars. Figures of speech add many dimensions of richness to our reading and understanding of a poem; they also provide many opportunities for worthwhile analysis.

Essential terminology and literary devices germane to literary analysis include the following.

Alliteration: Alliteration occurs when the initial sounds of a word, beginning either with a consonant or a vowel, are repeated in close succession. Examples include "Athena and Apollo," "Nate never knows," "people who pen poetry."

Note that the words only have to be close to one another: Alliteration that repeats and attempts to connect a number of words is little more than a tongue twister.

The function of alliteration, like rhyme, might be to accentuate the beauty of language in a given context, or to unite words or concepts through a kind of repetition. Alliteration, like rhyme, can follow specific patterns. Sometimes the consonants aren't always the initial ones, but they are generally the stressed syllables. Alliteration is less common than rhyme, but because it is less common, it can call our attention to a word or line in a poem that might not have the same emphasis otherwise.

In its simplest form, it reinforces one or two consonant sounds. An example is from Shakespeare's Sonnet #12:

> When I do count the clock that tells the time.

Some poets have used more complex patterns of alliteration by creating consonants both at the beginning of words and at the beginning of stressed syllables within words. An example is from Shelley's "Stanzas Written in Dejection Near Naples"

> The City's voice itself is soft like Solitude's

Antithesis: Balanced writing about conflicting ideas, usually expressed in sentence form. Some examples are "expanding from the center," "shedding old habits," and "searching never finding."

Aphorism: A focused, succinct expression about life from a sagacious viewpoint. Writings by Ben Franklin, Sir Francis Bacon, and Alexander Pope contain many aphorisms. "Whatever is begun in anger ends in shame" is an aphorism by Benjamin Franklin.

Apostrophe: Literary device of addressing an absent or dead person, an abstract idea, or an inanimate object. Sonneteers, such as Sir Thomas Wyatt, John Keats, and William Wordsworth,

> For more information, consult
> **Glossary of Poetry Terms**
> http://www.infoplease.com/spot/
> pmglossary1.html

address the moon, stars, and the dead Milton. For example, in William Shakespeare's *Julius Caesar*, Mark Antony addresses the corpse of Caesar in the speech that begins: "O, pardon me, thou bleeding piece of earth / That I am meek and gentle with these butchers! / Thou art the ruins of the noblest man / That ever lived in the tide of times. / Woe to the hand that shed this costly blood!"

Assonance: If alliteration occurs at the beginning of a word and rhyme at the end, assonance takes the middle territory. Assonance occurs when the vowel sound within a word matches the same sound in a nearby word, but the surrounding consonant sounds are different. "Tune" and "June" are rhymes; "tune" and "food" are assonant. The function of assonance is frequently the same as end rhyme or alliteration; all serve to give a sense of continuity or fluidity to the verse. Assonance might be especially effective when rhyme is absent: It gives the poet more flexibility, and it is not typically used as part of a predetermined pattern. Like alliteration, it does not so much determine the structure or form of a poem but rather it is more ornamental.

Bathos: A ludicrous attempt to portray pathos—that is, to evoke pity, sympathy, or sorrow. It may result from inappropriately dignifying the commonplace, elevated language to describe something trivial, or greatly exaggerated pathos.

Blank Verse: Poetry written in iambic pentameter but unrhymed. Works by Shakespeare and Milton are epitomes of blank verse. Milton's *Paradise Lost* states, "Illumine, what is low raise and support, / That to the highth of this great argument I may assert Eternal Providence / And justify the ways of God to men."

Caesura: A pause, usually signaled by punctuation, in a line of poetry. The earliest usage occurs in *Beowulf*, the first English epic dating from the Anglo-Saxon era. "To err is human, // to forgive, divine" (Pope).

Climax: A number of phrases or sentences are arranged in ascending order of rhetorical forcefulness. Example from Melville's *Moby Dick*:

> All that most maddens and torments; all that stirs up the lees of things; all truth with malice in it; all that cracks the sinews and cakes the brain; all the subtle demonisms of life and thought; all evil, to crazy Ahab, were visibly personified and made practically assailable in Moby Dick.

Conceit: A comparison, usually in verse, between seemingly disparate objects or concepts. John Donne's metaphysical poetry contains many clever conceits. For instance, Donne's "The Flea" (1633) compares a flea bite to the act of love; and in "A Valediction: Forbidding Mourning" (1633) separated lovers are likened to the legs of a compass, the leg drawing the circle eventually returning home to "the fixed foot."

Connotation: The ripple effect surrounding the implications and associations of a given word, distinct from the denotative or literal meaning. For example, the word "rest" in *Hamlet's* "Good night, sweet prince, and flights of angels sing thee to thy rest," refers to a burial.

Consonance: The repeated usage of similar consonant sounds, most often used in poetry. "Sally sat sifting seashells by the seashore" is a familiar example.

Couplet: Two rhyming lines of poetry. Shakespeare's sonnets end in heroic couplets written in iambic pentameter. Pope is also a master of the couplet. His *Rape of the Lock* is written entirely in heroic couplets.

Denotation: What a word literally means, as opposed to its connotative meaning.

Diction: The right word in the right place for the right purpose. The hallmark of a great writer is precise, unusual, and memorable diction.

Epiphany: The moment when the something is realized and comprehension sets in. James Joyce used this device in his short story collection *The Dubliners*.

Euphemism: The substitution of an agreeable or inoffensive term for one that might offend or suggest something unpleasant. Many euphemisms are used to refer to death such as "passed away," "crossed over," or nowadays "passed."

Exposition: Fill-in or background information about characters meant to clarify and add to the narrative; the initial plot element that precedes the buildup of conflict.

Free Verse: Poetry that does not have any predictable meter or patterning. Margaret Atwood, e. e. cummings, and Ted Hughes write in this form.

Hyperbole: Exaggeration for a specific effect. An example from Shakespeare's *The Merchant of Venice*:

> Why, if two gods should play some heavenly match
> And on the wager lay two earthly women,
> And Portia one, there must be something else
> Pawned with the other, for the poor rude world
> Hath not her fellow.

Iambic Pentameter: The two elements in a set five-foot line of poetry. An iamb is two syllables, unaccented and accented, per foot or measure. Pentameter means five feet of these iambs per line or ten syllables.

Imagery: Imagery can be described as a word or sequence of words that refers to any sensory experience—that is, anything that can be seen, tasted, smelled, heard, or felt on the skin or fingers. While prose writers may also use these images, they are most distinctive of poetry. The poet intends to make an experience available to the reader. In order to do that, the poet must appeal to one of the senses. The most-often-used one, of course, is the visual sense. The poet will deliberately paint a scene in such a way that the reader can see it. However, the purpose is not simply to stir the visceral feeling but also to stir the emotions. A good example is "The Piercing Chill" by Taniguchi Buson (1715-1783):

> The piercing chill I feel:
> My dead wife's comb, in our bedroom,
> Under my heel . . .

In only a few short words, the reader can feel many things: the shock that might come from touching the corpse, a literal sense of death, the contrast between her death and the memories he has of her when she was alive. Imagery might be defined as speaking of the abstract in concrete terms, a powerful device in the hands of a skillful poet.

Inversion: An atypical sentence order to create a given effect or interest. Francis Bacon and Milton's work use inversion successfully. Emily Dickinson was fond of arranging words outside of their familiar order. For example in "Chartless" she writes "Yet know I how the heather looks" and "Yet certain am I of the spot." Instead of saying "Yet I know" and "Yet I am certain" she reverses the usual order and shifts the emphasis to the more important words.

Irony: An unexpected disparity between what is written or stated and what is really meant or implied by the author. Verbal, dramatic and situational are the three literary ironies. Verbal irony is when an author says one thing and means something else. Dramatic irony is when an audience perceives something that a character in the literature does not know. Irony of situation is a discrepancy between the expected result and actual results. Shakespeare's plays contain numerous and highly effective use of irony. O. Henry's short stories have ironic endings.

In poetry, it is often used as a sophisticated or resigned awareness of contrast between what is and what ought to be and expresses a controlled pathos without sentimentality. It is a form of indirection that avoids overt praise or censure. An early example: the Greek comic character Eiron, a clever underdog who by his wit repeatedly triumphs over the boastful character Alazon.

Kenning: Another way to describe a person, place, or thing so as to avoid prosaic repetition. The earliest examples can be found in Anglo-Saxon literature such as *Beowulf* and "The Seafarer." Instead of writing King Hrothgar, the anonymous monk wrote great Ring-Giver, or Father of his people. A lake becomes the swans' way, and the ocean or sea becomes the great whale's way. In ancient Greek literature, this device was called an "epithet."

Malapropism: A verbal blunder in which one word is replaced by another similar in sound but different in meaning. This derives from Sheridan's Mrs. Malaprop in *The Rivals* (1775). Thinking of the geography of contiguous countries, she spoke of the "geometry" of "contagious countries." Meaning the "pinnacle of perfection," she describes someone as "the pineapple of perfection."

Metaphor: Indirect comparison between two things. It is the use of a word or phrase denoting one kind of object or action in place of another to suggest a comparison between them. While poets use them extensively, they are also integral to everyday speech. For example, chairs are said to have "legs" and "arms" although we know that humans and other animals have these appendages.

Metaphysical Poetry: Verse characterization by ingenious wit, unparalleled imagery, and clever conceits. The greatest metaphysical poet is John Donne. Henry Vaughn and other 17th century British poets contributed to this movement as in *Words*, "I saw eternity the other night, like a great being of pure and endless light."

Metonymy: Use of an object or idea closely identified with another object or idea to represent the second. "Hit the books" means "go study." Washington, D.C. means the U.S. government and the White House means the U.S. president.

Motif: A key, oft-repeated phrase, name, or idea in a literary work. Dorset/Wessex in Hardy's novels and the moors and the harsh weather in the Bronte sisters' novels are effective use of motifs. Shakespeare's *Romeo and Juliet* represents the ill-fated young lovers' motif.

Octava Rima: A specific eight-line stanza of poetry whose rhyme scheme is abababcc. Lord Byron's mock epic *Don Juan* is written in this poetic way.

> Share this website with your students
> **NewsHour Extra: Poetry**
> http://www.pbs.org/newshour/
> extra/poetry/#

Onomatopoeia: Word used to evoke the sound in its meaning. The early Batman series used "pow," "zap," "whop," "zonk," and "eek" in an onomatopoetic way. The naming of a thing or action by a vocal imitation of the sound associated with it such as buzz or hiss or the use of words whose sound suggests the sense. A good example: from "The Brook" by Tennyson:

> I chatter over stony ways,
> In little sharps and trebles,
> I bubble into eddying bays,
> I babble on the pebbles.

Oxymoron: A contradiction in terms deliberately employed for effect. It is usually seen in a qualifying adjective whose meaning is contrary to that of the noun it modifies such as "wise folly." Other examples include jumbo shrimp, unkindly kind, or singer John Mellencamp's "It hurts so good."

Paradox: Seemingly untrue statement, which when examined more closely proves to be true. John Donne's sonnet "Death Be Not Proud" postulates that death shall die and humans will triumph over death, at first thought not true, but ultimately explained and proven in this sonnet.

Parallelism: A type of close repetition of clauses or phrases that emphasize key topics or ideas in writing. The arrangement of ideas in phrases, sentences, and paragraphs that balance one element with another of equal importance and similar wording.

An example from Francis Bacon's *Of Studies:* "Reading maketh a full man, conference a ready man, and writing an exact man." The psalms in the King James Version of the Bible contain many examples.

Personification: Human characteristics are attributed to an inanimate object, an abstract quality, or animal. Examples: John Bunyan wrote characters named Death, Knowledge, Giant Despair, Sloth, and Piety in his *Pilgrim's Progress.* The metaphor of an arm of a chair is a form of personification. Carl Sandburg, in his poem "Fog," writes "The fog comes / on little cat feet. // It sits looking / over harbor and city / on silent haunches / and then moves on."

Quatrain: A poetic stanza composed of four lines. A Shakespearean or Elizabethan sonnet is made up of three quatrains and ends with a heroic couplet.

Scansion: The two-part analysis of a poetic line. Count the number of syllables per line and determine where the accents fall. Divide the line into metric feet. Name the meter by the type and number of feet. Much is written about scanning poetry. Try not to inundate your students with this jargon; rather allow them to feel the power of the poets' words, ideas, and images instead.

Slant Rhyme: This occurs when the final consonant sounds are the same but the vowels are different. Occurs frequently in Irish, Welsh, and Icelandic verse. Examples include "green and gone," "that and hit," "ill and shell."

Simile: Direct comparison between two things using "like," "as," such as." For example: "My love is like a red-red rose."

Soliloquy: A highlighted speech, in drama, usually delivered by a major character expounding on the author's philosophy or expressing, at times, universal truths. This is done with the character alone on the stage, as in Hamlet's famous "To be or not to be" soliloquy.

Spenserian Stanza: Invented by Sir Edmund Spenser for use in *The Faerie Queene*, his epic poem honoring Queen Elizabeth I. Each stanza consists of nine lines, eight in iambic parameter. The ninth line, called an alexandrine, has two extra syllables or one additional foot.

Sprung Rhythm: Invented and used extensively by the poet, Gerard Manley Hopkins. It consists of variable meter, which combines stressed and unstressed syllables fashioned by the author. See "Pied Beauty" or "God's Grandeur."

Stream of Consciousness: A style of writing which reflects the mental processes of the characters expressing, at times, jumbled memories, feelings, and dreams. James Joyce, Virginia Woolf, and William Faulkner use stream of consciousness in their writings.

Symbolism: A **symbol** is an object or action that can be observed with the senses in addition to its suggesting many other things. The lion is a symbol of courage; the cross a symbol of Christianity; the color green a symbol of envy.

These can almost be defined as metaphors because society agrees on the one-to-one meaning of them. Symbols used in literature are usually of a different sort. They tend to be private and personal; their significance is only evident in the context of the work where they are used. A good example of a symbol in poetry is the mending wall in Frost's poem "Mending Wall."

A symbol can certainly have more than one meaning, and the meaning may be as personal as the memories and experiences of the particular reader. In analyzing a poem or a story, students should identify the symbols and their possible meanings.

Looking for symbols is often challenging, especially for novice poetry readers. However, these suggestions may be useful: First, pick out all the references to concrete objects such as a newspaper, black cats, or other nouns. Note any that the poet emphasizes by describing in detail, by repeating, or by placing at the very beginning or ending of a poem.

Ask yourself, what is the poem about? What does it add up to? Paraphrase the poem and determine whether the meaning depends upon certain concrete objects. Then ponder what the concrete object symbolizes in this particular poem.

Look for a character with the name of a prophet who does little but utter prophecy or a trio of women who resemble the Three Fates. A symbol may be a part of a person's body such as the eye of the murder victim in Poe's story "The Tell-Tale Heart" or a look, a voice, or a mannerism.

Some things a symbol is not: an abstraction such as truth, death, and love; in narrative, a well-developed character who is not at all mysterious; the second term in a metaphor. In Emily Dickenson's "The Lightning Is a Yellow Fork," the symbol is the lightning, not the fork.

Synecdoche: A synecdoche is a figure of speech in which the word for part of something is used to mean the whole; for example, "sail" for "boat," or vice versa.

Terza Rima: A series of poetic stanzas use the recurrent rhyme scheme of aba, bcb, cdc, ded, and so forth. The second-generation Romantic poets—Keats, Byron, Shelley, and, to a lesser degree, Yeats—used this Italian verse form, especially in their odes. Dante used this stanza in *The Divine Comedy*.

Tone: The discernible attitude inherent in an author's work regarding the subject, readership, or characters. Jonathan Swift or Pope's tone is satirical. James Boswell's tone toward Samuel Johnson is admiring.

> Read about **Tone and Style**
> http://www.delmar.edu/engl/wrtctr/
> handouts/ToneStyle.pdf

Wit: Writing of genius, keenness, and sagacity expressed through clever use of language. Alexander Pope and the Augustans wrote about and were said to possess wit.

Poets use figures of speech to sharpen the effect and meaning of their poems and to help readers see things in ways they have never seen them before. Marianne Moore observed that a fir tree has "an emerald turkey-foot at the top." Her poem makes us aware of something we probably had never noticed before. The sudden recognition of the likeness yields pleasure in the reading. The approach to take in analyzing a poem on the basis of its figures of speech is to ask the question: What does it do for the poem? Does it underscore meaning? Does it intensify understanding? Does it increase the intensity of our response?

Literary Elements

The elements of fiction vary in importance and development from story to story. Some stories are mainly plot-driven while others are character studies. Stories can be so tightly constructed that all elements work together to develop the theme and entertain the reader. Although readers can certainly enjoy a story without an in-depth understanding of these elements, they can develop a deeper appreciation for those works which display the author's talent and writing skill.

Plot is sometimes called action, or the sequence of the events. If the plot does not move, the story quickly dies. Therefore, the successful writer of stories uses a wide variety of active verbs in creative and unusual ways. If a reader is kept interested by the movement of the story, the experience of reading it will be pleasurable. That reader will probably want to read more of this author's work. Careful, unique, and unusual choices of active verbs will bring about that effect.

William Faulkner is a good example of a successful writer whose stories are lively and memorable because of his use of unusual active verbs. In analyzing the development of plot, analytical readers will look at the verbs. However, the development of believable conflicts is also vital. If there is no conflict, there is no story. In critical thinking readers should ask: What devices does a writer use to develop the conflicts, and are they real and believable?

Character is portrayed in many ways: description of physical characteristics, dialogue, interior monologue, the thoughts of the character, the attitudes of other characters toward this one, and so on. Descriptive language depends on the ability to recreate a sensory experience for the reader.

If the description of the character's appearance is a visual one, then the reader must be able to see the character. What's the shape of the nose? What color are the eyes? How tall or how short is this character? Thin or chubby? How does the character move? How does the character walk? Writers choose terms that will create a picture for the reader. It's not enough to say the eyes are blue, for example. What kind of blue? Often the color of eyes is compared to something else to enhance the readers' ability to visualize the character.

A good test of characterization is the level of emotional involvement of the reader in the character. If the reader is to become involved, the description must provide an actual experience—seeing, smelling, hearing, tasting, or feeling. In the following example, Isaac Asimov deftly describes a character both directly and indirectly.

> "Undersecretary Albert Minnim was a small, compact man, ruddy of skin, and graying, with the angles of his body smoothed down and softened. He exuded an air of cleanliness and smelled faintly of tonic. It all spoke of the good things of life that came with the liberal rations obtained by those high in Administration."
>
> Isaac Asimov, *The Robot Series: The Naked Sun*

Dialogue will reflect characteristics. Is it clipped? Is it highly dialectal? Does a character rely on colloquialisms (*dis me, bling*)? The ability to portray the speech of a character can make or break a story.

The kind of person the character is in the mind of the reader is dependent on impressions created by description and dialogue. How do other characters feel about this one as revealed by their treatment of him/her, their discussions of him/her with each other, or their overt descriptions of the character? For example, "John, of course, can't be trusted with another person's possessions." In analyzing a story, it's useful to discuss the devices used to produce character.

Setting may be visual, temporal, psychological, or social. Descriptive words are often used here also. In Edgar Allan Poe's description of the house in "The Fall of the House of Usher" as the protagonist/narrator approaches it, the air of dread and gloom that pervades the story is caught in the setting and sets the stage for the story. A setting may also be symbolic, as it is in Poe's story, where the house is a symbol of the family that lives in it. As the house disintegrates, so does the family.

The language used in all of these aspects of a story—plot, character, and setting—work together to create the **mood** of a story. Poe's first sentence establishes the mood of the story: "During the whole of a dull, dark, and soundless day in the autumn of the year, when the clouds hung oppressively low in the heavens, I had been passing alone, on horseback, through a singularly dreary tract of country; and at length found myself, as the shades of the evening drew on, within view of the melancholy House of Usher."

Why did the author write this story? This question will lead to the **theme**—the underlying main idea. Whether a story is escapist or interpretive, it will have a controlling idea that is integral to its development. This idea is more than a topic (love, anger, guilt, jealousy); it is the author's view of the moral.

Sometimes the title of a story will help reveal the theme. For example, in "The Tell-Tale Heart," Poe tells us a story about guilt and the effect it has on one's conscience. The title foreshadows the outcome and helps the reader understand how all these elements contribute to an effective story.

Skill 4.2   Identify the characteristics of various literary genres, movements, and critical approaches.

Prose is divided into two main genres: fiction and nonfiction. Fiction is based on an author's imagination, and nonfiction is based on factual information,

Genres

The Difference Between Fiction and Nonfiction

Fiction is the opposite of fact and, simple as that may seem, it's the major distinction between fictional works and nonfictional works.

> Learn more about
> **Writing Fiction**
> http://crofsblogs.typepad.com/fiction/
> 2003/07/narrative_voice.html

A work of fiction typically has a central character, called the protagonist, and a character that stands in opposition, called the antagonist. The antagonist might be something other than a person. In Stephen Crane's short story, "The Open Boat," for example, the antagonist is a hostile environment, a stormy sea.

Conflicts between protagonist and antagonist are typical of a work of fiction, and climax is the turning point when those conflicts are resolved. The plot is the sequence of events during which the conflicts occur as the characters and plot move toward resolution.

A fiction writer artistically uses devices labeled characterization to reveal character. Characterization can depend on dialogue, description, or the attitude or attitudes of one or more characters toward another.

Enjoying fiction depends upon the ability of the readers to suspend disbelief. Readers make a deal with the writer that, for the time the readers take to read the story, the readers will replace their own beliefs with the convictions expressed by the writer and will accept the reality created by the writer.

This is not true in nonfiction. The writer of nonfiction must stick to verifiable facts. Thus, a writer of nonfiction is not free to create a character from imagination, no matter how realistic the author makes that character seem. All nonfiction characters have actually lived. The writer of nonfiction declares in the choice of that genre that the work is reliably based upon reality.

Types of Fiction (not all):

- Action-adventure
- Erotica
- Mystery
- Thriller
- Crime
- Fantasy
- Romance
- Western
- Detective
- Horror
- Science fiction

A *bildungsroman* (from the German) means "novel of education" or "novel of formation" and is a novel that traces the spiritual, moral, psychological, or social development and growth of the main character from childhood to maturity.

Dickens' *David Copperfield* (1850) represents this genre as does Thomas Wolfe's *Look Homeward Angel* (1929).

Types of Nonfiction (not all):

- Almanac
- Blueprint
- Dictionary
- Essay
- Letter
- Textbook
- Autobiography
- Book report
- Documentary film
- History
- Philosophy
- User manual
- Biography
- Diary
- Encyclopedia
- Journal
- Science book

Poetry

Poetry, one of the densest forms of communications, is embedded with meaning. It is the use of heightened language to convey meaning and music.

Traditionally, a poem is created in language using literary conventions such as meter, rhyme, alliteration, imagery, allusion, and versification such as stanza form. In modern times, the definition of poetry has been expanded to use metaphor, unmetered poetry, poetry written like prose but broken into short lines on a page, free verse, and unrhymed poetry. Subjects now include personal and autobiographical topics.

Subgenres include the sonnet, elegy, ode, pastoral, and villanelle. Unfixed types of literature include blank verse and dramatic monologue.

Drama

In its most general sense, a drama is any work that is designed to be performed by actors onstage. It can also refer to a literary genre broadly divided into comedy and tragedy.

Contemporary usage, however, denotes drama as a work that treats serious subjects and themes but does not aim for the same grandeur as tragedy. Drama usually deals with characters of a less stately nature than tragedy. A classical example is Sophocles' tragedy *Oedipus Rex,* while a modern example is Eugene O'Neill's *The Iceman Cometh.*

Movements

There are four major time periods of writings: Neoclassicism, Romanticism, Realism, and Naturalism. Certain authors, among these Chaucer, Shakespeare, and Donne, though writing during a particular literary period, are considered to have a style all their own.

Neoclassicism

Patterned after the greatest writings of classical Greece and Rome, this type of writing is characterized by balanced, graceful, well-crafted, refined, elevated style. Major proponents of this style are poet laureates John Dryden and Alexander Pope. The eras in which they wrote are called the Ages of Dryden and Pope. The self is not exalted and focus is on the group, not the individual, in neoclassic writing.

Romanticism

These writings emphasize the individual. Emotions and feelings are validated. Nature acts as an inspiration for creativity; it is a balm of the spirit. Romantics hearken back to medieval, chivalric themes and ambiance. They also emphasize supernatural, Gothic themes and settings, which are characterized by gloom and darkness. Imagination is stressed. New types of writings include detective and horror stories and autobiographical introspection (William Wordsworth).

There are two generations in British Literature: First Generation includes William Wordsworth and Samuel Taylor Coleridge whose collaboration, *Lyrical Ballads,* defines romanticism and its exponents. Wordsworth maintained that the scenes and events of everyday life and the speech of ordinary people were the raw material with which poetry could and should be made. Romanticism spread to the United States, where Ralph Waldo Emerson and Henry David Thoreau adopted it in their transcendental romanticism, emphasizing reasoning. Further extensions of this style are found in Edgar Allan Poe's Gothic writings.

Second Generation romantics include the ill-fated Englishmen Lord Byron, John Keats, and Percy Bysshe Shelley. Byron and Shelley, who for some most epitomize the romantic poet (in their personal lives as well as in their work), wrote resoundingly in protest against social and political wrongs and in defense of the struggles for liberty in Italy and Greece. The Second Generation romantics stressed personal introspection and the love of beauty and nature as requisites of inspiration.

Realism

Unlike classical and neoclassical writing, which often deal with aristocracies and nobility or the gods, realistic writers deal with the common man and his socio/economic problems in a non-sentimental way. Muckraking, social injustice, domestic abuse, and inner city conflicts are examples of writings by writers of realism. Realistic writers include Thomas Hardy, George Bernard Shaw, and Henrik Ibsen.

Naturalism

This is realism pushed to the maximum, writing which exposes the underbelly of society, usually the lower class struggles. This is the world of penury, injustice, abuse, ghetto survival, hungry children, single parenting, and substance abuse. Émile Zola was inspired by his readings in history and medicine and attempted to apply methods of scientific observation to the depiction of pathological human character, notably in his series of novels devoted to several generations of one French family.

Teachers should be familiar with professional resources that aid them in recognizing reader responses and teaching students the process of assessing their responses. One exceptional tool is Laurence Perrine's *Sound and Sense*, cited in the bibliography. Both the text itself and the teacher manual that accompanies it provide excellent activities that contribute to the student's ability to make interpretive and evaluative responses.

In addition, a variety of good student resources are available in most school and public libraries that provide models of critical analyses. The Twayne publications are book-length critiques of individual titles or of the body of work of a given author. *The Modern Critical Interpretations* series, edited by Harold Bloom, offers a collection of critical essays on individual titles in each book. Gale Research Company also provides several series: *Nineteenth Century Literature Criticism, Twentieth Century Literature Criticism*, and *Contemporary Literary Criticism*, to name a few. These encyclopedic sets contain reprints of literary magazine articles that date from the author's own lifetime to the present. Students doing independent research will find these are invaluable tools.

Critical Approaches

The New Criticism

New Criticism treats literary texts as independent entities requiring little or no consideration of external factors such as the identity of the author or the society in which he or she lives. Proponents of the New Criticism believe that the literary text itself is the paramount concern.

Works are analyzed, evaluated, and interpreted through what is called "close reading." Close reading emphasizes genre and literary form; a work's theme and a writer's rendition of it; plot and character development; poetic meter, rhythm, and, if applicable, rhyme; metaphor, simile, and other figurative or literal imagery; evaluation of literary quality; analysis and interpretation of a work's meaning.

The goal of close reading is to arrive, without biographical or sociological distractions, at an objective understanding and appreciation of a literary work

> **Resources for Literary Theory**
> http://vos.ucsb.edu/browse.asp?id=2718

The New Criticism's approach is summed up in two key literary anthologies: *Understanding Poetry* (4th ed.) and *Understanding Fiction*, both edited by Cleanth Brooks and Robert Penn Warren. Either one of these would be suitable as assigned texts for high school literature courses.

Structuralism and Deconstructionism

The structural approach is to examine the structure of a literary work without regard for external influences. This is an attempt to quantify objectively certain criteria that a work must follow. Emphasis is placed on the work as a whole and its place within its genre.

In deconstruction theory, only the text itself is examined. This is done through a very close reading. Formulated by Jacques Derrida in the 1960s, it has been unjustly called "destruction criticism" because of its detailed analytical approach.

Both of these theories are much more complex than explained here and require further study.

Marxist Criticism

Based on the ideas of Karl Marx, some of the key components of this critical theory follow:

- Class conflict drives the history of human civilization.

- The capitalists or bourgeoisie (those who possess and control economic capital) exploit and oppress the proletariat (the working classes) for their own economic and political benefit.

-

- The workers must therefore unite to overthrow the capitalists and their socio-economic system. This will result in a "dictatorship of the proletariat" that will create a classless society in which most, if not all, private property is abolished in favor of collective ownership. The result will be a "workers' paradise"; eventually the nation-states themselves will dissolve and be replaced by a unitary, worldwide communist society free of class conflict.

- Marxist orthodoxy holds that the triumph of communism is inevitable, and that Marxist doctrine is validated by its scientific and materialist approach to history.

- Therefore the Marxist critic uses these ideas to scrutinize literary works, which are analyzed and interpreted to determine their "revolutionary" or "proletarian," "bourgeois" or "reactionary," character.

- Works focused primarily on social injustice and abuses of power have drawn sustained attention from Marxist critics. These include: *The Jungle* by Upton Sinclair; Stephen Crane's *Maggie, a Girl of the Streets*; Theodore Dreiser's *Sister Carrie* and *An American Tragedy*; John Steinbeck's *Grapes of Wrath*; Virginia Woolf's *A Room of One's Own*; and Dostoevsky's *Crime and Punishment* and *The Brothers Karamazov*.

Feminist Criticism

Feminist critics emphasize the ways that literary works are informed and inspired by an author's gender, by an author's ideas about gender and gender roles, and by social norms regarding gender. Of prime concern to the feminist critical enterprise is the advocacy of women as intellectual, social, and artistic equals to men. Feminist criticism is not limited to works by women, nor is it hostile or opposed to male writers or males in general.

"Feminism" could just as easily be referred to as "feminisms." There are a variety of schools of thought that make the plural form more accurate than the singular. Some feminists emphasize class, others race, still others sexual orientation, when critiquing texts or social norms and conditions affecting women's lives.

When introducing feminist writing and criticism to high school students, teachers should consider giving a comprehensive summary of what feminism is, and when, where, and why it arose. Some students will likely have the impression that feminism originated in the 1960s, despite the fact that it has existed for over 200 years. To counter any such misconceptions, teachers can assign excerpts or entire works by these 18th or 19th century authors:

-
- Mary Wollstonecraft
- Margaret Fuller
- Sojourner Truth
- Susan B. Anthony
- Elizabeth Cady Stanton
- Frederick Douglass

Some popular 20th century works relevant to feminist thought and suitable for high school students are listed below.

- *A Room of One's Own* by Virginia Woolf (nonfiction)
- *The Yellow Wallpaper* by Charlotte Perkins Gilman (novella)
- *The Color Purple* by Alice Walker (novel)
- *Beloved* by Toni Morrison (novel)
- *Good Woman* by Lucille Clifton (poems)
- *She Had Some Horses* by Joy Harjo (poems)
- *The Joy Luck Club* by Amy Tan (novel)
- *The Secret Life of Bees* by Sue Monk Kidd (novel)

Numerous up-to-date anthologies of women's literature and feminist criticism are available through major publishers. The groundbreaking anthology, *The New Feminist Criticism*, edited by Elaine Showalter, offers an excellent variety of feminist essays on Western literature. Some of these essays are rather dated but the collection does give a solid overview of key concerns that animated "second wave" feminism in the 1960s and 70s.

Students who seem uninterested in feminist thought might benefit from teachers giving written assignments based on questions such as: Should men and women have equality in today's society? How has life in America been affected by women's campaigns for equal rights? What are your thoughts about gender-based roles, norms, and social expectations in today's America? Once such assignments have been completed, teachers can assign readings and essays in which students compare and contrast their ideas with some of those expressed in a literary work or works listed above.

Psychoanalytic, or Freudian, Criticism

Based initially on the works of Sigmund Freud, this theory has been expanded to include the ideas of other psychoanalysts.

Freudian psychoanalysis holds that the human mind is a tripartite structure composed of the id, which generates and seeks to satisfy all of a person's urges and desires; the superego, which "polices" and counters the id; and the ego, which is the psychic result of the id/superego conflict. The ego is characterized by a person's thoughts and behaviors.

The formation of human character—including sexual behavior—begins at birth. The infant is said to pass through various stages—the oral stage, the anal stage, and so on—as its needs and urges arise and are either satisfied or frustrated; and as it learns (or doesn't learn) to master human relationships and bodily functions.

All humans are said to have inexorable conflicts between drives such as Eros and Thanatos (the sex drive and the death wish), which are also played out in the contests between id and superego.

Neurotic behavior results from fixations on one of the above physical factors, or from an imbalance in the powers of the id and superego, or from deeply embedded (unconscious) memories of pleasant or unpleasant experiences, or from a combination of these. Neurosis is usually rooted in infancy or early childhood.

To discover the nature of a person's mind, the psychoanalyst looks for recurrent thoughts, images, speech patterns, and behaviors evident in the person being analyzed. By carefully observing (especially listening to) a patient, the psychoanalyst uncovers previously unknown truths about the hows and whys of the patient's predicament.

The psychoanalytic literary critic applies Freudian theories to writings and authors in order to better understand the psychological underpinnings of literary works, writers, and, sometimes, society itself.

Writers that have garnered much attention from Freudian critics include Edgar Allen Poe, the Marquis de Sade, Moses, Madame de Stahl, and William S. Burroughs. Not surprisingly, sex and violence feature prominently in these writers' works. Representative examples of psychoanalytic criticism include "Moses and Monotheism" by Sigmund Freud, and *Edgar Allen Poe* by Marie Bonaparte.

Note: For high school-level literature courses, short works would probably be best for any psychoanalytic critical ventures. Especially "Freud-friendly" are stories and poems by Poe that directly relate to one or another facet of Freudian thought: "The Tell-Tale Heart," "The Black Cat," "The Fall of the House of Usher," "The Premature Burial," "The Cask of Amontillado," "The Raven," and "Annabelle Lee," among others. Some of these works share subject matter that makes it appropriate to cluster them in single assignments.

Reader-Response

In this critical theory, the readers create meaning through their individual understandings and responses. Some critics focus solely on the readers' experiences; other critics experiment on defined groups to determine reader response.

Skill 4.3   Identify how allusions from a variety of sources (e.g., literary, mythological, religious, historical) contribute to literature.

Mythology and Oral Tradition

Literary allusions are drawn from classic mythology, national folklore, and religious writings that are supposed to have such familiarity to the reader that he can recognize the comparison between the subject of the allusion and the person, place, or event in the current reading. Children and adolescents who have knowledge of proverbs, fables, myths, epics, and the Bible can understand these allusions and thereby appreciate their reading to a greater degree than those who cannot recognize them.

Classical Mythology

Much of the mythology that produces allusions in world literature is a product of ancient Greece and Rome because Greek and Roman myths have been liberally translated. Some Norse myths are also well known.

Children are fond of myths because those ancient people sought explanations for what happened in their lives in a manner accessible and familiar to children. These stories provide insight into the order and ethics of life. In them, ancient heroes overcome the terrors of the unknown, and explanations are given for thunder and lightning, the changing seasons, the origin and function of magical creatures of the forests and seas, and frightening natural phenomena. There is often a childlike directness in the emotions of supernatural beings. Many good translations of myths exist, but Edith Hamilton's *Mythology* is the definitive choice for adolescents.

Drama

In its most general sense, a drama is any work that is designed to be performed by actors onstage. It can also refer to a literary genre broadly divided into comedy and tragedy.

Contemporary usage, however, denotes drama as a work that treats serious subjects and themes but does not aim for the same grandeur as tragedy. Drama usually deals with characters of a less stately nature than tragedy. A classical example is Sophocles' tragedy *Oedipus Rex* while a modern example is Eugene O'Neill's *The Iceman Cometh*.

Comedy: The comedic form of dramatic literature is meant to amuse and often ends happily. It uses techniques such as satire or parody and can take many forms, from farce to burlesque. Examples include Dante Alighieri's *The Divine Comedy,* Noel Coward's play *Private Lives,* some of Geoffrey Chaucer's *Canterbury Tales,* and some of William Shakespeare's plays, such as *A Midsummer's Night Dream*.

Read more about
Greek Tragedy
http://depthome.brooklyn.cuny.e
du/classics/dunkle/studyguide/
tragedy.htm

Tragedy: Tragedy is comedy's other half. It is defined as a work of drama written in either prose or poetry, telling the story of a brave, noble hero who, because of some tragic character flaw (*hamartia*), brings ruin upon himself. It is characterized by serious, poetic language that evokes pity and fear.

In modern times, dramatists have tried to update drama's image by drawing its main characters from the middle class and showing their nobility through their nature instead of their standing. Sophocles' *Oedipus Rex* is the classic example of tragedy, while works of Henrik Ibsen (*Hedda Gabler*) and Arthur Miller (*Death of a Salesman*) epitomize modern tragedy.

A **dramatic monologue** is a speech given by an actor as if talking to himself or herself, but actually intended for the audience. It reveals key aspects of the character's psyche and sheds insight on the situation at hand. The audience takes the part of the silent listener, passing judgment and giving sympathy at the same time. This form was invented and used predominantly by Victorian poet Robert Browning.

Fairy Tales

Fairy tales are lively fictional stories involving children or animals that come in contact with super beings via magic. They provide happy solutions to human dilemmas. The fairy tales of many nations are peopled by trolls, elves, dwarfs, and pixies, child-sized beings capable of fantastic accomplishments.

Among the most famous are "Beauty and the Beast," "Cinderella," "Hansel and Gretel," "Snow White and the Seven Dwarfs," "Rumplestiltskin," and "Tom Thumb." In each tale, the

> Check out
> **Sur La Lune Fairy Tales and Folklore**
> http://www.surlalunefairytales.com/
> introduction/index.html

protagonist survives prejudice, imprisonment, ridicule, and even death to receive justice in a cruel world.

Older readers encounter a kind of fairy tale world in Shakespeare's *The Tempest* and *A Midsummer Night's Dream*, which use pixies and fairies as characters. Adolescent readers today are as fascinated by the creations of fantasy realms in the works of Piers Anthony, Ursula LeGuin, and Anne McCaffrey. An extension of interest in the supernatural is the popularity of science fiction that allows us to use current knowledge to predict the possible course of the future.

Angels (or sometimes fairy godmothers) play a role in some fairy tales, and Milton in *Paradise Lost* and *Paradise Regained* also used symbolic angels and devils.

Biblical stories provide many allusions. Parables, moralistic-like fables but with human characters, include the stories of the Good Samaritan and the Prodigal Son. References to the treachery of Cain and the betrayal of Christ by Judas Iscariot are oft-cited examples.

Fables and Folktales

This literary group of stories and legends was originally orally transmitted to the common populace to provide models of exemplary behavior or deeds worthy of recognition and homage.

In fables, animals talk, feel, and behave like human beings. Fables always have a moral, and the animals depict specific people or groups indirectly. For example, in Aesop's *Fables,* the lion represents the king and the wolf represents the cruel, often unfeeling, nobility. In *The Lion and the Mouse, the* moral is that "little friends may prove to be great friends." In *The Lion's Share*, it is "might makes right." British folktales (*How Robin Became an Outlaw* and *St. George Slaying of the Dragon*) investigate the interplay between power and justice.

American Folk Tales

American folktales are divided into two categories: tall tales and legends.

Imaginary tales, also called **tall tales,** are humorous tales based on non-existent, fictional characters developed through blatant exaggeration.

- John Henry is a two-fisted steel driver who beats out a steam drill in competition.

- Rip Van Winkle sleeps for twenty years in the Catskill Mountains and upon awakening cannot understand why no one recognizes him.

- Paul Bunyan, a giant lumberjack, owns a great blue ox named Babe and has extraordinary physical strength. He is said to have plowed the Mississippi River while the impression of Babe's hoof prints created the Great Lakes.

Real tales, also called **legends,** are based on real persons who accomplished the feats that are attributed to them even if they are slightly exaggerated.

- For more than forty years, Johnny Appleseed (John Chapman) roamed Ohio and Indiana planting apple seeds.

- Daniel Boone, scout, adventurer, and pioneer, blazed the Wilderness Trail and made Kentucky safe for settlers.

- Paul Revere, a colonial patriot, rode through the New England countryside warning of the approach of British troops.

- George Washington cut down a cherry tree, which he could not deny. Or did he?

Skill 4.4   Identify major authors representative of the diversity of American culture.

American Indian Literature

The foundation of American Indian writing is found in story-telling, oratory, autobiographical and historical accounts of tribal village life, reverence for the environment, and the postulation that the earth with all of its beauty was given in trust, to be cared for and passed on to future generations.

Early American Indian Writers
- Hal Barland, *When the Legends Die*
- S.M. Barrett, Editor, *Geronimo: His Own Story - Apache*
- C. Eastman & E. Eastman, *Wigwam Evenings: Sioux Folktales Retold*
- L. Riggs, *Cherokee Night* - drama

Twentieth Century American Indian Writers
- V. Deloria, *Custer Died for your Sins* (Sioux)
- M. Dorris, *The Broken Cord: A Family's On-going Struggle with Fetal Alcohol Syndrome* (Modoc)
- L. Hogan, *Mean Spirited* (Chickasaw)
- C.F. Taylor, *Native American Myths and Legends*

Afro-American Literature

The three phases of Afro-American Literature can be broken down as follows:

- Oppression, slavery, and the re-construction of the post-Civil War/rural South

- Inner city strife/single parenting, drug abuse, lack of educational opportunities and work advancement that was controlled by biased and disinterested factions of society.

- Post-Civil Rights and the emergence of the Black movement focusing on biographical and autobiographical Black heroes and their contribution to Black and American culture.

Pre-Civil War
Mary McLeod Bethune, *Voice of Black Hope*
Howard Fast, *Freedom Road*
James Haskins, *Black Music in America: A History Through Its People*
Nathan Irving Huggins, *Black Odyssey*
Nicholas Lemann, *The Promised Land*
Harriet Beecher Stowe, *Uncle Tom's Cabin*
Phyllis Wheatley, *Memoirs and Poems*

Post-Civil War and Reconstruction
William Armstrong, *Sounder*
Frank Bonham, *Durango Street*
Alice Childress, *A Hero Ain't Nothin' But a Sandwich*
Ernest Gaines, *The Autobiography of Miss Jane Pittman*

Post-Civil War to the Present
Maya Angelou, *I Know Why the Caged Bird Sings*
James Baldwin, *Go Tell It on the Mountain*
Alex Haley, *Roots*
Lorraine Hansberry, *A Raisin in the Sun*
Harper Lee, *To Kill a Mockingbird*
Langston Hughes, *I, Too, Sing America*
Richard Wright, *White Man Listen!* and *Native Son*

Latino/a Literature

In the field of literature, we have two new expanding areas, Latino/a and feminist writers. These authors write to retain cultural heritage; share their people's struggle for recognition, independence, and survival; and express their hopes for the future.

Latino/Latina Writers
Lora Dee Cervantes (Chicana), *The First Quartet*
Sandra Cisneros (Hispanic), *The House on Mango Street* and short story collections
Gabriel Garcia Marquez (Colombian), *One Hundred Years of Solitude*
A. López Muñoz (Spanish), *Programas Para Días Especiales*
Pablo Neruda (Chile), Nobel Prize Winner - Collections of poetry
Leslie Marmon Silko (Mexican), *Garden in the Dunes* and short story collections
Gary Soto (Mexican), *Tale of Sunlight*

Feminist / Gender-Concern Literature Written by Women in the United States

American women authors have contributed notably to literature in all genres. Edith Wharton's *Ethan Frome* is a heartbreaking tale of lack of communication, lack of funds, the unrelenting cold of the Massachusetts winter, and a toboggan ride which gnarls Ethan and Mattie just like the old tree which they smash into. The *Age of Innocence*, in contrast to *Ethan Frome*, is set in the upper echelons of fin-de-siècle New York and explores marriage without stifling social protocols.

Willa Cather's work moves the reader to the prairies of Nebraska and the harsh eking out of existence by the immigrant families who choose to stay there and farm. Her most acclaimed works include *My Antonia* and *Death Comes for the Archbishop*.

Kate Chopin's regionalism and local color takes her readers to the upper-crust Creole society of New Orleans and resort isles off the Louisiana coast. "The Story of an Hour" is lauded as one of the greatest of all short stories. Her feminist liberation novel *The Awakening* is still hotly debated.

Eudora Welty's regionalism and dialect shine in her short stories of rural Mississippi, especially in "The Worn Path."

Modern black female writers who explore the world of feminist/gender issues as well as class prohibitions are Alice Walker (*The Color Purple*), Zora Neale Hurston (*Their Eyes Were Watching God*), and Toni Morrison (*Beloved, Jazz,* and *Song of Solomon*).

Feminists
Louisa May Alcott, *Little Women*
Betty Friedan, *The Feminine Mystique* and *The Second Stage*
Elizabeth Janeway, *Man's World, Woman's Place: A Study in Social Mythology*
Adrienne Rich, *Of Woman Born: Motherhood As Experience and Institution* and *Driving into the Wreck*

Skill 4.5   Identify principal periods of British literature and American literature, major authors, and representative works.

British Literature

Anglo-Saxon

The Anglo-Saxon period spans six centuries but produced only a smattering of literature. The first British epic is *Beowulf,* anonymously written by Christian monks many years after the events in the narrative

> Review a
> **Timeline of British Literature**
> http://www.studyguide.org/
> brit_lit_timeline.htm

supposedly occurred. This Teutonic saga relates the triumph three times over monsters by the hero, Beowulf. "The Seafarer," a shorter poem, some history, and some riddles are the rest of the Anglo-Saxon canon.

Medieval

The Medieval period introduces Geoffrey Chaucer, the father of English literature, whose *Canterbury Tales* are written in the vernacular, or street language of England, not in Latin. Thus, the tales are said to be the first work of British literature.

Next, Thomas Malory's *Le Morte d'Arthur* calls together the extant tales from Europe as well as England concerning the legendary King Arthur, Merlin, Guenevere, and the Knights of the Round Table. This work is the generative work that gave rise to the many Arthurian legends that stir the chivalric imagination.

Renaissance and Elizabethan Periods

The Renaissance, the most important period since it is synonymous with William Shakespeare, begins with importing the idea of the Petrarchan or Italian sonnet into England. Sir Thomas Wyatt and Sir Philip Sydney wrote English versions. Next, Sir Edmund Spenser invented a variation on this Italian sonnet form, aptly called the Spenserian sonnet. His masterpiece is the epic, *The Faerie Queene*, honoring Queen Elizabeth I's reign. He also wrote books on the Red Cross Knight, St. George and the Dragon, and a series of Arthurian adventures. Spencer was dubbed the Poet's Poet. He created a nine-line stanza, eight lines iambic pentameter and an extra-footed ninth line, an alexandrine. Thus, he invented the Spenserian stanza as well.

William Shakespeare, the Bard of Avon, wrote 154 sonnets, 39 plays, and two long narrative poems. The sonnets are justifiably called the greatest sonnet sequence in all literature. Shakespeare dispensed with the octave/sestet format of the Italian sonnet and invented his three quatrains, one heroic couplet format.

His plays are divided into comedies, history plays, and tragedies. Great lines from these plays are more often quoted than from any other author. The Big Four tragedies, *Hamlet*, *Macbeth*, *Othello*, and *King Lear* are acknowledged to be the most brilliant examples of this genre.

Seventeenth Century

John Milton's devout Puritanism was the wellspring of his creative genius that closes the remarkable productivity of the English Renaissance. His social commentary in such works as *Aereopagitica*, *Samson Agonistes*, and his elegant sonnets would be enough to solidify his stature as a great writer. It is his masterpiece based in part on the Book of Genesis that places Milton very near the top of the rung of a handful of the most renowned of all writers. *Paradise Lost*, written in balanced, elegant neoclassic form, truly does justify the ways of God to man.

The greatest allegory about man's journey to the Celestial City (Heaven) was written at the end of the English Renaissance, as was John Bunyan's *The Pilgrim's Progress*, which describes virtues and vices personified. This work is, or was for a long time, second only to the Bible in numbers of copies printed and sold.

The Jacobean Age gave us the marvelously witty and cleverly constructed conceits of John Donne's metaphysical sonnets as well as his insightful meditations and his version of sermons or homilies.

"Ask not for whom the bell tolls" and "No man is an island unto himself" are famous epigrams from Donne's *Meditations*. His most famous conceit is that which compares lovers to a footed compass traveling seemingly separate, but always leaning towards one another and conjoined in "A Valediction: Forbidding Mourning."

Eighteenth Century

Ben Jonson, author of the wickedly droll play *Volpone,* and the Cavalier *carpe diem* poets Robert Herrick, Sir John Suckling, and Richard Lovelace also wrote during King James I's reign.

The Restoration and Enlightenment reflect the political turmoil of the regicide of Charles I, the Interregnum Puritan government of Oliver Cromwell, and the restoring of the monarchy to England by the coronation of Charles II, who had been given refuge by the French King Louis. Neoclassicism became the preferred writing style, especially for Alexander Pope. New genres, such as *The*

Diary of Samuel Pepys, the novels of Daniel Defoe, the periodical essays and editorials of Joseph Addison and Richard Steele, and Alexander Pope's mock epic *The Rape of the Lock* demonstrate the diversity of expression during this time.

Writers who followed were contemporaries of Dr. Samuel Johnson, the lexicographer of *The Dictionary of the English Language*. Fittingly, this Age of Johnson, which encompasses James Boswell's biography of Dr. Johnson, Robert Burns' Scottish dialect and regionalism in his evocative poetry and the mystical pre-Romantic poetry of William Blake usher in the Romantic Age and its revolution against Neoclassicism.

Romantic Period

The Romantic Age encompasses what is known as the First Generation Romantics, William Wordsworth and Samuel Taylor Coleridge, who collaborated on *Lyrical Ballads,* which defines and exemplifies the tenets of this style of writing. The Second Generation includes George Gordon, Lord Byron, Percy Bysshe Shelley, and John Keats. These poets wrote sonnets, odes, epics, and narrative poems, most dealing with homage to nature.

Read about
The Romantic Period
http://www.wwnorton.com/college/
english/nael/romantic/welcome.htm

Wordsworth's most famous other works are "Intimations on Immortality" and "The Prelude." Byron's satirical epic *Don Juan* and his autobiographical *Childe Harold's Pilgrimage* are irreverent, witty, self-deprecating and, in part, cuttingly critical of other writers and critics. Shelley's odes and sonnets are remarkable for sensory imagery. Keats' sonnets, odes, and longer narrative poem *The Eve of St. Agnes* are remarkable for their introspection and the tender age of the poet, who died when he was only twenty-five.

In fact, all of the Second Generation died before their times. Wordsworth, who lived to be eighty, outlived them all, including Coleridge, his friend and collaborator.

Others who wrote during the Romantic Age are the essayist Charles Lamb and the novelist Jane Austin. The Brontë sisters, Charlotte and Emily, wrote one novel each, which are noted as two of the finest ever written, *Jane Eyre* and *Wuthering Heights*. Mary Anne Evans, also known as George Eliot, wrote several important novels: her masterpiece, *Middlemarch*, and *Silas Marner, Adam Bede,* and *Mill on the Floss*.

Nineteenth Century

The Victorian Period is remarkable for the diversity and proliferation of work in three major areas. Poets who are typified as Victorians include Alfred, Lord Tennyson,

The Victorian Web
http://www.victorianweb.org/

who wrote *Idylls of the King*, twelve narrative poems about the Arthurian legend, and Robert Browning, who wrote chilling, dramatic monologues, such as "My Last Duchess," as well as long poetic narratives such as *The Pied Piper of Hamlin*. His wife Elizabeth wrote two major works, the epic feminist poem, *Aurora Leigh*, and her deeply moving and provocative *Sonnets from the Portuguese,* in which she details her deep love for Robert and his startling, to her, reciprocation.

Gerard Manley Hopkins, a Catholic priest, wrote poetry with sprung rhythm. A. E. Housmann, Matthew Arnold, and the Pre-Raphaelites, especially the brother and sister duo, Dante Gabriel Rosetti and Christina Rosetti, contributed much to round out the Victorian Era poetic scene. The Pre-Raphaelites, a group of 19th-century English painters, poets, and critics, reacted against Victorian materialism and the neoclassical conventions of academic art by producing earnest, quasi-religious works. Medieval and early Renaissance painters up to the time of the Italian painter Raphael inspired the group.

Robert Louis Stevenson, the great Scottish novelist, wrote his adventure/history lessons for young adults. Victorian prose ranges from the incomparable, keenly woven plot structures of Charles Dickens to the deeply moving Dorset/Wessex novels of Thomas Hardy, in which women are repressed and life is more struggle than euphoria. Rudyard Kipling wrote about Colonialism in India in works like *Kim* and *The Jungle Book* that create exotic locales and a distinct main point concerning the Raj, the British Colonial government during Queen Victoria's reign. Victorian drama is a product mainly of Oscar Wilde, whose satirical masterpiece *The Importance of Being Earnest* farcically details and lampoons Victorian social mores.

Twentieth Century

The early twentieth century is represented mainly by the towering achievement of George Bernard Shaw's dramas: *St. Joan, Man and Superman, Major Barbara,* and *Arms and the Man,* to name a few. Novelists are too numerous to list, but Joseph Conrad, E. M. Forster, Virginia Woolf, James Joyce, Nadine Gordimer, Graham Greene, George Orwell, and D. H. Lawrence comprise some of the century's very best.

Twentieth century poets of renown and merit include W. H. Auden, Robert Graves, T. S. Eliot, Edith Sitwell, Stephen Spender, Dylan Thomas, Philip Larkin, Ted Hughes, Sylvia Plath, and Hugh MacDarmid. This list is by no means complete.

American Literature

When compared to other countries, America has had a relatively brief history and thus a comparatively smaller canon of literature. Nevertheless, its fiction and nonfiction have the depth and breadth to tell the story of its people. To study American literature is to study also American history. Students will discover the interconnectedness of writing as a reflection of the historical, social, ethnic, political and economic environment of the time.

American Literature is defined by a number of clearly identifiable periods.

Native American Works from Various Tribes

These were originally part of a vast oral tradition that spanned most of continental America from as far back as before the 15th century.

Characteristics of native Indian literature include
- Reverence for and awe of nature.
- The interconnectedness of the elements in the life cycle.

Themes of Indian literature often reflect
- The hardiness of the native body and soul.
- Remorse for the destruction of their way of life.
- The genocide of many tribes by the encroaching settlement and Manifest Destiny policies of the U. S. government.

The Colonial Period in both New England and the South

Stylistically, early colonists' writings were neo-classical, emphasizing order, balance, clarity, and reason. Because the people had been schooled in England, their writing and speaking were still decidedly British even as their thinking became entirely American.

Early American literature reveals the lives and experiences of the New England expatriates who left England to find religious freedom.

William Bradford's excerpts from *The Mayflower Compact* relate vividly the hardships of crossing the Atlantic in such a tiny vessel, the misery and suffering of the first winter, the approaches of the American Indians, the decimation of their ranks, and the establishment of the Bay Colony of Massachusetts.

Anne Bradstreet's poetry relates colonial New England life. From her journals, modern readers learn of the everyday life of the early settlers, the hardships of travel, and the responsibilities of different groups and

> *"If ever two were one, then surely we.*
> *If ever man were loved by wife, then thee."*
> Read more about
> **Anne Bradstreet**
> http://www.annebradstreet.com/Default.htm

individuals in the community, Early American literature also reveals the commercial and political adventures of the Cavaliers who came to the New World with King George's blessing.

William Byrd's journal, *A History of the Dividing Line,* concerning his trek into the Dismal Swamp separating the Carolinian territories from Virginia and Maryland makes quite lively reading. A privileged insider to the English Royal Court, Byrd, like other Southern Cavaliers, was given grants to pursue business ventures.

The Revolutionary Period

The Revolutionary Period contains non-fiction genres: essay, pamphlet, speech, famous document, and epistle.

Thomas Paine's pamphlet, *Common Sense*, though written by a recently transplanted Englishman, spoke to the American patriots' common sense in dealing with the issues in the cause of freedom.

Other contributions are Benjamin Franklin's essays from *Poor Richard's Almanac* and satires such as "How to Reduce a Great Empire to a Small One" and "A Letter to Madame Gout."

There were great orations such as Patrick Henry's *Speech to the Virginia House of Burgesses* (the "Give me liberty or give me death" speech) and George Washington's *Farewell to the Army of the Potomac.* Less memorable are Washington's inaugural addresses, which strike modern readers as lacking sufficient focus.

The *Declaration of Independence*, the brainchild predominantly of Thomas Jefferson (along with some prudent editing by Ben Franklin), is a prime example of neoclassical writing—balanced, well crafted, and focused.

Epistles include the exquisitely written, moving correspondence between John Adams and Abigail Adams. The poignancy of their separation—she in Boston, he in Philadelphia—is palpable and real.

The Romantic Period

Early American folktales, and the emergence of a distinctly American writing, not just a stepchild to English forms, constitute the next period.

Washington Irving's characters, Icabod Crane and Rip Van Winkle, represent a uniquely American folklore devoid of English influences. The characters are indelibly marked by their environment and the superstitions of the New Englander. The early American writings of James Fenimore Cooper and his *Leatherstocking Tales* provide a window into their uniquely American world through the stirring accounts of drums along the Mohawk, the French and Indian Wars, the futile British defense of Fort William Henry and the brutalities of this period. Natty Bumppo, Chingachgook, Uncas, and Magua are unforgettable characters who reflect the American spirit in thought and action.

The poetry of Fireside Poets—James Russell Lowell, Oliver Wendell Holmes, Henry Wadsworth Longfellow, and John Greenleaf Whittier— was recited by American families and read in the long New England winters. In "The Courtin'," Lowell used Yankee dialect to tell the story. Spellbinding epics by Longfellow (such as *Hiawatha*, *The Courtship of Miles Standish*, and *Evangeline*) told of adversity, sorrow, and ultimate happiness in a uniquely American fashion. "Snowbound" by Whittier relates the story of a captive family isolated by a blizzard, stressing family closeness.

Nathaniel Hawthorne and Herman Melville are the preeminent early American novelists, writing on subjects definitely regional, specific, and American, yet sharing insights about human foibles, fears, loves, doubts, and triumphs.

Hawthorne's writings range from children's stories, like the Cricket on the Hearth series, to adult fare of dark, brooding short stories such as "Dr. Heidegger's Experiment," "The Devil and Tom Walker," and "Rapuccini's Daughter." His masterpiece, *The Scarlet Letter*, takes on the society of hypocritical Puritan New Englanders, who ostensibly left England to establish religious freedom but who have become entrenched in judgmental finger wagging. They ostracize Hester and condemn her child Pearl as a child of Satan. Great love, sacrifice, loyalty, suffering, and related epiphanies add universality to this tale. *The House of the Seven Gables* deals with kept secrets, loneliness, societal pariahs, and love ultimately triumphing over horrible wrong.

Herman Melville's great opus *Moby Dick* follows a crazed Captain Ahab on his Homeric odyssey to conquer the great white whale that has outwitted him and his whaling crews time and again. The whale has even taken Ahab's leg and, according to Ahab, wants all of him. Melville recreates in painstaking detail and with insider knowledge of the harsh life of a whaler out of New Bedford by way of Nantucket.

For those who don't want to learn about every guy rope or all parts of the whaler's rigging, Melville offers up the succinct tale of *Billy Budd* and his Christ-like sacrifice to the black-and-white maritime laws on the high seas. An accident results in the death of one of the ship's officers, a slug of a fellow, who had taken a dislike to the young, affable, shy Billy. Captain Vere must hang Billy for the death of Claggert but knows that this is not right. However, an example must be given to the rest of the crew so that discipline can be maintained.

The Life and Works of Herman Melville
http://www.melville.org/

Edgar Allan Poe creates a distinctly American version of romanticism with his 16-syllable line in "The Raven," the classical "To Helen," and his Gothic "Annabelle Lee." The horror short story can be said to originate from Poe's pen. "The Tell-Tale Heart," "The Cask of Amontillado," "The Fall of the House of Usher," and "The Masque of the Red Death" are exemplary short stories. In addition, the genre of detective story emerges with Poe's "Murders in the Rue Morgue."

American Romanticism has its own offshoot in the Transcendentalism of Ralph Waldo Emerson and Henry David Thoreau. One wrote about transcending the complexities of life; the other, who wanted to get to the marrow of life, immersed himself in nature at Walden Pond and wrote an inspiring autobiographical account of his sojourn, aptly titled *On Walden Pond*. Thoreau also wrote passionately regarding his objections to the interference of government imposed on the individual in "On the Duty of Civil Disobedience."

Emerson's elegantly-crafted essays and war poetry still validate several important universal truths. Probably most remembered for his address to Thoreau's Harvard graduating class, "The American Scholar," he defined the qualities of hard work and intellectual spirit required of Americans in their growing nation.

The Transition Between Romanticism and Realism

The Civil War period ushers in the poignant poetry of Walt Whitman and his homage to all who suffer from the ripple effects of war and

> Find more sites about
> **American Literature**
> http://www.wsu.edu/~campbelld/amlit/sites.htm

presidential assassination. His "Come up from the Fields, Father" about a Civil War soldier's death and his family's reaction and "When Lilacs Last in the Courtyard Bloom'd" about the effects of Abraham Lincoln's death on the poet and the nation should be required readings in any American literature course. Further, his *Leaves of Grass* gave America its first poetry truly unique in form, structure, and subject matter.

Emily Dickinson, like Walt Whitman, leaves her literary fingerprints on a vast array of poems, all but three of which were never published in her lifetime. Her themes of introspection and attention to nature's details and wonders are, by any measurement, world-class works. Her posthumous recognition reveals the timeliness of her work. American writing had most certainly arrived!

Mark Twain also left giant footprints with his unique blend of tall tale and fable. "The Celebrated Jumping Frog of Calaveras County" and "The Man who Stole Hadleyburg" are epitomes of short story writing. Move to novel creation, and Twain again rises above others by his bold, still disputed, oft-banned *The Adventures of Huckleberry Finn*, which examines such taboo subjects as a white person's love of a slave, the issue of leaving children with abusive parents, and the outcomes of family feuds. Written partly in dialect and southern vernacular, *The Adventures of Huckleberry Finn* is touted by some as the greatest American novel.

The Realistic Period

The late nineteenth century saw a reaction against the tendency of romantic writers to look at the world through rose-colored glasses. Writers like Frank Norris (*The Pit*) and Upton Sinclair (*The Jungle*) used their novels to decry conditions for workers in slaughterhouses and wheat mills.

Upton Sinclair
http://www.online-literature.com/upton_sinclair/

In *The Red Badge of Courage*, Stephen Crane writes of the daily sufferings of the common soldier in the Civil War. Realistic writers wrote of common, ordinary people and events using realistic detail to reveal the harsh realities of life. They broached taboos by creating protagonists whose environments often destroyed them. Romantic writers would have only protagonists whose indomitable wills helped them rise above adversity. Crane's *Maggie: A Girl of the Streets* deals with a young woman forced into prostitution to survive. In "The Occurrence at Owl Creek Bridge," Ambrose Bierce relates the unfortunate hanging of a Confederate soldier.

Short stories, like Bret Harte's "The Outcasts of Poker Flat" and Jack London's "To Build a Fire," deal with unfortunate people whose luck in life has run out. Many writers, sub-classified as naturalists, believed that man was subject to a fate over which he had no control.

Contemporary American Literature

Twentieth century American writing can be divided into the following three genres: drama, fiction, and poetry.

American Drama: The greatest and most prolific of American playwrights include these playwrights:

- Eugene O'Neill, *Long Day's Journey into Night*, *Mourning Becomes Electra*, and *Desire Under the Elms*
- Arthur Miller, *The Crucible*, *All My Sons*, and *Death of a Salesman*
- Tennessee Williams. *Cat on a Hot Tin Roof*, *The Glass Menagerie*, and *A Street Car Named Desire*
- Edward Albee, *Who's Afraid of Virginia Woolf? Three Tall Women*, and *A Delicate Balance*

American Fiction: The renowned American novelists of this century include these authors:

- Eudora Welty, *The Optimist's Daughter*
- John Updike, *Rabbit Run* and *Rabbit Redux*
- Sinclair Lewis, *Babbit* and *Elmer Gantry*
- F. Scott Fitzgerald, *The Great Gatsby* and *Tender Is the Night*
- Ernest Hemingway, *A Farewell to Arms* and *For Whom the Bell Tolls*
- William Faulkner, *The Sound and the Fury* and *Absalom, Absalom*
- Bernard Malamud, *The Fixer* and *The Natural*

American Poetry: The poetry of the twentieth century is multifaceted, as represented by Edna St. Vincent Millay, Marianne Moore, Richard Wilbur, Langston Hughes, Maya Angelou, and Rita Dove. Above all others are the many-layered poems of Robert Frost. His New England motifs of snowy evenings, birches, apple picking, stone wall mending, hired hands, and detailed nature studies relate universal truths in exquisite diction, polysyllabic words, and rare allusions to mythology and the Bible.

Skill 4.6   Identify representative works and major authors of world literature.

North American Literature

North American literature is divided between the United States, Canada, and Mexico. Canadian writers of note include feminist Margaret Atwood, (*The Hand Maiden's Tale*); Alice Munro, a remarkable short story writer; and W. P. Kinsella, another short story writer whose two major subjects are North American Indians and baseball.

Mexican writers include 1990 Nobel Prize winning poet Octavio Paz (*The Labyrinth of Solitude*) and feminist Rosario Castillanos (*The Nine Guardians*).

Central American/Caribbean Literature

The Caribbean and Central America encompass a vast area and cultures that reflect oppression and colonialism by England, Spain, Portugal, France, and

> **The Norton Anthology of World Literature**
> http://www.wwnorton.com/college/english/nawol/

The Netherlands. The Caribbean writers include Samuel Selvon from Trinidad and Armando Valladares of Cuba. Central American authors include dramatist Carlos Solorzano, from Guatemala, whose plays include *Dona Beatriz, The Hapless, The Magician,* and *The Hands of God*.

South American Literature

Chilean Gabriela Mistral was the first Latin American writer to win the Nobel Prize for literature. She is best known for her collections of poetry, *Desolation and Feeling*.

Chile was also home to Pablo Neruda, who, in 1971, also won the Nobel Prize for literature for his poetry. His 29 volumes of poetry have been translated into more than 60 languages, attesting to his universal appeal. *Twenty Love Poems* and *Song of Despair* are justly famous. Isabel Allende is carrying on the Chilean literary standards with her acclaimed novel, *House of Spirits*. Argentine Jorge Luis Borges is considered by many literary critics to be the most important writer of his century from South America. His collections of short stories, *Ficciones*, brought him universal recognition. Also from Argentina, Silvina Ocampo, a collaborator with Borges on a collection of poetry, is famed for her poetry and short story collections, which include *The Fury* and *The Days of the Night*.

Horacio Quiroga represents Uruguay, and Brazil has Joao Guimaraes Rosa, whose novel, *The Devil to Pay*, is considered first-rank world literature.

Continental European Literature

With its long history of great writers, continental European literature expands the world of students and broadens their exposure to different cultures and values. This category as discussed below excludes British literature as it was covered previously.

Germany

German poet and playwright Friedrich von Schiller is best known for his history plays *William Tell* and *The Maid of Orleans*. He is a leading literary figure in Germany's Golden Age of Literature. Also from Germany, Rainer Maria Rilke, the great lyric poet, is one of the poets of the unconscious, or stream of consciousness. Germany also has given the world Herman Hesse, (*Siddartha*), Gunter Grass (*The Tin Drum*), and the greatest of all German writers, Goethe.

Scandinavia

Scandinavian literature includes the work of Hans Christian Andersen of Denmark, who advanced the fairy tale genre with such wistful tales as "The Little Mermaid" and "Thumbelina." The social commentary of Henrik Ibsen in Norway startled the world through drama exploring such issues as feminism (*The Doll's House* and *Hedda Gabler*) and the effects of sexually-transmitted diseases (*The Wild Duck* and *Ghosts*).

Read more about
Henrik Ibsen
http://www.hf.uio.no/
ibsensenteret/
index_eng.html

Sweden's Selma Lagerlof is the first woman to win the Nobel Prize for literature. Her novels include *Gosta Berling's Saga* and the world-renowned *The Wonderful Adventures of Nils*, a children's work.

Russia

Russian literature is vast and monumental. Who has not heard of Fyodor Dostoyevski's *Crime and Punishment* and *The Brothers Karamazov* or of Count Leo Tolstoy's *War and Peace*? These are examples of psychological realism. Dostoyevski's influence on modern writers cannot be overstressed.

Tolstoy's *War and Peace* is the sweeping account of the invasion of Russia and Napoleon's taking of Moscow. This novel is called the national novel of Russia. Further advancing Tolstoy's greatness is his ability to create realistic and unforgettable female characters, especially Natasha in *War and Peace* and Anna in *Anna Karenina*. Pushkin is famous for great short stories; Anton Chekhov for drama (*Uncle Vanya*, *The Three Sisters*, *The Cherry Orchard*); and Yevgeny Yevtushenko for poetry (*Babi Yar*). Boris Pasternak won the Nobel Prize (*Dr. Zhivago*). Aleksandr Solzhenitsyn (*The Gulag Archipelago*) returned to Russia after years of expatriation in Vermont. Ilya Varshavsky, who creates fictional societies that are dystopias, or the opposite of utopias, represents the genre of science fiction.

France

France has a multifaceted canon of great literature that is universal in scope and usually champions some social cause. Examples include the poignant short stories of Guy de Maupassant; the fantastic poetry of Charles Baudelaire (*Fleurs du Mal*); the groundbreaking lyrical poetry of Rimbaud and Verlaine; and the existentialism of Jean-Paul Sartre (*No Exit*, *The Flies*, *Nausea*), Andre Malraux (*The Fall*) and Albert Camus (*The Stranger* and *The Plague*), the recipient of the 1957 Nobel Prize for literature. Feminist writings include those of Sidonie-Gabrielle Colette, known for her short stories and novels, as well as Simone de Beauvoir.

Drama in France is best represented by Rostand's *Cyrano de Bergerac* and the neo-classical dramas of Racine and Corneille (*El Cid*).

Learn more about
Jean Paul Sartre
http://www.users.muohio.e
du/shermalw/honors_2001
_fall/honors_papers_2001/
detwilerj_Sartre.htm

The great French novelists include Andre Gide, Honore de Balzac (*Cousin Bette*), Stendel (*The Red and the Black*), and Alexandre Dumas (*The Three Musketeers* and *The Man in the Iron Mask*). Victor Hugo is the Charles Dickens of French literature, having penned the masterpieces *The Hunchback of Notre Dame* and *Les Miserables*. The stream of consciousness of Proust's *Remembrance of Things Past* and the Absurdist theatre of Samuel Beckett and Eugene Ionesco (*The Rhinoceros*) attest to the groundbreaking genius of the French writers.

Slavic Nations

Austrian writer Franz Kafka (*The Metamorphosis*, *The Trial*, and *The Castle*) is considered by many to be the literary voice of the first-half of the twentieth century. Poet Vaclav Havel represents the Czech Republic. Slovakia has dramatist Karel Capek (*R.U.R.*). Romania is represented by Elie Weisel (*Night*), a Nobel Prize winner.

Spain

Spain's great writers include Miguel de Cervantes (*Don Quixote*) and Juan Ramon Jimenez. The anonymous national epic, *El Cid*, has been translated into many languages.

Italy

Italy's greatest writers include Virgil (*The Aeneid)*, Giovanni Boccaccio (*The Decameron*), Dante Alighieri (*The Divine Comedy*) and the more contemporary Alberto Moravia.

Ancient Greece

Greece will always be foremost in literary stature because of Homer's epics, *The Iliad* and *The Odyssey*. No one except Shakespeare is more often cited. The works of Plato and Aristotle in philosophy; of Aeschylus, Euripides, and Sophocles in tragedy, and of Aristophanes in comedy further solidify Greece's pre-eminence. Greece is the cradle not only of democracy but of literature as well.

Africa

African literary greats include South Africans Nadine Gordimer (Nobel Prize for literature) and Peter Abrahams (*Tell Freedom: Memories of Africa*), an autobiography of life in Johannesburg. Chinua Achebe (*Things Fall Apart*) and the poet, Wole Soyinka, hail from Nigeria. Mark Mathabane wrote an autobiography *Kaffir Boy* about growing up in South Africa. Egyptian writer Naguib Mahfouz and Doris Lessing from Rhodesia, now Zimbabwe, write about race relations in their respective countries. Lessing won the 2007 Nobel Prize for Literature. Because of her radical politics, Lessing was once banned from her homeland and the Union of South Africa, as was Alan Paton whose seemingly simple story, *Cry, the Beloved Country*, brought the plight of blacks and the whites' fear of blacks under apartheid to the rest of the world.

> Learn more about
> **Postcolonial Literature in English**
> http://www.thecore.nus.edu.sg/post/misc/africov.html

Far East Literature

Asia has many modern writers who are being translated for the western reading public. India's Krishan Chandar has authored more than 300 stories. Rabindranath Tagore won the Nobel Prize for literature in 1913 (*Song Offerings*). R. K. Narayan, India's most famous writer (*The Guide*), is interested in mythology and legends of India. Santha Rama Rau's work *Gifts of Passage* is her true story of life in a British school where she tries to preserve her Indian culture and traditional home.

Revered as Japan's most famous female author, Fumiko Hayashi (*Drifting Clouds*) by the time of her death had written more than 270 literary works.

In 1968 the Nobel Prize for literature was awarded to Yasunari Kawabata (*The Sound of the Mountain*, *The Snow Country*). His Palm-of-the-Hand Stories take the essentials of Haiku poetry and transform them into the short story genre.

Katai Tayama (*The Quilt*) is touted as the father of the Japanese confessional novel. His works, characterized as naturalism, are definitely not for the squeamish. The "slice of life" psychological writings of Ryunosuke Akutagawa gained him acclaim in the western world. His short stories, especially "Rashamon" and "In a Grove," are greatly praised for style as well as content.

China, too, has given to the literary world. Li Po, the T'ang dynasty poet from the Chinese Golden Age, revealed his interest in folklore by preserving the folk songs and mythology of China. Po further enables his readers to enter into the Chinese philosophy of Taoism and to understand feelings against expansionism during the T'ang dynastic rule. The T'ang dynasty, which was one of great diversity in the arts, saw Jiang Fang help create the Chinese version of a short story. His themes often express love between a man and a woman.

Modern feminist and political concerns are written eloquently by Ting Ling, who used the pseudonym Chiang Ping-Chih. Her stories reflect her concerns about social injustice and her commitment to the women's movement.

Skill 4.7   Identify a variety of appropriate materials, techniques, and methods for teaching literature.

In analyzing literature and in looking for ways to bring a work to life for an audience, the use of comparable themes and ideas from other pieces of literature and from one's own life experiences, including from reading the daily newspaper, is very important and useful.

It's human nature to compare objects, ideas, and even people to look for commonalities. We can't take our eyes off someone who reminds us of a lost love, for example. This naturally-occurring phenomenon can be very useful in literary analysis.

> Check out these links on
> **Teaching Literature:**
> **Story Response/ Writing**
> http://www.teachingliterature.org/
> teachingliterature/response.htm

For example, in *The Five People You Meet in Heaven*, Mitch Albom's theme of giving one's life to save another alludes to the biblical teaching that the greatest love is to give up one's life for a friend. This is called a biblical allusion. The same theme can be found in newspapers as well. For example, a man in New York City risked his life to rescue a homeless man from the wheels of a train. Stories of animals that show extraordinary bravery to save their masters or mistresses are very popular.

War is a very popular theme for literature of all kinds. For example, Ernest Hemingway's novels, written based on his experience in the Spanish Civil War, make familiar and poignant statements about the effects of war. Much poetry has been written about this theme: "Johnny, I Hardly Know Ye," an anonymous eighteenth-century Irish ballad; Wilfred Owen's World War I poem, "Dulce et Decorum Est," and Richard Lovelace's seventeenth century "To Lucasta," for examples. Comparing the treatment of such a common theme or its treatment by different writers adds depth and interest to an interpretation of a literary work. One's own experience is useful in interpreting war literature. Few of us have had the privilege of living our lives out without experiencing our country at war and of seeing its destructive effects on human beings.

It's always important to think about and draw conclusions about a writer's purpose in creating a work of fiction in attempting to understand and appreciate it. Why did this writer write this particular work at this particular time?

We know that John Steinbeck wrote *Grapes of Wrath* out of his own concern that his fellow Americans were suffering and that their suffering could be traced to greed and indifference on the parts of those who brought on and perpetuated the state of affairs that had led to the Great Depression. Prior learning about the history and political situation in the decade of the thirties is very useful in interpreting writing from that period of time, including Steinbeck's masterpiece. What led him to these conclusions? Was it his brief education at Stanford? Was it because of reading that he had done? These are important questions for an interpreter to ask about a writer and the literature he or she produces.

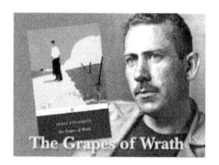

Check out this detailed lesson plan on
The Grapes of Wrath
http://www.neabigread.org/books/grapesofwrath/

In reading descriptive writing, the questions to ask are whether you can experience what the writer is attempting to share with you. Can you see what the writer is describing? Can you hear it, can you smell it, and so on? Are the descriptions complete enough for comprehension and reaction? A good example of effective and powerful descriptive writing is Wilfred Owen's poem "Dulce et Decorum Est." Read some of the lines:

> Bent double, like old beggars under sacks,
> Knock-kneed, coughing like hags, we cursed through sludge,
> Till on the haunting flares we turned our backs
> And towards our distant rest began to trudge.
> Men marched asleep. Many had lost their boots
> But limped on, blood-shod. All went lame; all blind;
> Drunk with fatigue; deaf even to the hoots
> Of tired, outstripped Five-Nines (gas shells) that dropped behind.

Someone has said, "War is hell," but this poem lets us see and feel how bad it truly is from those who have experienced it first hand, fulfilling the purpose of descriptive language.

In reading a narrative, the questions to ask are whether the incidents lead to a resolution. What is the purpose of the story? What is the meaning? Why did the writer write it?

Encourage students to react honestly to literature. Allow them to choose their reading selections; if the choice is their own, their reactions can be more spontaneous and comfortable. With middle school/junior high students, keeping a reading diary may be as much as they can handle. High school students can be encouraged to write analytical reviews but try to keep them informal. Encourage students to read book reviews in current periodicals to see how critics express their responses.

Encourage students to attempt to write in certain genres. Have middle school students compose their own myths. High school students can try their hands at poems, short stories, and one-act plays. By attempting to write in a particular form, the student will gain a greater appreciation of the author's task.

Remember that teaching for appreciation and the encouragement of life-long reading means that instruction must be student centered. If you ever sat through a lecture in a college literature survey class, you can identify with the problems students have with lecturing in secondary schools. Teach the elements of literature and the process of learning through lecture, but avoid lecturing on the meaning of the literature at all costs. If you really want to inspire your students, perform the Lady Macbeth soliloquy or give your own book review—gratis.

Read and write when they do and share your creativity with them. High school students are especially appreciative of teachers who would never ask them to do something the teachers themselves cannot or will not do.

Skill 4.8   Identify representative young adult literature and its contribution to personal, social, and academic development.

Prior to twentieth century research on child development and child/adolescent literature's relationship to that development, books for adolescents were primarily didactic. They were designed to address history, manners, and morals.

Middle Ages

As early as the eleventh century, Anselm, the Archbishop of Canterbury, wrote an encyclopedia designed to instill in children the beliefs and principles of conduct acceptable to adults in medieval society. Early monastic translations of the Bible and other religious writings were written in Latin for the edification of the upper class.

Fifteenth century hornbooks were designed to teach reading and religious lessons. William Claxton printed English versions of *Aesop's Fables*, Mallory's *Le Morte d'Arthur,* and stories from Greek and Roman mythology. Though printed for adults, tales of adventures of Odysseus and the Arthurian knights were also popular with literate adolescents.

Renaissance

The Renaissance saw the introduction of the inexpensive chapbooks, small in size and 16-64 pages in length. Chapbooks were condensed versions of mythology and fairy tales. Designed for the common people, chapbooks were imperfect grammatically but were immensely popular because of their adventurous contents. Though most of the serious, educated adults frowned on the sometimes vulgar little books, they received praise from Richard Steele of *Tattler* fame for inspiring his grandson's interest in reading and in pursuing his other studies.

Meanwhile, the Puritans' three most popular reads were the Bible, John Foe's *Book of Martyrs*, and John Bunyan's *Pilgrim's Progress*. Though venerating religious martyrs and preaching the moral propriety which was to lead to eternal happiness, the stories of the *Book of Martyrs* were often lurid in their descriptions of the fate of the damned. In contrast, *Pilgrim's Progress*, not written for children and difficult reading even for adults, was as attractive to adolescents for its adventurous plot as for its moral outcome. In Puritan America, the *New England Primer* set forth the prayers, catechisms, Bible verses, and illustrations meant to instruct children in the Puritan ethic. The seventeenth-century French used fables and fairy tales to entertain adults, but children found them enjoyable as well.

Seventeenth Century

The late seventeenth century brought the first concern with providing literature that specifically targeted the young. Pierre Peril's *Fairy Tales*, Jean de la Fontaine's retellings of famous fables, Mme. d'Aulnoy's novels based on old folktales, and Mme. de Beaumont's Beauty and the Beast were written to delight as well as instruct young people. In England, publisher John Newbury was the first to publish a line for children. These included a translation of Perrault's *Tales of Mother Goose; A Little Pretty Pocket-Book*, "intended for instruction and amusement" but decidedly moralistic and bland in comparison to the previous century's chapbooks; and *The Renowned History of Little Goody Two Shoes*, allegedly written by Oliver Goldsmith for a juvenile audience.

Eighteenth Century

Largely, eighteenth century adolescents were finding their reading pleasure in adult books: Daniel Defoe's *Robinson Crusoe*, Jonathan Swift's *Gulliver's Travels*, and Johann Wyss's *Swiss Family Robinson*. More books were being written for children, and moral didacticism, though less religious, was nevertheless ever present.

The short stories of Maria Edgeworth, the four-volume *The History of Sandford and Merton* by Thomas Day, and Martha Farquharson's twenty-six volume *Elsie Dinsmore* series dealt with pious protagonists who learned restraint, repentance, and rehabilitation from sin.

Two bright spots in this period of didacticism were Jean Jacques Rousseau's *Emile* and *The Tales of Shakespeare*, and Charles and Mary Lamb's simplified versions of Shakespeare's plays. Rousseau believed that a child's abilities were enhanced by a free, happy life, and the Lambs subscribed to the notion that children were entitled to entertaining literature written in language comprehensible to them.

Nineteenth Century

Child/adolescent literature truly began its modern rise in nineteenth century Europe. Hans Christian Andersen's *Fairy Tales* were fanciful adaptations of the somber revisions of the Grimm brothers in the previous century. Andrew Lang's series of colorful fairy books contain the folklores of many nations and are still part of the collections of many modern libraries. Clement Moore's "A Visit from St. Nicholas" is a cheery, non-threatening child's view of the night before Christmas. The humor of Lewis Carroll's books about Alice's adventures, Edward Lear's poems with caricatures, and Lucretia Nole's stories of the Philadelphia Peterkin family are full of fancy and not a smidgen of morality.

Other popular Victorian novels introduced the modern fantasy and science fiction genres: William Makepeace Thackeray's *The Rose and the Ring*, Charles Dickens' *The Magic Fishbone*, and Jules Verne's *Twenty Thousand Leagues Under the Sea*. Adventure to exotic places became a popular topic: Rudyard Kipling's *Jungle Books*, Verne's *Around the World in Eighty Days*, and Robert Louis Stevenson's *Treasure Island* and *Kidnapped*. In 1884, the first English translation of Johanna Spyri's *Heidi* appeared.

North America was also finding its voices for adolescent readers. American Louisa May Alcott's *Little Women* and Canadian L.M. Montgomery's *Anne of Green Gables* ushered in the modern age of realistic fiction. American youth were enjoying the adventures of Tom Sawyer and Huckleberry Finn. For the first time, children were able to read books about real people just like themselves.

Twentieth Century

The literature of the twentieth century is extensive and diverse and, as in previous centuries, much influenced by the adults who write, edit, and select books for youth consumption. In the first third of the century, suitable adolescent literature dealt with children from good homes with large families. These books projected an image of a peaceful, rural existence.

Though the characters and plots were more realistic, the stories maintained focus on topics that were considered emotionally and intellectually proper. Popular at this time

> For more information, read
> **Introductory Lecture on Children's**
> **& Adolescent Literature**
> http://homepages.wmich.edu/~tarboxg/
> Introductory_Lecture_on_Children's_&_Adol_Lit.html

were Laura Ingalls Wilder's *Little House on the Prairie* series and Carl Sandburg's biography *Abe Lincoln Grows Up*. English author J.R.R. Tolkein's fantasy, The Hobbit, prefaced modern adolescent readers' fascination with the works of Piers Antony, Madelaine L'Engle, and Anne McCaffery.

Adolescent Development

The social changes of post-World War II significantly affected adolescent literature. The Civil Rights movement, feminism, the protest of the Vietnam Conflict, and issues surrounding homelessness, neglect, teen pregnancy, drugs, and violence have bred a new vein of contemporary fiction that helps adolescents understand and cope with the world in which they live.

Popular books for preadolescents deal more with establishing relationships with members of the opposite sex (Sweet Valley High series) and learning to cope with their changing bodies, personalities, or life situations, as in Judy Blume's *Are You There, God? It's Me, Margaret*. Adolescents are still interested in the fantasy and science fiction genres as well as popular juvenile fiction. Middle school students still read the Little House on the Prairie series and the mysteries of the Hardy Boys and Nancy Drew.

Teens value the works of Emily and Charlotte Brontë, Willa Cather, Jack London, William Shakespeare, and Mark Twain as much as those of Piers Anthony, S.E. Hinton, Madeleine L'Engle, Stephen King, and J.R.R. Tolkein because they're fun to read whatever their underlying worth may be.

Older adolescents enjoy the writers in these genres.

Fantasy: Piers Anthony, Ursula LeGuin, Ann McCaffrey

Horror: V.C. Andrews, Stephen King

Juvenile Fiction: Judy Blume, Robert Cormier, Rosa Guy, Virginia Hamilton, S.E. Hinton, M.E. Kerr, Harry Mazer, Norma Fox Mazer, Richard Newton Peck, Cynthia Voight, and Paul Zindel.

Science Fiction: Isaac Asimov, Ray Bradbury, Arthur C. Clarke, Frank Herbert, Larry Niven, H.G. Wells.

Child Development Theories Influence on Literature

The studies by behaviorists and developmental psychologists in the late nineteenth and early twentieth affected the manner in which the education community and parents approached the selection of literature for children.

The cognitive development studies of Piaget, the epigenetic view of personality development by Erik Erikson, the formulation of Abraham Maslow's hierarchy of basic needs, and the social learning theory of behaviorists like Alfred

> Learn more about
> **Piaget's Cognitive Development**
> http://courses.dsu.edu/epsy330/
> theorists/cognitive.htm

Bandura contributed to a greater understanding of child/adolescent development even as these theorists contradicted each others' findings.

Though few educators today totally subscribe to Piaget's inflexible stages of mental development, his principles of both qualitative and quantitative mental capacity, his generalizations about the parallels between physical growth and thinking capacity, and his support of the adolescent's heightened moral perspective are still used as measures to evaluate child/adolescent literature.

Piaget's Four Stages of Mental Development:

Sensimotor intelligence (birth to age two) deals with the pre-language period of development. The child is most concerned with coordinating movement and action. Words begin to represent people and things.

Preoperational thought is the period spanning ages 2-12. It is broken into several substages.

- Preconceptual (2-4) phase—most behavior is based on subjective judgment.

- Intuitive (4-7) phase—children use language to verbalize their experiences and mental processes.

Concrete operations (7-11) occur when children begin to apply logic to concrete things and experiences. They can combine performance and reasoning to solve problems.

Formal operations (12-15) occur when adolescents begin to think beyond the immediate and to theorize. They apply formal logic to interpreting abstract constructions and to recognizing experiences that are contrary to fact.

Though Piaget presented these stages as progressing sequentially, a child might enter any period earlier or later than most children. Furthermore, a child might perform at different levels in different situations. Thus, a fourteen-year-old female might be able to function at the formal operations stage in a literature class but function at a concrete operations level in mathematical concepts.

Piaget's Theories Influence Literature

Most middle school students have reached the concrete operations level. By this time they have left behind their egocentrism for a need to understand the physical and social world around them. They become more interested in ways to relate to other people. Their favorite stories become those about real people rather than animals or fairy tale characters. The conflicts in their literature are internal as well as external.

Books like Paula Fox's *The Stone-Faced Boy*, Betsy Byards' *The Midnight Fox*, and Lois Lenski's *Strawberry Girl* deal with a child's loneliness, confusion about identity or loyalty, and poverty. Pre-adolescents are becoming more aware of and interested in the past, thus their love of adventure stories about national heroes like Davy Crockett, Daniel Boone, and Abe Lincoln and biographies and autobiographies of real life heroes, like Jackie Robinson and Cesar Chevas. At this level, children also become interested in the future—thus, their love of both fantasy (most medieval in spirit) and science fiction.

The seven- to eleven-year-olds also internalize moral values. They are concerned with their sense of self and are willing to question rules and adult authority. In books such as Beverly Cleary's *Henry Huggins* and *Mitch and Amy*, the protagonists are children pursuing their own desires with the same frustrations as other children. When these books were written in the 1960s, returning a found pet or overcoming a reading disability were common problems.

From twelve to fifteen, adolescents advance beyond the concrete operations level to begin developing communication skills that enable them to articulate attitudes and opinions and exchange knowledge. They can recognize and contrast historical fiction from pure history and biography. They can identify the elements of literature and their relationships within a specific story. As their thinking becomes more complex, early adolescents become more sensitive to others' emotions and reactions. They become better able to suspend their disbelief and enter the world of literature, thus expanding their perceptions of the real world.

In discussing the adolescent's moral judgment, Piaget noted that after age eleven, children stopped viewing actions as either "right" or "wrong." The older child considers both the intent and the behavior in its context. A younger child would view an accidental destruction of property in terms of the amount of damage. The older child would find the accident less wrong than minor damage done with intended malice.

Kohlberg's Theories of Moral Development

Expanding on Piaget's thinking, Lawrence Kohlberg developed a hierarchy of values. Though progressive, the stages of Kohlberg's hierarchy are not clearly aligned to chronological age. The six stages of development correlate to three levels of moral judgment.

Level I. Moral values reside in external acts rather than in persons or standards.

Stage 0. Premoral. No association of actions or needs with sense of right or wrong.

Stage 1. Obedience and punishment orientation. Child defers to adult authority. Child's actions are motivated by a desire to stay out of trouble.

Stage 2. Right action/self-interest orientation. Performance of right deeds results in needing satisfaction.

Level II. Moral values reside in maintaining conventions of right behavior.

> Stage 3. Good person orientation. The child performs right actions to receive approval from others, conforming to the same standards.

> Stage 4. Law and order orientation. Doing one's duty and showing respect for authority contributes to maintaining social order.

Level III. Moral values reside in principles separate in association from the persons or agencies that enforce these principles.

> Stage 5. Legalistic orientation. The rules of society are accepted as correct but alterable. Privileges and duties are derived from social contact. Obedience to society's rules protects the rights of self and others.

> Stage 6. Conscience orientation. Ethical standards, such as justice, equality, and respect for others, guide moral conduct more than legal rules.

Though these stages represent a natural progression of values to actions relationships, persons may regress to an earlier stage in certain situations. An adolescent already operating at Stage 5 may regress to Stage 3 in a classroom where consequences of non-conformity are met with disapproval or punishment.

An adult operating at Stage 6 may regress to Stage 4 when obligated by military training or confronted with a conflict between self-preservation and the protection of others.

Values clarification education based on Piaget's and Kohlberg's theories imply that development is inherent in human socialization. Becoming a decent person is a natural result of human development.

Social Learning Theory

Much of traditional learning theory resulted from the work of early behaviorists, like B. F. Skinner, and has been refined by modern theorists such as Albert Bandura. Behaviorists believe that intellectual, and therefore behavioral, development cannot be divided into specific stages. They believe that behavior is the result of conditioning experiences, a continuum of rewards and punishments. Environmental conditions are viewed as greater stimuli than inherent qualities. Thus in social learning theory the consequences of behavior—that is, the rewards or punishments—are more significant in social development than are the motivations for the behavior.

Bandura also proposed that a child learns vicariously through observing the behavior of others whereas the developmental psychologists presumed that children developed through the actual self-experience.

The Humanistic Theory of Development

No discussion of child development would be complete without a review of Abraham Maslow's hierarchy of needs, from basic physiological needs to the need for self-actualization. The following list represents those needs from the hierarchy that most affect children.

- **Need for Physical Wellbeing**. In young children the provisions for shelter, food, clothing, and protection by significant adults satisfy this need. In older children, this satisfaction of physical comforts translates to a need for material security and may manifest itself in struggles to overcome poverty and maintain the integrity of home and family.

- **Need for Love**. The presumption is that every human being needs to love and be loved. With young children, this reciprocal need is directed at and received from parents and other family members, pets, and friends. In older children and adolescents, this need for love forms the basis for romance and peer acceptance.

-
- **Need to Belong**. Beyond the need for one-on-one relationships, a child needs the security of being an accepted member of a group. Young children identify with family, friends, and schoolmates. They are concerned with having happy experiences and being accepted by people they love and respect. Later, they associate with community, country, and perhaps world groups. Adolescents become more aware of a larger world order and thus develop concerns about issues facing society, such as political or social unrest, wars, discrimination, and environmental issues. They seek to establish themselves with groups who accept and share their values. They become more team oriented.

- **Need to Achieve Competence**. A human's need to interact satisfactorily with his environment begins with the infant's exploration of the immediate surroundings. Visual and tactile identification of objects and persons provides confidence to perform further explorations. To become well adjusted, the child must achieve competence to feel satisfaction. Physical and intellectual achievements become measures of acceptance. Frustrations resulting from physical or mental handicaps are viewed as hurtles to be overcome if satisfaction is to be achieved. Older children view the courage-overcome obstacles as part of the maturing process.

- **Need to Know**. Curiosity is the basis of intelligence. The need to learn is persistent. To maintain intellectual security, children must be able to find answers to their questions in order to stimulate further exploration of information to satisfy that persistent curiosity.

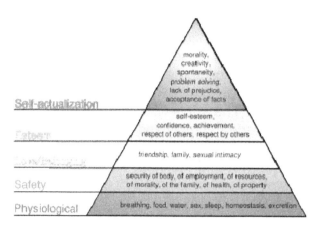

- **Need for Beauty and Order**. Aesthetic satisfaction is as important as the need for factual information. Intellectual stimulation comes from satisfying curiosity about the fine, as well as the practical, arts. Acceptance for one's accomplishments in dance, music, drawing, writing, performing or appreciating any of the arts leads to a sense of accomplishment and self-actualization.

Theory of Psychosocial Development

Erik Erikson, a follower of Sigmund Freud, presented the theory that human development consists of maturation through a series of psychosocial crisis. The struggle to resolve these crises helps a person achieve individuality as the person learns to function in society.

Maturation occurs as the individual moves through a progression of increasingly complex stages. The movement from one stage to the next hinges on the successful resolution of the conflicts encountered in each stage, and each of the stages represents a step in identity formation. Stage 1 (trust versus distrust), stage 2 (achieving autonomy), and stage 3 (developing initiative) relate to infants and young/middle children. Stages 4 and 5 relate to late childhood through adolescents.

Stage 4—**Becoming Industrious**. Late childhood, according to Erikson, occurs between seven to eleven. They have already mastered conflicts that helped them overcome mistrust of unfamiliar persons, places, and things; that made them more independent in caring for themselves and their possessions; and that overcame their sense of guilt at behavior that creates opposition with others. Now children are ready to assert themselves in suppressing feelings of inferiority. Children at this stage learn to master independent tasks as well as to work cooperatively with other children. They increasingly measure their own competence by comparing themselves to their peers.

Stage 5—**Establishing Identity**. From age eleven through the teen years, a person's conflicts arise from the search for identity, as an individual and a member of society. Because internal demands for independence and peer acceptance sometimes oppose external demands for conformity to rules and standards, friction with family, school, and society in general occur during these years. The adolescent must resolve issues such as the amount of control to concede to family and other rule-enforcing adults as the teen searches for other acceptance models. In the quest for self-identity, the teen experiments with adult behavior and attitudes. At the end of the teen years, this person should have a well established sense of identity.

Theory of Multiple Intelligences

Howard Gardner's research in the 1980s has been recently influential in helping teachers understand that human beings process information differently and, therefore, communicate their knowledge through different modes of operation. It is important to present language and literature in visual, auditory, tactile, and kinesthetic ways to allow every child to develop good skills through that child's own mode of learning. Then, the child alone must be allowed to perform through the strength of intelligence. The movement toward learning academies in the practical and fine arts and in the sciences is a result of our growing understanding of all aspects of child development.

Modern Society's Role in Child Development

Despite their differences, the theories of child development have many similarities. However, most of these theories were developed prior to the social unrest of the 1970s. In industrialized Western society, children are increasingly excluded from the activities of work and play with adults, and education has become their main occupation. This exclusion tends to prolong childhood and adolescents and thus inhibit development as visualized by theorists. For adolescents in America, this prolongs results in slower social and intellectual maturation contrasted to increasing physical maturity. Adolescents today deal with drugs, violence, communicable diseases, and a host of social problems that were of minimal concerns thirty years ago. Even pre-adolescent children are dealing with poverty, disease, broken homes, abuse, and drugs.

Influence of Theories on Literature

All of these development theories and existing social conditions influence the literature created and selected for and by child/adolescent readers.

Child/adolescent literature has always been to some degree didactic, whether nonfiction or fiction. Until the twentieth century, "kiddie" lit was also morally prescriptive. Written by adults who determined either what they believed children needed or liked or what they should need or like, most books, stories, poems, and essays dealt with experiences or issues that would make children into better adults. The fables, fairy tales, and epics of old set the moral and social standards of their times while entertaining the child in every reader/listener. These tales are still popular because they have a universal appeal. Except for the rare exceptions discussed earlier in this section, most books were written for literate adults. Educated children found their pleasure in the literature that was available.

Benefits of Research

One benefit of the child development and learning theory research is that they provide guidelines for writers, publishers, and educators to follow in the creation, marketing, and selection of good reading materials. MacMillan introduced children's literature as a separate publishing market in 1918. By the 1930s, most major publishers had a children's department. Though arguments have existed throughout this century about quality versus quantity, there is no doubt that children's literature is a significant piece of the publishing market.

Another influence is that children's books are a reflection of both developmental theories and social changes. Reading provides children with the opportunity to become more aware of societal differences, to measure their behavior against the behavior of realistic fictional characters or the subjects of biographies, to become informed about events of the past and present that will affect their futures, and to acquire a genuine appreciation of literature.

Furthermore, adults are obligated to provide instruction and entertainment that all children in our democratic society can use. Parents and educators have a further obligation to guide children in the selection of books that are appropriate to their reading ability and interest levels. Of course, there is a fine line between guidance and censorship. As with discipline, parents learn that to make forbidden is to make more desirable. To publish a list of banned books is to make them suddenly attractive. Most children and adolescents, left to their own selections, will choose books on topics that interest them and are written in language they can understand.

Impact of Research on Teachers

Adolescent literature, because of the age range of readers, is extremely diverse. Fiction for the middle group, usually ages ten/eleven to fourteen/fifteen, deals with issues of coping with internal and external changes in their lives. Because children's writers in the twentieth century have produced increasingly realistic fiction, adolescents can now find problems dealt with honestly in novels.

Teachers of middle/junior high school students see the greatest change in interests and reading abilities. Fifth and sixth graders, included in elementary grades in many schools, are viewed as older children while seventh and eighth graders are preadolescent.

Ninth graders included sometimes as upper tier in junior high school and sometimes as underlings in high school, definitely view themselves as teenagers. Their literature choices will often be governed more by interest than by ability—thus, the wealth of high-interest, low readability books that have flooded the market in recent years. Tenth through twelfth graders will still select high-interest books for pleasure reading but are also easily encouraged to stretch their literature muscles by reading more classics.

Because of the rapid social changes, topics that once did not interest young people until they reached their teens—suicide, gangs, and homosexuality—are now subjects of books for even younger readers. The plethora of high-interest books reveals how desperately schools have failed to produce on-level readers and how the market has adapted to that need.

However, these high-interest books are now readable for younger children whose reading levels are at or above normal. No matter how tastefully written, some contents are inappropriate for younger readers. The problem becomes not so much steering them toward books that they have the reading ability to handle but encouraging them toward books whose content is appropriate to their levels of cognitive and social development. A fifth-grader may be able to read V.C. Andrews book *Flowers in the Attic* but not possess the social or moral development to handle the deviant behavior of the characters.

At the same time, because of the complex changes affecting adolescents, the teacher must be well versed in learning theory and child development as well as competent to teach the subject matter of language and literature.

Skill 4.9 Identify a variety of appropriate methods for assessing the understanding of literature.

To assess student comprehension of reading materials, teachers employ a wide variety of diagnostic tools.

Skills to Evaluate

> Check out these
> **Online Resources for K-12 Teachers: Children's and Adolescent Literature**
> http://www.indiana.edu/~reading/ieo/digests/d149.html

- Ability to understand what is happening in a story.

- Ability to use more than one example or piece of information when responding to the reading.

- Ability to ask questions regarding the reading to show analytical thinking.

- Ability to make predictions based on information from the story or from personal experiences that are similar to events in the story.

- Ability to make clear and understandable connections between the literature and personal experiences as well as other literature the student has read.

Methods of Evaluation

- Have students keep reading journals that document their reactions to the literature they are reading.

- Assign both free writing exercises, in which they respond to any element of the story, as well as prompt-driven responses, in which they respond to a specified topic you assign. Make sure the prompts are created to get the students thinking deeply about the reading. An example might be, "Write about the main conflict in the story. Tell why it is so important and how it is solved."

- Ask that students back up any assertions or assumptions they make with evidence from the text. This clearly demonstrates their mental comprehension processes.

For Fifth and Sixth Grades

These classic and contemporary works combine the characteristics of multiple theories. Functioning at the concrete operations stage (Piaget), being of the "good person," orientation (Kohlberg), still highly dependent on external rewards (Bandura), and exhibiting all five needs previously discussed from Maslow's hierarchy, these eleven- to twelve-year-olds should appreciate the following titles, grouped by reading level. These titles are also cited for interest at that grade level and do not reflect high-interest titles for older readers who do not read at grade level. Some high interest titles will be cited later.

Reading Level 6.0 to 6.9

Barrett, William. *Lilies of the Field*
Cormier, Robert. *Other Bells for Us to Ring*
Dahl, Roald. *Danny, Champion of the World; Charlie and the Chocolate Factory*
Lindgren, Astrid. *Pippi Longstocking*
Lindbergh, Anne. *Three Lives to Live*
Lowry, Lois. *Rabble Starkey*
Naylor, Phyllis. *The Year of the Gopher, Reluctantly Alice*
Peck, Robert Newton. *Arly*
Speare, Elizabeth. *The Witch of Blackbird Pond*
Sleator, William. *The Boy Who Reversed Himself*

For Seventh and Eighth Grades

Most seventh and eight grade students, according to learning theory, are still functioning cognitively, psychologically, and morally as sixth graders. As these are not inflexible standards, some twelve- and thirteen-year-olds are much more mature socially, intellectually, and physically than the younger children who share the same school. They are becoming concerned with establishing individual and peer group identities that presents conflicts with breaking from authority and the rigidity of rules. Some at this age are still tied firmly to the family and its expectations while others identify more with those their own age or older.

Enrichment reading for this group must help them cope with life's rapid changes or provide escape and thus must be either realistic or fantastic depending on the child's needs. Adventures and mysteries (the Hardy Boys and Nancy Drew series) are still popular today. These preteens also become more interested in biographies of contemporary figures rather than legendary figures of the past.

Reading Level 7.0 to 7.9
Armstrong, William. *Sounder*
Bagnold, Enid. *National Velvet*
Barrie, James. *Peter Pan*
London, Jack. *White Fang, Call of the Wild*
Lowry, Lois. *Taking Care of Terrific*
McCaffrey, Anne. *The Dragonsinger* series
Montgomery, L. M. *Anne of Green Gables* and sequels
Steinbeck, John. *The Pearl*
Tolkien, J. R. R. *The Hobbit*
Zindel, Paul. *The Pigman*

Reading Level 8.0 to 8.9
Cormier, Robert. *I Am the Cheese*
McCullers, Carson. *The Member of the Wedding*
North, Sterling. *Rascal*
Twain, Mark. *The Adventures of Tom Sawyer*
Zindel, Paul. *My Darling, My Hamburger*

For Ninth Grade
Depending upon the school environment, ninth graders may be the rank the highest in a junior high school or the lowest in a high school. Much of their social development and thus their reading interests become motivated by peer associations. They are technically adolescents operating at the early stages of formal operations in cognitive development. Their perceptions of their own identities are becoming well-defined, and they are fully aware of the ethics required by society. Ninth graders are more receptive to the challenges of classic literature but still enjoy popular teen novels.

Reading Level 9.0 to 9.9
Brown, Dee. *Bury My Heart at Wounded Knee*
Defoe, Daniel. *Robinson Crusoe*
Dickens, Charles. *David Copperfield*
Greenberg, Joanne. *I Never Promised You a Rose Garden*
Kipling, Rudyard. *Captains Courageous*
Mathabane, Mark. *Kaffir Boy*
Nordhoff, Charles. *Mutiny on the Bounty*
Shelley, Mary. *Frankenstein*
Washington, Booker T. *Up From Slavery*

For Tenth to Twelfth Grades

All high school sophomores, juniors and seniors can handle almost all other literature except for a few of the very most difficult titles like *Moby Dick* or *Vanity Fair*. However, since many high school students do not progress to the eleventh or twelfth grade reading level, they will still have their favorites among authors whose writings they can understand. Many will struggle with assigned novels but still read high interest books for pleasure. A few high interest titles are listed below without reading level designations, though most are 6.0 to 7.9.

Bauer, Joan. *Squashed*
Borland, Hal. *When the Legends Die*
Danzinger, Paula. *Remember Me to Harold Square*
Duncan, Lois. *Stranger with My Face*
Hamilton, Virginia. *The Planet of Junior Brown*
Hinton, S. E. *The Outsiders*
Paterson, Katherine. *The Great Gilly Hopkins*

COMPETENCY 5.0   KNOWLEDGE OF LISTENING, VIEWING, AND SPEAKING AS METHODS FOR ACQUIRING CRITICAL LITERACY

Skill 5.1   Identify effective speaking skills for various occasions, audiences, and purposes.

Different Methods of Oral Communication

Different from the basic writing forms of discourse is the art of **debating, discussion, and conversation**. The ability to use language and logic to convince the audience to accept your reasoning and to side with you is an art. This form of writing/speaking is extremely confined or structured, and logically sequenced with supporting reasons and evidence. At its best, it is the highest form of propaganda. A position statement, evidence, reason, evaluation and refutation are integral parts of this writing schema.

> Learn more about
> **Oral Communication Skills**
> http://www.glencoe.com/sec/teachingtoday/weeklytips.phtml/88

Interviewing provides opportunities for students to apply expository and informative communication. It teaches them how to structure questions to evoke fact-filled responses. Compiling the information from an interview into a biographical essay or speech helps students list, sort, and arrange details in an orderly fashion.

Speeches that encourage them to describe persons, places, or events in their own lives or oral interpretations of literature help them sense the creativity and effort used by professional writers.

Useful resources

Price, Brent. *Basic Composition Activities Kit* provides practical suggestions and student guide sheets for use in the development of student writing.

Simmons, John S., R.E. Shafer, and Gail B. West. (1976). *Decisions About The Teaching of English - "Advertising, or Buy It, You'll Like It."* Allyn & Bacon.

Additional resources may be found in the library, social studies, economic, debate and journalism textbooks and locally published newspapers.

Delivery Techniques

As a teacher, you recognize the importance of delivering your message. While written communications is discussed in later sections, let's consider oral communications now. Instruct your students on the ways that verbal and non-verbal communication can affect the way a presentation is understood. You can model these techniques.

Posture: Maintain a straight, but not stiff posture. Instead of shifting weight from hip to hip, point your feet directly at the audience and distribute your weight evenly. Keep shoulders towards the audience. If you have to turn your body to use a visual aid, turn 45 degrees and continue speaking towards the audience.

Movement: Instead of staying glued to one spot or pacing back and forth, stay within four to eight feet of the front row of your audience. Take a step or half-step to the side every once in a while. If you are using a lectern, feel free to move to the front or side of it to engage your audience more. Avoid distancing yourself from the audience; you want them to feel involved and connected.

Gestures: Gestures can maintain a natural atmosphere when speaking publicly. Use them just as you would when speaking to a friend. They shouldn't be exaggerated, but they should be used for added emphasis. Avoid keeping your hands in your pockets or locked behind your back, wringing your hands and fidgeting nervously, or keeping your arms crossed.

Eye Contact: Many people are intimidated by using eye contact when speaking to large groups. Interestingly, eye contact usually *helps* the speaker overcome speech anxiety by connecting with the attentive audience and easing feelings of isolation. Instead of looking at a spot on the back wall or at your notes, scan the room and make eye contact for one to three seconds per person.

In addition to the content of your presentation, you want to use a strong delivery. As with most skills, the key is practice, practice, practice. Record and play back your presentation to hear how you sound.

Voice: Many people fall into one of two traps when speaking: using a monotone or talking too fast. These are both caused by anxiety. A monotone restricts your natural inflection but can be remedied by releasing tension in upper and lower body muscles. Subtle movement will keep you loose and natural.

| Learn more about |
| **Using Your Voice** |
| http://www.longview.k12.wa.us/mmhs /wyatt/pathway/voice.html |

Talking too fast, on the other hand, is not necessarily bad if you are exceptionally articulate. If you are not a strong speaker or if you are talking about very technical items, the audience will easily become lost.

When you talk too fast and begin tripping over your words, consciously pause after every sentence you say. Don't be afraid of brief silences. The audience needs time to absorb what you are saying.

Volume: Problems with volume, whether too soft or too loud, can usually be overcome with practice. If you tend to speak too softly, have someone stand in the back of the room and signal you when your volume is strong enough. If possible, have someone in the front of the room as well to make sure you're not overcompensating with excessive volume.

Conversely, if you have a problem with speaking too loud, have the person in the front of the room signal you when your voice is soft enough and check with the person in the back to make sure it is still loud enough to be heard. In both cases, note your volume level for future reference. Don't be shy about asking your audience, "Can you hear me in the back?" Suitable volume is beneficial for both you and the audience.

Pitch: Pitch refers to the length, tension, and thickness of your person's vocal bands. As your voice gets higher, the pitch gets higher. In oral performance, pitch reflects the emotional arousal level. More variation in pitch typically corresponds to more emotional arousal but can also be used to convey sarcasm or highlight specific words.

While these skills are essential for you to be an effective teacher, you want your students to develop these techniques as well. By encouraging the development of proper techniques for oral presentations, you are enabling your students to develop self-confidence for higher levels of communication.

Guidelines for Assessing your Audience

Now that you know your purpose and have the information, you need to assess your audience. What does your audience know and what does it need to know? Here are some questions to consider.

Values: What is important to this group of people? What is their background and how will that affect their perception of your speech?

Needs: Find out in advance what the audience's needs are. Why are they listening to you? Find a way to satisfy their needs.

Constraints: What might hold the audience back from being fully engaged in what you are saying, or agreeing with your point of view, or processing what you are trying to say? These could be political reasons, which make them wary of your presentation's ideology from the start, or knowledge reasons, in which the audience lacks the appropriate background information to grasp your ideas.

Avoid this last constraint by staying away from technical terminology, slang, or abbreviations that may be unclear to your audience.

Demographic Information: Take the audience's size into account as well as the location of the presentation. Demographics could include age, gender, education, religion, income level and other such countable characteristics.

Start where the listeners are, and then take them where you want to go!

Skill 5.2 **Identify effective strategies and techniques for listening.**

Listening

Communication skills are crucial in a collaborative society. In particular, a person cannot be a successful communicator without being an active listener.

Focus on what others say, rather than planning on what to say next. By listening to everything another person is saying, you may pick up on natural cues that lead to the next conversation move without so much added effort.

Reasons to Improve Listening Skills
To avoid saying the wrong thing, being tactless
To dissipate strong feelings
To learn to accept feelings (yours and others)
To generate a feeling of caring
To help people start listening to you
To increase the other person's confidence in you
To make the other person feel important and recognized
To be sure you both are on the same wavelength
To be sure you both are focused on the same topic
To check that you are both are on target with one another
http://www.coping.org/dialogue/listen.htm

Skill 5.3 **Determine appropriate methods and strategies to analyze persuasive techniques used to convey messages in mass media.**

The art of rhetoric was first developed in Ancient Greece. Its pioneer was Socrates, who recognized the crucial role that rhetoric played in education, politics, and story telling. Socrates argued that, presently effectively, speech could evoke any desired emotion or opinion. His method of dialectic syllogism, known today as the Socratic Method,

Check out more
Strategies for Developing Listening Skills
http://www.nclrc.org/essentials/ listening/stratlisten.htm

pursued truth through a series of questions. Socrates established three types of appeals used in persuasive speech:

Types of Appeal

Ethos: Refers to the credibility of the speaker. It establishes the speaker as a reliable and trustworthy authority by focusing on the speaker's credentials.

Pathos: Refers to the emotional appeal made by the speaker to the listeners. It emphasizes the fact that the audience responds to ideas with emotion. For example, when the government is trying to persuade citizens to go to war for the sake of "the fatherland," it is using the appeal to pathos to target their love of their country.

Logos: Refers to the logic of the speaker's argument. It uses the idea that facts, statistics, and other forms of evidence can convince an audience to accept a speaker's argument. Remember that information can be just as, if not more, persuasive than appeal tactics.

Today, rhetoric's evolution can be traced back to ancient Athens in many facets of our society. The structure of many governments and judicial systems reflect rhetorical tactics established by the Greeks so long ago. The media has taken rhetoric to a whole new level and has refined it to a very skilled art. Every word as well as the method of presentation is carefully planned. The audience is taken into account and speech tailored to their needs and motivations. Though the content has changed, this concept has been around since Socrates contemplated it thousands of years ago.

Advertising Techniques

Because students are very interested in the types of approaches advertisers use, you can develop high-interest assignments requiring them to analyze commercial messages. What is powerful about Nike's "Just Do It" campaign? What is the appeal of Jessica Simpson's eponymous perfume?

Beauty Appeal: Beauty attracts us; we are drawn to beautiful people, places, and things.

Celebrity Endorsement: This technique associates product use with a well-known person. By purchasing this product we are led to believe that we will attain characteristics similar to the celebrity.

Compliment the Consumer: Advertisers flatter the consumer who is willing to purchase their product. By purchasing the product the consumer is recognized by the advertisers for making a good decision with the selection.

Escape: Getting away from it all is very appealing; you can imagine adventures you cannot have; the idea of escape is pleasurable.

Independence/Individuality: This technique associates product with people who can think and act for themselves. Products are linked to individual decision making.

Intelligence: This technique associates product with smart people who can't be fooled.

Lifestyle: This technique associates product with a particular style of living/way of doing things.

Nurture: Every time you see an animal or a child, the appeal is to your paternal or maternal instincts, so this technique associates products with taking care of someone.

Peer Approval: This technique associates product use with friendship/acceptance. Advertisers can also use this negatively to make you worry that you'll lose friends if you don't use a certain product.

Rebel: This technique associates products with behaviors or lifestyles that oppose society's norms.

Rhetorical Question: This technique poses a question to the consumer that demands a response. A question is asked and the consumer is supposed to answer in such a way that affirms the product's goodness.

Scientific/Statistical Claim: This provides some sort of scientific proof or experiment, very specific numbers, or an impressive sounding mystery ingredient.

Unfinished Comparison/Claim: This technique uses phrases such as "Works better in poor driving conditions!" Works better than what?

Deductive and Inductive Reasoning

The two forms of reasoning to support an argument are *inductive* or *deductive.* Inductive reason goes from the particular to the general. In other words, I observe that all the green apples I have ever tasted are sour. 1) I have tasted some from my grandfather's orchard, 2) I have tasted the Granny Smiths that my mother buys in the grocery store and makes pies from, 3) I taste the green apples in my friend's kitchen. (All particular instances or bits of evidence.) All are sour (conclusion). Then I can *generalize* that all green apples are sour. This is inductive reasoning, a very prevalent aspect of the way we think and deal with each other and essential to persuasive discourse.

Deductive reasoning, on the other hand, reverses the order by going from general to particular. The generalization drawn in the previous illustration, "All green apples are sour" can be used to make a statement about

Learn more about
Deductive and Inductive Argument
http://www.iep.utm.edu/d/ded-ind.htm

a particular apple. A new variety of green apples has appeared in the grocery store. Arguing from the generalization that all green apples are sour, I may reject this new variety because I am sure that they are going to be sour. Deductive reasoning is based on the syllogism:

All green apples are sour.
This apple is green.
Therefore, this apple is sour.

When a prosecutor presents a trial in a courtroom, he typically puts forth the statement of fact: On November 2 in an alley between Smith and Jones Street at the 400 block, Stacy Highsmith was brutally raped and murdered. The coroner has concluded that she was bludgeoned with a blunt instrument at or around midnight and her body was found by a shopkeeper the next morning. (There may be other "knowns" presented in the statement of fact.)

Following the laying out of the facts of the case, the prosecutor will use inductive reasoning (a series of particulars) to accuse the person on trial for the crime. For example, Terry Large, the accused, 1) was seen in the neighborhood at 11:30 p.m. on November 2. 2) He was carrying a carpenter's tool kit, which was later recovered, and 3) a hammer with evidence of blood on it was found in that tool kit. 4) The blood was tested and it matched the victim's DNA. (All particulars leading to a conclusion.) Ultimately, the prosecutor will reach the generalization: Terry Large murdered Stacy Highsmith in the alley in the middle of the night on November 2.

Skill 5.4 Analyze media messages to interpret meaning, method, and intent.

More money is spent each year on advertising to children than educating them. Thus, the media's strategies are considerably well thought out and effective. They employ large, clear letters, bold colors, simple line drawings, and popular symbols to announce upcoming events, push ideas and advertise products. By using attractive photographs, brightly colored cartoon characters, or instructive messages, they increase sales, win votes, or stimulate learning. The graphics are designed to communicate messages clearly, precisely, and efficiently. Some even target subconscious yearnings for sex and status.

Because so much effort is being spent on influencing students through media tactics, just as much effort should be devoted to educating those students about media awareness. A teacher should explain that artists and the aspects they choose to portray as well as the ways in which they portray them reflect their attitude and understanding of those aspects. The artistic choices are not entirely based on creative license—they also reflect an embedded meaning the artist wants to represent. Colors, shapes, and positions are meant to arouse basic instincts for food, sex, and status, and are often used to sell cars, clothing, or liquor.

To stimulate analysis of media strategies, ask students questions such as:

- Where/when do you think this picture was taken/film was shot/piece was written?

- Would you like to have lived at this time in history, or in this place?

- What objects are present?

- What do the people presented look like? Are they happy or sad?

- Who is being targeted?

- What can you learn from this piece of media?

- Is it telling you something is good or bad?

- What message is being broadcasted?

Skill 5.5 Evaluate the elements, uses and effects of media.

Media's impact on today's society is immense and ever increasing. As children, we watch programs on television that are amazingly fast-paced and visually rich. Parents' roles as verbal and moral teachers are diminishing in response to the much

> Learn more about
> **Integrating Technology
> in the Classroom**
> http://www.glencoe.com/sec/
> teachingtoday/tiparchive.phtml/3

more stimulating guidance of the television set. Adolescence, which used to be the time for going out and exploring the world first hand, is now consumed by the allure of MTV, popular music, and video games. Young adults are exposed to uncensored sex and violence.

But media's effect on society is beneficial and progressive at the same time. Its effect on education in particular provides special challenges and opportunities for teachers and students.

Thanks to satellite technology, urban classrooms and rural villages can receive instructional radio and television programs. CD-ROMs enable students to learn information through a virtual reality experience. The Internet allows instant access to unlimited data and connects people across all cultures through shared interests. Educational media, when used in a productive way, enriches instruction and makes it more individualized, accessible, and economical.

Aesthetic Effects of a Media Presentation

- Use of moving pictures and video to document events
- Use of sound clips in addition to written text
- Use of music/sound effects not printed in text
- Links to other web resources and to other archived articles

A common classroom assignment that applies to this skill is to view the movie version of a book studied by a particular class, to compare and contrast the two media, and to argue which did the better job of conveying the intended message(s).

It is difficult to convey the same message across different media because of the dynamics specific to those media. The degree of difficulty increases as the complexity of the message does. Nonetheless, certain general observations inform the discussion.

Check out the
**Language of Media Literacy:
A Glossary of Terms**
http://www.medialit.org/reading_room/
article565.html

A print message has two kinds of unique features. Some seem to be positive. For instance, print messages have longevity; they are also easily portable. Print messages appeal almost exclusively to the mind and enable students to recursively read sections that warrant more thought. Other features of print seem potentially negative. For instance, a print message requires an active reader; without such a reader, print messages are not very effective. Print messages are not accessible to non-readers.

A graphic message in the hands of an artistic genius can produce images that seem to be Jungian archetypes. More commonly, a graphic message gives a quick overview of some quantifiable situation. Some learners find that graphic information works for them better than print, and many struggling readers find graphic messages more helpful, too. However, compared to print, graphic messages convey a much shorter range of information. If the particular graphic is inspiring, the inspirations it conveys are subject to the descriptions of the various readers who view it. With print, the inspired scripts are already there for the reader, provided the reader is applying active reading skills.

An audio message allows for messages delivered with attention to prosody. Students who can't read can access the material. Audio messages invite the listener to form mental images consistent with the topic of the audio. Audio messages allow the learners to close their eyes for better mental focus. Listening to an audio message is a more passive modality than reading a print message. As a rule, people read faster than normal speech patterns, so print conveys more information in a given time span.

An audiovisual message offers the easiest accessibility for learners. It has the advantages of each, the graphic and the audio, medium. Learners' eyes and ears are engaged. Non-readers get significant access to content. On the other hand, viewing an audiovisual presentation is an even more passive activity than listening to an audio message because information is coming to learners effortlessly through two senses. Activities to foster a critical perspective on an audiovisual presentation serve as valuable safeguards against any overall and unwelcome passivity.

Skill 5.6 Identify a variety of methods for assessing listening, viewing, and speaking.

For the benefit of the students, you will want to evaluate the proficiency of their listening, viewing, and speaking skills. With constructive feedback from you, they will be proud of those areas they have mastered and identify the specific areas that need improvement.

You can evaluate them holistically with a score that encompasses the entire activity or you can use a rubric, such as the one below from the Utah Education Network, to analyze a more specific range of skills.

LISTENING SKILLS RUBRIC
EXCELLENT—5. The student is attentive, courteous and sensitive to the ideas, tone and purpose of the presentation; intellectual curiosity, attention to the task, and sensitivity to others help to create a productive climate in and for the group.
PROFICIENT—4. The student is attentive and courteous; purposefully and confidently listens to the presentation.
SATISFACTORY—3. The student is courteous and willing to listen to others; accepts ideas of others.
LIMITED—2. The student is easily distracted; lacks confidence to receive ideas easily and clearly; may use language, tone, or nonverbal behavior inappropriate for the occasion; is an insecure member of the group.
POOR—1. The student is uninvolved in the activity and lacks courtesy.

Another evaluation method is a student-managed assessments such as a checklist. Distributed with the assignment, students are aware of the expectations. Both the student and the teacher can use this checklist to monitor and evaluate progress.

Student portfolios, one-on-one assessment interviews, and national proficiency tests are other methods.

Facilitating Conversation

It is quite acceptable to use standard opening lines to facilitate a conversation. Don't agonize trying to come up with witty "one-liners" as the main obstacle in initiating conversation is just getting the first statement over with. After that, the real substance begins. A useful technique may be to make a comment or ask a question about a shared situation. This may be anything from the weather to the food you are eating to a new policy at work. Use an opener you are comfortable with because your partner in conversation will be comfortable with it as well.

Stimulating Higher Level Critical Thinking Through Inquiry

Many people rely on questions to communicate with others. However, most fall back on simple clarifying questions rather than open-ended inquiries. For example, if you paraphrase a response by asking "Did you mean this…" you may receive merely a "yes" or "no" answer. On open-ended inquiry would ask "What did you mean when you said…?"

Try to ask open-ended, deeper-level questions since those tend to have the greatest reward and lead to a greater understanding. With answers to those questions, you can make more complex connections and achieve more significant information.

The successful conversationalist is a person who keeps up with what's going on in the world and ponders the meanings of events and developments. That person also usually reads about the interesting topics, both in print and online. In addition, the effective conversationalist has probed certain areas some depth. An interest in human behavior is usually one of this person's most particular interests. Why do people behave as they do? Why do some succeed and some fail? This person will also be interested in and concerned about social issues, particularly in the immediate community but also on a wider scale and will have ideas for solving some of those problems.

Skill 5.7 **Select appropriate technological resources for instructional purposes.**

The use of technology has broadened and enriched the entire communication process. Teachers and students who learn to use these resources effectively will expand their capabilities inside and outside the classroom.

Multimedia refers to a technology for presenting material in both visual and verbal forms. This format is especially conducive to the classroom, since it reaches both visual and auditory learners.

Knowing how to select effective teaching software is the first step in efficient multi-media education. First, decide what you need the software for (creating spreadsheets, making diagrams, or creating slideshows). Consult magazines such as *Popular Computing, PC World, MacWorld,* and *Multimedia World* to learn about the newest programs available.

Go to a local computer store and ask a customer service representative to help you find the exact media you need. If possible, test the programs you are interested in. Check reviews in magazines such as *Consumer Reports, PCWorld, Electronic Learning* or *Multimedia Schools* to ensure the software's quality.

Software Programs for Producing Teaching Material
- Adobe
- CorelDRAW!
- Claris Works
- Harvard Graphics
- Microsoft Word
- Aldus Freehand
- DrawPerfect
- PC Paintbrush
- Visio
- Microsoft Power Point

Requiring extensive revision in writing classrooms nowadays is not unreasonable and can be an important stage in the production of papers. Microsoft Word has had a "tracking" capability in its last several upgrades, which carries revision a step further. Now the teacher and student can carry on a dialogue on the paper itself. The teacher's deletions and additions can be tracked, the student can respond, and the tracking will be facilitated by automatically putting the changes in a different color. The "comment" function makes it possible for both teacher and student to write notes at the exactly relevant point in the manuscript.

While a spelling checker is an appropriate first step, students should be reminded that they should not rely solely on spell checkers for proofreading. Noted for their failure to understand context, spell checkers will not help with incorrect homonyms or typos.

Tips for Creating Visual Media

- Limit your graph to just one idea or concept
- Keep the content simple and concise (avoid too many lines, words, or pictures)
- Balance substance and visual appeal
- Make sure the text is large enough for the class to read
- Match the information to the format that will fit it best

COMPETENCY 6.0   KNOWLEDGE OF THE METHODS FOR INTEGRATION OF THE LANGUAGE ARTS

Skill 6.1   Identify methods of integrating language arts.

The last twenty years have seen great change in instruction in the English classroom. Gone are the days when literature is taught on Monday, grammar is taught on Wednesday, and writing is assigned on Friday. Integrating reading, writing, speaking, listening and viewing enables students to make connections between each aspect of language development during each class.

Suggestions for Integrating Language Arts

- Use prereading activities such as discussion, writing, research, and journals. Use writing to tap into prior knowledge before students read; engage students in class discussions about themes, issues, and ideas explored in journals, predicting the outcome and exploring related information.

- Use prewriting activities such as reading model essays, researching, interviewing others, combining sentences and other prewriting activities. Remember that developing language proficiency is a recursive process and involves practice in reading, writing, thinking, speaking, listening and viewing.

- Create writing activities that are relevant to students by having them write and share with real audiences.

- Connect correctness—including developing skills of conventional usage, spelling, grammar, and punctuation—to the revision and editing stage of writing. Review of mechanics and punctuation can be done with mini-lessons that use sentences from student papers, sentence combining strategies, and modeling passages of skilled writers.

- Connect reading, writing, listening, speaking, and viewing by using literature read as a springboard for a variety of activities.

Skill 6.2   Identify elements of cooperative learning, including grouping strategies, group interactions, and collaboration.

Research shows that students who work together in groups or teams develop their skills in organization, leadership, research, communication, and problem solving. Working in teams can help students overcome anxiety in distance learning courses and contribute a sense of community and belonging for the students.

What Is Cooperative/Collaborative Learning?

Research shows that when students work together in small groups they tend to learn more material and retain the information longer than when the same information is taught using different methods. The process used in both cooperative and collaborative learning is that students work in groups or teams to reach a goal. Cooperative and collaborative discussions actively involve the students interacting with faculty, other students, and the material in meaningful ways. Providing opportunities for students to communicate with each other what they are learning in an online environment is one highly effective way to engage students in the active learning process.

Some collaborative or cooperative learning strategies include the following:

- **Panel discussion:** A panel/group of students is given a set of questions from which they prepare a group response.

- **Case study:** A group of students is given a narrative description of a problematic situation and then asked to identify and/or solve the problem.

- **Action maze:** A group of students is given a description of an incident that requires analysis and action. They provide a brief response and then forward it to another group. The group that received that response must determine the consequences of the first group's response and either agree or come up with a better response. This process can go on through as many levels as the instructor feels is meaningful.

- **Role-playing:** A team of students is asked to take on the parts of characters in a dramatic representation of a real situation or organizational unit. Role-playing can take place in a chat room or via bulletin board response to questions. Students respond as their character would respond throughout the planned dialog.

- **Students as teachers:** A group of students develops the presentation of a course topic for the rest of the class, perhaps posing one or more interesting questions for class discussion.

- **Formal debate:** Students are divided into teams to present opposing viewpoints; some students may act as respondents or judges.

- **Writing groups:** Students present drafts of written assignments to one another for critique and then revise their drafts based on other student comments.

Group Interactions

Assign a student in each group a specific role he/she will take on for the duration of the activity:

- Leader—the leader directs the action for the day once the teacher has given the instructions.

- Recorder—this group member does the writing for the entire group; he or she uses one sheet, which saves paper.

- Encourager—the encourager gives compliments related to how the group is working, such as "That was a great answer!"

- Checker—this member checks and hands in the work for the group.

Collaboration

- Students decide on goals and the means to accomplish those goals.

- Students decide which roles to play to reach goals.

- Students practice negotiation and social skills and evaluate both their own contributions and those of the other group members.

- Students learn to collaborate and reinforce one another's strengths and observe that people with different strengths may accomplish goals differently or more efficiently.

A good activity to enforce the importance of collaboration breaks the students into groups of four. They use a problem-solving plan and work together during class time as well as outside of class. A recent problem: Would it be cheaper to get to New York City from Long Island by car, bus, or plane? The students show their plans and all their work for each mode of transportation so there are no questions about their answers. The groups may have a little trouble getting started and getting all parties involved, but the outcome will ensure improved cooperation skills as well as real world training.

Skill 6.3   Identify appropriate interdisciplinary activities.

Ideas for Interdisciplinary Classroom Activities:

- Have students produce a newspaper that incorporates many different subject areas (sports, weather, crossword puzzles, books reviews, pictures, poetry, advertisements).

-

- Connect each student with an "adoptive grandparent" at a nearby nursing home. Have students write their "grandparent" letters and stories, make timelines of their lives, and learn about life during the time they grew up in.

- Have students create a PowerPoint presentation on a career they are interested in pursuing. Research pros and cons, salary information, skills necessary for the job.

- Using a book the class is reading as a whole, have students pick out any words they are unfamiliar with. Research the origin of those words, their definitions, and then have them write a creative story using each word.

Skill 6.4   Identify various elements of an integrated lesson.

Gone are the days when students engage in skill practice with grammar worksheets. Grammar needs to be taught in the context of the students' own work. Listed below is a series of classroom practices that encourage meaningful context-based grammar instruction, combined with occasional mini-lessons and other language strategies that can be used on a daily basis.

- Connect grammar with the student's own writing while emphasizing grammar as a significant aspect of effective writing.

- Emphasize the importance of editing and proofreading as an essential part of classroom activities.

- Provide students with an opportunity to practice editing and proofreading cooperatively.

- Give instruction in the form of 15-20 minute mini-lessons.

- Emphasize the sound of punctuation by connecting it to pitch, stress, and pause.

- Involve students in all facets of language learning including reading, writing, listening, speaking and thinking. Good use of language comes from exploring all forms of it on a regular basis.

Try a variety of activities that involve grammar instruction in the context of the writing.

Sentence Combining: Try to use the student's own writing as much as possible. Emphasize the theory behind combining ideas and the correct punctuation.

Sentence and Paragraph Modeling: Provide students with the opportunity to practice imitating the style and syntax of professional writers.

Sentence Transforming: Give students an opportunity to change sentences from one form to another, i.e. from passive to active, inverting the sentence order, change forms of the words used.

Daily Language Practice: Introduce or clarify common errors using daily language activities. Use actual student examples whenever possible. Correct and discuss the problems with grammar and usage.

COMPETENCY 7.0   ABILITY TO WRITE WELL ON A SELECTION FROM POETRY OR PROSE, INCLUDING FICTION OR NONFICTION

Skill 7.1   Analyze a given selection.

Studying literature requires more student involvement than traditional discussion/lecture processes have allowed. Literature, whether fiction, non-fiction, poetry, or drama, should not be studied for comprehension alone nor should detailed analyses of the elements of literature be an end in themselves. Literature is to be experienced if it is to be appreciated. Having students write about literature provides an avenue for self-expression and critical analysis.

Teaching Strategy: Reading/Discussion

Reading, whether aloud or silently, evokes responses that can be verbalized. For young or below grade level readers, some sight reading may be necessary. This should be done in small groups of two or three without teacher intervention. Students should feel free to discuss the text as they read.

Most high school students should be able to participate in small group discussions of literature that has been read outside of class. During silent or at-home reading, the students should take notes of key elements as they read to enable them to contribute to subsequent discussions.

Teacher-guided discussion should transpire only after students have had a chance to think through the elements of the literature that they are studying. Teacher-led discussions should evolve from student responses to the reading not from preconceived interpretations by the teacher or recognized critics. Perceptive assessment of student comments will lead to questioning that probes the student's personal reactions and can ultimately be as analytical as any discussion the teacher might have planned.

Rather than involving the whole class, which favors the loquacious and inhibits the shy, let the students get into four or five discussion groups. After the initial discussion, combine two groups to share their reactions.

Skill 7.2   Demonstrate the ability to organize ideas around a focal point.

In teaching students to write about literature, you can provide them with the basic skills they will need for any writing activity.

General Strategies for Writing an Essay

The strategies below which apply to your own experience in writing essays for the certification exam can be adapted for your students.

- Budget your time. You will not have time to revise your essay. It is important that you write a good first draft.

- Read the question carefully. Make sure you understand what the question is asking you to do.

- Review basic literary terms.

- Take time to pre-write.

- Write a thesis statement by restating the question.

- Keep your purpose in mind as you write your essay.

- Connect the ideas of your essay in a brief conclusion.

- Leave enough time to quickly proofread and edit your essay.

The essay that you are to write must demonstrate the ability to write on a literary topic. As you practice the steps provided to prepare for this test, please keep in mind that this review will not teach you how to analyze literature. It is expected that analyzing literature has been a focus of your course of study. The following steps in writing an essay in a timed situation will aid you in preparing to write the essay in the most time efficient manner possible. Keep in mind that a good essay has focus, organization, support, and correct usage.

Understanding the Question

When you receive your question, the first thing you need to do is decide what the question is asking you to do. Look for key words that will establish the purpose of your essay. Examine the following chart and review the key words and purpose each word establishes. Please note that for each key word the purpose and an example are illustrated.

KEY WORD	PURPOSE	EXAMPLE
Analyze	To examine the parts of a literary selection	Read a passage and analyze how the author achieves tone using diction and imagery
Compare	To identify the similarities	Read "I Hear America Singing" by Walt Whitman and "Chicago" by Carl Sandburg and compare each poet's attitude about America.
Contrast	To identify the differences	Read "Thanatopsis" by Bryant and "Do Not Go Gentle Into That Good Night" by Dylan Thomas and contrast how each poet uses imagery to express his distinct views of death.
Discuss	Examine in detail	Read a poem and discuss how the poet establishes the mood using imagery and word choice.
Explain	Provide reasons, examples or clarify the meaning	Read the opening passage of *The Great Gatsby* and explain how the author establishes the tone of the novel.

When writing an essay on literature, consider the following before you begin to prewrite.

Identifying the elements for analysis. If you are asked to examine the tone of poem, you might need to look at imagery and word choice. If you are asked to examine prose and explain how a writer creates mood, you should examine the diction, style, imagery, syntax, structure, and selection of detail.

Deciding on your main idea. Use the question as a guideline. However, do not merely restate the question. Make sure that in restating the topic you have taken a position on how you will answer the prompt. For example, you might be asked to read Whitman's poem "I Hear America Singing" and discuss not only the tone of the poem but also how Whitman creates the tone. It is important, if you wish to receive a high score on the essay, that your main idea clearly states what you think is the tone and how it is created.

A well-crafted thesis statement can help both writers and readers. Writers can stay on topic and develop their thesis statement with appropriate and relevant details. Readers can better understand the main idea and the supporting ideas. By following these steps, writers can develop the skill to formulate clear and strong thesis statements.

Write the Thesis Statement

First, you should identify the topic.

> I am going to write about the tone and how it is created in the poem "I Hear America Singing" by Walt Whitman.

Second, state your point of view about the topic.

> The upbeat and optimistic tone of Whitman's poem is created by his word choice, structure and imagery.

Third, summarize the main points you will make in your essay.

> Whitman creates an optimistic tone through his choice of words, parallel structure, and images.

State the Main Point of Each Body Paragraph and Organize Support

Using a five-paragraph essay format is one of many ways to respond to literature. It is a basic structure that encourages development and coherence. As writers become more sophisticated, they will progress beyond this formula.

PARAGRAPH	PURPOSE	SUPPORT
1st Intro	Main idea statement	
2nd 1st body paragraph	Main point 1	Quotes or specifics from the text with analysis or explanation of how each detail supports your main point.
3rd 2nd body Paragraph	Main point 2	Quotes or specifics from the text with analysis or explanation of how each detail supports your main point.
4th 3rd body paragraph	Main point 3	Quotes or specifics from the text with analysis or explanation of how each detail supports Your main point.
5th Closing	Summarize ideas	

Consider Audience, Purpose, and Tone

Keep in mind as you write this essay that your purpose is to demonstrate literary skill by reading an unfamiliar passage or poem and examining its elements. It is crucial to avoid giving a summary of the piece or writing your personal reaction to the work. Your audience is familiar with the piece and thus does not need to have the work summarized. In fact, the readers of your essay have been trained to look for focus, organization, support, and correct usage. Finally, the tone is formal.

Techniques to Maintain Focus

- **Focus on a main point.** The point should be clear to readers, and all sentences in the paragraph should relate to it.

- **Start the paragraph with a topic sentence.** This should be a general, one-sentence summary of the paragraph's main point, relating back to the thesis and forward to the content of the paragraph. (A topic sentence is sometimes unnecessary if the paragraph continues a developing idea clearly introduced in a preceding paragraph, or if the paragraph appears in a narrative of events where generalizations might interrupt the flow of the story.)

- **Stick to the point.** Eliminate sentences that do not support the topic sentence.

- **Be flexible.** If you do not have enough evidence to support the claim of your topic sentence, do not fall into the trap of wandering or introducing new ideas within the paragraph. Either find more evidence, or adjust the topic sentence to corroborate with the evidence that is available.

Skill 7.3   Exhibit conventions of standard written English.

For formal writing, writers should use the standards of written English. This includes following the rules of capitalization, spelling, and punctuation.

Capitalization

Capitalize all proper names of persons (including specific organizations or agencies of government); places

> Check out this
> **Guide to Grammar and Writing**
> http://grammar.ccc.commnet.edu/grammar/

(countries, states, cities, parks, and specific geographical areas); and things (political parties, structures, historical and cultural terms, and calendar and time designations); and religious terms (any deity, revered person or group, sacred writings).

> Percy Bysshe Shelley, Argentina, Mount Rainier National Park,
> Grand Canyon, League of Nations, the Sears Tower, Birmingham,
> Lyric Theater, Americans, Midwesterners, Democrats, Renaissance,
> Boy Scouts of America, Easter, God, Bible, Dead Sea Scrolls, Koran

Capitalize proper adjectives and titles used with proper names.

> California gold rush, President John Adams, French fries, Homeric epic,
> Romanesque architecture, Senator John Glenn

Note: Some words that represent titles and offices are not capitalized unless used with a proper name.

Capitalized	Not Capitalized
Congressman McKay	the congressman from Florida
Commander Alger	commander of the Pacific Fleet
Queen Elizabeth	the queen of England

Capitalize all main words in titles of works of literature, art, and music.
> *For Whom the Bell Tolls*, a novel by Ernest Hemingway
> *Dancers at the Bar*, a painting by Edgar Degas
> *Sgt. Pepper's Lonely Hearts Club Band*, an album by the Beatles

Spelling

Concentration in this section will be on spelling plurals and possessives. If the multiplicity and complexity of spelling rules based on phonics, letter doubling, and exceptions to rules are not mastered by adulthood, writers should use a good dictionary to achieve correctness. As spelling mastery is usually difficult for adolescents, our recommendation for them is the same. Learning the use of a dictionary and thesaurus will be a more rewarding use of time than laboring to master each obscure rule and exception.

Most plurals of nouns that end in hard consonants or hard consonant sounds followed by a silent *e* are made by adding *s*. Some words ending in vowels only add *s*.

fingers, numerals, banks, bugs, riots, homes, gates, radios, bananas

Nouns that end in soft consonant sounds *s, j, x, z, ch,* and *sh,* add *es*. Some nouns ending in *o* add *es*.

dresses, waxes, churches, brushes, tomatoes, potatoes

Nouns ending in *y* preceded by a vowel just add *s*.

boys, alleys

Nouns ending in *y* preceded by a consonant change the *y* to *i* and add *es*.

babies, corollaries, frugalities, poppies

Some nouns plurals are formed irregularly or remain the same.

sheep, deer, children, leaves, oxen

Some nouns derived from foreign words, especially Latin, may make their plurals in two different ways—one of them Anglicized. Sometimes, the meanings are the same; other times, the two plurals are used in slightly different contexts. It is always wise to consult the dictionary.

appendices, appendixes   criterion, criteria
indexes, indices   crisis, crises

Make the plurals of closed (solid) compound words in the usual way except for words ending in *ful* which make their plurals on the root word.

timelines, hairpins, cupsful

Make the plurals of open or hyphenated compounds by adding the change in inflection to the word that changes in number.

> fathers-in-law, courts-martial, masters of art, doctors of medicine

Make the plurals of letters, numbers, and abbreviations by adding *s*.

> fives and tens, IBMs, 1990s, *p*s and *q*s (Note that letters are italicized.)

When in doubt, consult a dictionary.

Punctuation

A basic way to show relationship of ideas in sentences is to use punctuation correctly and effectively. You should be aware of the proper rules and conventions of punctuation, capitalization, and spelling. Competency exams will generally test the ability to apply the more advanced skills; thus, a limited number of more frustrating rules are presented here. Rules should be applied according to the American style of English, i.e. spelling *theater* instead of *theatre* and placing terminal marks of punctuation almost exclusively within other marks of punctuation.

Quotation Marks

The more troublesome punctuation marks involve the use of quotations.

Using Terminal Punctuation in Relation to Quotation Marks: In a quoted statement that is either declarative or imperative, place the period inside the closing quotation marks.

> "The airplane crashed on the runway during takeoff."

If the quotation is followed by other words in the sentence, place a comma inside the closing quotations marks and a period at the end of the sentence.

> "The airplane crashed on the runway during takeoff," said the announcer.

In most instances in which a quoted title or expression occurs at the end of a sentence, the period is placed before either the single or double quotation marks.

> The educator worried, "The middle school readers were unprepared to understand Bryant's poem 'Thanatopsis.'"

> Early book-length adventure stories like *Don Quixote* and *The Three Musketeers* are known as "picaresque novels."

There is an instance in which the final quotation mark would precede the period—if the content of the sentence were about a speech or quote so that the understanding of the meaning would be confused by the placement of the period.

> The first thing out of his mouth was "Hi, I'm home." *but*
> The first line of his speech began "I arrived home to an empty house".

In sentences that are interrogatory or exclamatory, the question mark or exclamation point should be positioned outside the closing quotation marks if the quote itself is a statement or command or cited title.

> Who decided to lead us in the recitation of the "Pledge of Allegiance"?

> Why was Tillie shaking as she began her recitation, "Once upon a midnight dreary..."?

> I was embarrassed when Mrs. White said, "Your slip is showing"!

In sentences that are declarative but the quotation is a question or an exclamation, place the question mark or exclamation point inside the quotation marks.

> The hall monitor yelled, "Fire! Fire!"

> "Fire! Fire!" yelled the hall monitor.

> Cory shrieked, "Is there a mouse in the room?" (In this instance, the question supersedes the exclamation.)

Using Double Quotation Marks with Other Punctuation: Quotations—whether words, phrases, or clauses—should be punctuated according to the rules of the grammatical function they serve in the sentence.

> The works of Shakespeare, "the bard of Avon," have been contested as originating with other authors.

> "You'll get my money," the old man warned, "when 'Hell freezes over'."

> Sheila cited the passage that began "Four score and seven years ago...." (Note the ellipsis followed by an enclosed period.)

> "Old Ironsides" inspired the preservation of the U.S.S. Constitution.

Use quotation marks to enclose the titles of shorter works: songs, short poems, short stories, essays, and chapters of books. (See "Using Italics" for punctuating longer titles.)

"The Tell-Tale Heart" - short story
"Casey at the Bat" - poem
"America the Beautiful" - song

Using Commas

Separate two or more coordinate adjectives modifying the same word and three or more nouns, phrases, or clauses in a list.

Maggie's hair was dull, dirty, and lice-ridden.

Dickens portrayed the Artful Dodger as skillful pickpocket, loyal follower of Fagin, and defendant of Oliver Twist.

Ellen daydreamed about getting out of the rain, taking a shower, and eating a hot dinner.

In Elizabethan England, Ben Jonson wrote comedy, Christopher Marlowe wrote tragedies, and William Shakespeare composed both.

Use commas to separate antithetical or complimentary expressions from the rest of the sentence.

The veterinarian, not his assistant, would perform the delicate surgery.

The more he knew about her, the less he wished he had known.

Randy hopes to, and probably will, get an appointment to the Naval Academy.

His thorough, though esoteric, scientific research could not easily be understood by high school students.

Using Semicolons

Use semicolons to separate independent clauses when the second clause is introduced by a transitional adverb. (These clauses may also be written as separate sentences, preferably by placing the adverb within the second sentence.)

> The Elizabethans modified the rhyme scheme of the sonnet; thus, it was called the English sonnet.
> *or*
> The Elizabethans modified the rhyme scheme of the sonnet. It thus was called the English sonnet.

Use semicolons to separate items in a series that are long and complex or have internal punctuation.

> The Italian Renaissance produced masters in the fine arts: Dante Alighieri, author of the *Divine Comedy;* Leonardo da Vinci, painter of *The Last Supper;* and Donatello, sculptor of the *Quattro Coronati*, the four saints.

> The leading scorers in the WNBA were Haizhaw Zheng, averaging 23.9 points per game; Lisa Leslie, 22; and Cynthia Cooper, 19.5.

Using Colons

Place a colon at the beginning of a list of items. (Note its use in the sentence about Renaissance Italians previously.)

> The teacher directed us to compare Faulkner's three symbolic novels: *Absalom, Absalom; As I Lay Dying;* and *Light in August.*

Do **not** use a comma if the list is preceded by a verb.

> Three of Faulkner's symbolic novels are *Absalom, Absalom; As I Lay Dying*, and *Light in August.*

Using Dashes

Place dashes (called an "em" dash) to denote sudden breaks in thought.

> Some periods in literature—the Romantic Age, for example—spanned different time periods in different countries.

Use dashes instead of commas if commas are already used elsewhere in the sentence for amplification or explanation.

> The Fireside Poets included three Brahmans—James Russell Lowell, Henry David Wadsworth, Oliver Wendell Holmes—and John Greenleaf Whittier.

Using Italics

Use italics to punctuate the titles of long works of literature, names of periodical publications, musical scores, works of art and motion picture television, and radio programs. (When unable to write in italics, you can instruct students to underline in their own writing where italics would be appropriate.)

> *The Idylls of the King*   *Hiawatha*   *The Sound and the Fury*
> *Mary Poppins*   *Newsweek*   *The Nutcracker Suite*

Skill 7.4   **Incorporate relevant content, using ample evidence.**

The resources used to support a piece of writing can be divided into two major groups: **primary** sources and **secondary** sources.

Primary sources are works, records, and the like that were created during the period being studied or immediately after it. Secondary sources are works written significantly after the period being studied and based upon primary sources. Primary sources are the basic materials that provide raw data and information. Secondary sources are the works that contain the explications of, and judgments on, this primary material.

Primary sources include the following kinds of materials.
- Documents that reflect the immediate, everyday concerns of people: memoranda, bills, deeds, charters, newspaper reports, pamphlets, graffiti, popular writings, journals or diaries, records of decision-making bodies, letters, receipts, snapshots, and others.
- Theoretical writings which reflect care and consideration in composition and an attempt to convince or persuade. The topic will generally be deeper and more pervasive values than is the case with "immediate" documents. These may include newspaper or magazine editorials, sermons, political speeches, or philosophical writings.
- Narrative accounts of events, ideas, and trends written with intentionality by someone contemporary with the events described.
- Statistical data, although statistics may be misleading.
- Literature and nonverbal materials, novels, stories, poetry and essays from the period, as well as coins, archaeological artifacts, and art produced during the period.

Secondary sources include the following kinds of materials.
- Books written on the basis of primary materials about the period of time.
- Books written on the basis of primary materials about persons who played a major role in the events under consideration.
- Books and articles written on the basis of primary materials about the culture, the social norms, the language, and the values of the period.
- Quotations from primary sources.
- Statistical data on the period.
- The conclusions and inferences of other historians.
- Multiple interpretations of the ethos of the time.

Questions for Analyzing Sources

To determine the authenticity or credibility of your sources, consider these questions:

> Learn more about **Assessing the Credibility of Online Sources**
> http://www.webcredible.co.uk/ user-friendly-resources/web-credibility/assessing-credibility-online-sources.shtml

1. Who created the source and why? Was it created through a spur-of-the-moment act, a routine transaction, or a thoughtful, deliberate process?
2. Did the recorder have firsthand knowledge of the event? Or, did the recorder report what others saw and heard?
3. Was the recorder a neutral party, or did the recorder have opinions or interests that might have influenced what was recorded?
   Did the recorder produce the source for personal use, for one or more individuals, or for a large audience?
4. Was the source meant to be public or private?
5. Did the recorder wish to inform or persuade others? (Check the words in the source. The words may tell you whether the recorder was trying to be objective or persuasive.) Did the recorder have reasons to be honest or dishonest?
6. Was the information recorded during the event, immediately after the event, or after some lapse of time? How large a lapse of time?

To *interpret* means essentially to read with understanding and appreciation. It is not as daunting as it might sound. Simple techniques for interpreting literature follow.

Context

Context includes the author's feelings, beliefs, past experiences, goals, needs, and physical environment. Incorporate an understanding of how these elements may have affected the writing to enrich an interpretation of it.

Symbols

Also referred to as a sign, a symbol designates something which stands for something else. In most cases, it is standing for something that has a deeper meaning than its literal denotation. Symbols can have personal, cultural, or universal associations. Use an understanding of symbols to unearth a meaning the author might have intended but not expressed, or even something the author never intended at all.

Inferential Comprehension Skills

A fallacy is, essentially, an error in reasoning. In persuasive speech, logical fallacies are instances of reasoning flaws that make an argument invalid. For example, a premature generalization occurs when you form a general rule based on only one or a few specific cases, which do not represent all possible cases. An illustration of this is the statement, "Bob Marley was a Rastafarian singer. Therefore, all Rastafarians sing."

A common fallacy in reasoning is the *post hoc ergo propter hoc* ("after this, therefore because of this") or the false-cause fallacy. These occur in cause/effect reasoning, which may either go from cause to effect or effect to cause.

They happen when an inadequate cause is offered for a particular effect; when the possibility of more than one cause is ignored; and when a connection between a particular cause and a particular effect is not made.

> Learn more about
> **Post Hoc Fallacy**
> http://www.sjsu.edu/depts/itl/graphics/ adhom/posthoc.html

An example of a *post hoc*: Our sales shot up thirty-five percent after we ran that television campaign; therefore the campaign caused the increase in sales.

It might have been a cause, of course, but more evidence is needed to prove it.

An example of an **inadequate cause for a particular effect**: An Iraqi truck driver reported that Saddam Hussein had nuclear weapons; therefore, Saddam Hussein is a threat to world security.

More causes are needed to prove the conclusion.

An example of **ignoring the possibility of more than one possible cause**: John Brown was caught out in a thunderstorm and his clothes were wet before he was rescued; therefore, he developed influenza the next day was because he got wet.

Being chilled may have played a role in the illness, but Brown would have had to contract the influenza virus before he would come down with it whether or not he had gotten wet.

> An example of **failing to make a connection between a particular cause and an effect** assigned to it. Anna fell into a putrid pond on Saturday; on Monday she came down with polio; therefore, the pond caused the polio.

This, of course, is not acceptable unless the poliovirus is found in a sample of water from the pond. A connection must be proven.

Reliability and Validity

Be sure your information is both reliable and valid.

To determine **reliability**, you should be able to find the same information in more than one source. If this doesn't happen, you will continue your research until you have resolved any discrepancies. Do not use information that cannot be verified or test results that cannot be repeated.

To determine **validity**, you should ensure that your research answers the questions you are posing. If you are researching how the English language developed and you locate information about the tower of Babel, your information is invalid for your research problem.

Reliability and validity are not mutually dependent. For example, when you test your students' understanding of a literary passage, your measurement of the results will be reliable if you used reliable methods to determine the results and you can repeat the same results every time you measure.

However, for those results to be valid, they have to measure the students' understanding of those particular concepts. If you hoped to measure comprehension of a literary passage but the students' responses discussed the author's life and environment, those results are not valid.

These same principles can be applied to writing. Your supporting points must come from reliable sources and must be interpreted with validity.

Paraphrasing

Paraphrasing is the art of rewording text. The goal is to maintain the original purpose of the statement while translating it into your own words. Your newly generated sentence can be longer or shorter than the original. Concentrate on the meaning, not on the words. Do not change concept words, special terms, or proper names. There are numerous ways to paraphrase effectively:

- Change the key words' form or part of speech. Example: "American news **coverage** is frequently **biased** in favor of Western views" becomes "When American journalists **cover** events, they often display a Western **bias**."

- Use synonyms of "relationship words." Look for a relationship word, such as **contrast, cause,** or **effect,** and replace it with a word that conveys a similar meaning, thus creating a different structure for your sentence. Example: "**Unlike** many cats, Purrdy can sit on command," becomes "Most cats are not able to be trained, **but** Purrdy can sit on command."

- Use synonyms of phrases and words. Example: "The Beatnik writers were relatively unknown at **the start of the decade**," becomes "**Around the early 1950s**, the Beatnik writers were still relatively unknown."

- Change passive voice to active voice or move phrases and modifiers. Example: "Not to be outdone by the third graders, the fourth grade class added a musical medley to their Christmas performance," becomes "The fourth grade class added a musical medley to their Christmas performance to avoid being showed up by the third graders."

- Use reversals or negatives that do not change the meaning of the sentence. Example: "That burger chain is only found in California," becomes "That burger chain is not found on the east coast."

Documentation

Documentation is an important skill in incorporating outside information into a piece of writing. Students must learn that research is more than cut and paste from the Internet and that plagiarism is a serious academic offense.

This skill pertains to recognizing that stealing intellectual property is an academic and, in some cases, a legal crime; because it is so, students need to learn how to give credit where credit is due.

Students need to be aware of the rules that apply to borrowing ideas from various sources. Increasingly, consequences for violations of these rules (plagiarism) are becoming more severe, and students are expected to be aware of how to avoid such problems. Pleading ignorance is less and less of a defense.

Such consequences include failing a particular assignment, losing credit for an entire course, expulsion from a learning environment, and civil penalties. Software exists that enables teachers and other interested individuals to determine quickly whether or not a given paper includes plagiarized material. As members of society in the information age, students are expected to recognize the basic justice of intellectual honesty and to conform to the systems meant to ensure it.

There are several style guides for documenting sources. Each guide has its own particular ways of signaling that information has been directly borrowed or paraphrased, and familiarity with at least where to find the relevant details of the major style guides is an essential for students. Many libraries publish overviews of the major style guides for students to consult, most bookstores will carry full guides for the major systems, and relevant information is readily available on the web as well.

Documentation of sources takes two main forms. The first form applies to citing sources in the text of the document or as footnotes or endnotes. In-text documentation is sometimes called parenthetical documentation and requires specific information within parentheses placed immediately after borrowed material. Footnotes or endnotes are placed either at the bottom of relevant pages or at the end of the document.

Beyond citing sources in the text, style guides also require a bibliography, a references section, or a works cited section at the end of the document. Sources for any borrowed material are to be listed according to the rules of the particular guide. In some cases, it may be required to include a works consulted listing even though no material is directly cited or paraphrased to the extent that an in-text citation would be required.

The major style guides to be familiar with include the *Modern Language Association Handbook (MLA), the Manual of the American Psychological Association (APA), the Chicago Manuel of Style, Turabian, and Scientific Style and Format: the CBE Manual.*

> Learn more about
> **MLA Works Cited Documentation**
> http://www.studyguide.org/
> MLAdocumentation.htm

Documentation of sources from the Internet is particularly involved and continues to evolve at a pace often requiring visiting the latest online update available for a particular style guide.

Tips for Documentation

- Keep a record of all sources consulted during the research process.

- As you take notes, avoid unintentional plagiarism. Summarize and paraphrase in your own words without the source in front of you. If you use a direct quote, copy it exactly as written and enclose in quotation marks.

- Cite anything that is not common knowledge. This includes direct quotes as well as ideas or statistics.

Within the body of your document follow this blueprint for standard attribution following MLA style.

1. Begin the sentence with, "According to _____,"

2. Proceed with the material being cited, followed by the page number in parentheses.

In-Text Citation Example

According to Steve Mandel, "our average conversational rate of speech is about 125 words per minute" (78).

Once students have mastered this basic approach, they can learn more sophisticated methods such as embedding information.

Each source used within the document will have a complete citation in a bibliography or works cited page.

Works Cited Entry

Mandel, Steve. *Effective Presentation Skills*. Menlo Park, California: Crisp Publications, 1993.

Skill 7.5 **Use elements of style that enhance the reader's interest and understanding.**

To accomplish their purpose, writers must maintain a reader's interest and ensure an understanding of the materials.

Enhancing Interest

- Start out with an attention-grabbing introduction. This sets an engaging tone for the entire piece and will be more likely to pull the reader in.

- Use dynamic vocabulary and varied sentence beginnings. Keep the readers on their toes. If they can predict what you are going to say next, switch it up.

- Avoid using clichés (*as cold as ice, the best thing since sliced bread, nip it in the bud*). These are easy shortcuts, but they are not interesting, memorable, or convincing.

Ensuring Understanding

- Avoid using the words *clearly, obviously,* and *undoubtedly.* Often, what is clear or obvious to the author is not as apparent to the reader. Instead of using these words, make your point so strongly that it is clear on its own.

- Use the word that best fits the meaning you intend for, even if it is longer or a little less common. Try to find a balance, and go with a familiar yet precise word.

- When in doubt, explain further.

In writing or speaking, you can be persuasive if you follow the three basic principles of unity, coherence, and emphasis.

Unity: All ideas must relate to the controlling thesis. At the simplest level, this means that all sentences must develop the topic sentence of a paragraph. By extension, then, all paragraphs must develop the thesis statement of the essay; all chapters must develop the main idea of the book. All ideas must develop the argument.

Coherence: One way to achieve unity is to show the relationship of ideas by using transitional words, phrases, sentences, and paragraphs. Using coordinating conjunctions (*for, and, nor, but, or, yet, so*), subordinating conjunctions (*because, since, whenever*), or transitional adverbs (*however, therefore*) is an effective way to show logical order and thus create coherence.

Another way to show the relationship of ideas is to use an appropriate strategy (spatial, chronological, cause and effect, classification, comparison/contrast) to arrange details.

Emphasis: By placing your stronger arguments in areas of importance, you emphasize the significance of the ideas. In direct order, the main ideas are stated first and then supported by reasons or details. In indirect order, the support is provided first (in either increasing or decreasing order of importance) so that the end is a well-defended argument.

Classical Argument

The classical argument structure below uses unity, coherence, and emphasis effectively. In its simplest form, the classical argument has five main parts:

The **introduction**, which warms up the audience, establishes goodwill and rapport with the readers, and announces the general theme or thesis of the argument.

The **narration**, which summarizes relevant background material, provides any information the audience needs to know about the environment and circumstances that produce the argument, and set up the stakes—what's at risk in this question.

The **confirmation**, which lays out in a logical order (usually strongest to weakest or most obvious to most subtle) the claims that support the thesis, providing evidence for each claim.

The **refutation** and concession, which looks at opposing viewpoints to the writer's claims, anticipating objections from the audience, and allowing as much of the opposing viewpoints as possible without weakening the thesis.

The **summation**, which provides a strong conclusion, amplifies the force of the argument, and shows the readers that this solution is the best at meeting the circumstances.

Resources

Abrams, M. H. ed. *The Norton Anthology of English Literature*. 6th ed. 2 vols. New York: Norton, 1979.

A comprehensive reference for English literature, containing selected works from *Beowulf* through the twentieth century and information about literary criticism.

Beach, Richard. "Strategic Teaching in Literature." *Strategic Teaching and Learning: Cognitive Instruction in the Content Areas*. Edited by Beau Fly Jones and others. ASCD Publications, 1987: 135-159.

A chapter dealing with a definition of and strategic teaching strategies for literature studies.

Brown, A. C. and others. *Grammar and Composition* 3rd Course. Boston: Houghton Mifflin, 1984.

A standard ninth-grade grammar text covering spelling, vocabulary, reading, listening, and writing skills.

Burmeister, L. E. *Reading Strategies for Middle and Secondary School Teachers*. Reading, MA: Addison-Wesley, 1978.

A resource for developing classroom strategies for reading and content area classes, using library references, and adapting reading materials to all levels of students.

Carrier, W. and B. Neumann, eds. *Literature from the World*. New York: Scribner, 1981.

A comprehensive world literature text for high school students, with a section on mythology and folklore.

Cline, R. K. J. and W. G. McBride. *A Guide to Literature for Young Adults: Background, Selection, and Use*. Glenview, IL: Scott Foresman, 1983.

A literature reference containing sample readings and an overview of adolescent literature and the developmental changes that affect reading.

Coater, R.B., Jr., ed. "Reading Research and Instruction." *Journal of the College Research Association*. Pittsburgh, PA: 1995.

A reference tool for reading and language arts teachers, covering the latest research and instructional techniques.

Corcoran, B. and E. Evans, eds. *Readers, Texts, Teachers.* Upper Montclair, NJ: Boynton/Cook, 1987.

A collection of essays concerning reader response theory, including activities that help students interpret literature and help the teacher integrate literature into the course study.

Cutting, Brian. *Moving on in Whole Language: The Complete Guide for Every Teacher.* Bothell, WA: Wright Group, 1992.

A resource of practical knowledge in whole language instruction.

Damrosch, L. and others. *Adventures in English Literature.* Orlando, FL: Harcourt, Brace, Jovanovich, 1985.

One of many standard high school English literature textbooks with a solid section on the development of the English language.

Davidson, A. *Literacy 2000 Teacher's Resource. Emergent Stages 1 & 2.* 1990.

Devine, T. G. *Teaching Study Skills: A Guide for Teachers.* Boston: Allyn and Bacon, 1981.

Duffy, G. G. and others. *Comprehension Instruction: Perspectives and Suggestions.* New York: Longman, 1984.

Written by researchers at the Institute of Research on Teaching and the Center for the Study of Reading, this reference includes a variety of instructional techniques for different levels.

Fleming, M. ed. *Teaching the Epic.* Urbana, IL: NCTE, 1974.

Methods, materials, and projects for the teaching of epics with examples of Greek, religious, national, and American epics.

Flood, J. Ed. *Understanding Reading Comprehension: Cognition, Language, and the Structure of Prose.* Newark, DE: IRA, 1984.

Essays by preeminent scholars dealing with comprehension for learners of all levels and abilities.

Fry, E. B. and others. *The Reading Teacher's Book of Lists.* Edgewood Cliffs, NJ: Prentice-Hall, 1984.

A comprehensive list of book lists for students of various reading levels.

Garnica, Olga K. and Martha L. King. *Language, Children, and Society.* New York: Pergamon Press, 1981.

Gere, A. R. and E. Smith. *Attitude, Language and Change.* Urbana, IL: NCTE, 1979.

A discussion of the relationship between standard English and grammar and the vernacular usage, including various approaches to language instruction.

Hayakawa, S. I. *Language in Thought and Action.* 4th ed. Orlando, Fl: Harcourt, Brace, Jovanovich, 1979.

Hook, J. N. and others. *What Every English Teacher Should Know.* Champaign, IL: NCTE, 1970.

Research-based text that summarizes methodologies and specific application for use with students.

Johnson, D. D. and P. D. Pearson. *Teaching Reading Vocabulary.* 2nd ed. New York: Holt, Rinehart, and Winston, 1984.

A student text that stresses using vocabulary study in improving reading comprehension, with chapters on instructional components in the reading and content areas.

Kaywell, I. F. Ed. *Adolescent Literature as a Complement to the Classics.* Norwood, MA: Christopher-Gordon Pub., 1993.

A correlation of modern adolescent literature to classics of similar themes.

Mack, M. Ed. *World Masterpieces.* 3rd ed. 2 vols. New York: Norton, 1973.

A standard world literature survey, with useful introductory material on a critical approach to literature study.

McLuhan, M. *Understanding Media: The Extensions of Man.* New York: Signet, 1964.

The most classic work on the effect media has on the public and the power of the media to influence thinking.

McMichael, G. ed. *Concise Anthology of American Literature.* New York: Macmillan, 1974.

A standard survey of American literature text.

Moffett, J. *Teaching the Universe of Discourse*. Boston: Houghton Mifflin, 1983.

A significant reference text that proposes the outline for a total language arts program, emphasizing the reinforcement of each element of the language arts curriculum to the other elements.

Moffett, James and Betty Jane Wagner. *Student-Centered Language Arts K-12*. 4th ed. Boston: Houghton Mifflin, 1992.

Nelms, B. F., ed. *Literature in the Classroom: Readers, Texts, and Contexts*. Urbana, IL: NCTE, 1988.

Essays on adolescent and multicultural literature, social aspects of literature, and approaches to literature interpretation.

Nilsen, A. P. and K. L. Donelson. *Literature for Today's Young Adults*. 2nd ed. Glenview, IL: Scott, Foresman, and Co., 1985.

An excellent overview of young adult literature—its history, terminologies, bibliographies, and book reviews.

Perrine, L. *Literature: Structure, Sound, and Sense*. 5th ed. Orlando, FL: Harcourt, Brace, Jovanovich, 1988.

A much revised text for teaching literature elements, genres, and interpretation.

Piercey, Dorothy. *Reading Activities in Content Areas: An Ideabook for Middle and Secondary Schools*. 2nd ed. Boston: Allyn and Bacon, 1982.

Pooley, R. C. *The Teaching of English Usage*. Urbana, IL: NCTE, 1974.

A revision of the important 1946 text, which discusses the attitudes toward English usage through history and recommends specific techniques for usage instruction.

Probst, R. E. *Response and Analysis: Teaching Literature in Junior and Senior High School*. Upper Montclair, NJ: Boynton/Cook, 1988.

A resource that explores reader response theory and discusses student-centered methods for interpreting literature. Contains a section on the progress of adolescent literature.

Pyles, T. and J. Alges. *The Origin and Development of the English Language.* 3rd ed. Orlando, FL: Harcourt, Brace, Jovanovich, 1982.

A history of the English language; sections on social, personal, historical, and geographical influences on language usage.

Readence, J. E. and others. *Content Area Reading: An Integrated Approach.* 2nd ed. Dubuque, IA: Kendall/Hunt, 1985.

A practical instruction guide for teaching reading in the content areas.

Robinson, H. Alan. *Teaching Reading and Study Strategies: The Content Areas.* Boston: Allyn and Bacon, 1978.

Roe, B. D. and others. *Secondary School Reading Instruction: The Content Areas.* 3rd ed. Boston: Houghton Mifflin, 1987.

A resource of strategies for the teaching of reading for language arts teachers with little reading instruction background.

Rosenberg, D. *World Mythology: An Anthology of the Great Myths and Epics.* Lincolnwood, IL: National Textbook, 1986.

Presents selections of main myths from which literary allusions are drawn. Thorough literary analysis of each selection.

Rosenblatt, L. M. *The Reader, the Text, the Poem. The Transactional Theory of the Literary Work.* Southern Illinois University Press, 1978.

A discussion of reader-response theory and reader-centered methods for analyzing literature.

Santeusanio, Richard P. *A Practical Approach to Content Area Reading.* Reading, MA.: Addison-Wesley Publishing Co., 1983.

Strickland, D. S. and others. *Using Computers in the Teaching of Reading.* New York: Teachers College Press, 1987.

Resource for strategies for teaching and learning language and reading with computers and recommendations for software for all grades.

Sutherland, Zena and others. *Children and Books*. 6th ed. Glenview, IL: Scott, Foresman, and Co., 1981.

Thorough study of children's literature, with sections on language development theory and chapters on specific genres with synopses of specific classic works for child/adolescent readers.

Tchudi, S. and D. Mitchell. *Explorations in the Teaching of English*. 3rd ed. New York: Harper Row, 1989.

A thorough source of strategies for creating a more student-centered involvement in learning.

Tompkins, Gail E. *Teaching Writing: Balancing Process and Product*. 2nd ed. New York: Macmillan, 1994.

A tool to aid teachers in integrating recent research and theory about the writing process, writing reading connections, collaborative learning, and across the curriculum writing with practices in the fourth through eighth grade classrooms.

Warriners, J. E. *English Composition and Grammar*. Benchmark ed. Orlando, FL: Harcourt, Brace, Jovanovich, 1988.

Standard grammar and composition textbook, with a six-book series for seventh through twelfth grades; includes vocabulary study, language history, and diverse approaches to writing process.

Sample Test

Section I: Essay Test

Given are several prompts, reflecting the need to exhibit a variety of writing skills. In most testing situations, 30 minutes would be allowed to respond to each of the prompts. Some tests may allow 60 minutes for the essay to incorporate more than one question or allow for greater preparation and editing time. Read the directions carefully and organize your time wisely.

Section II: Multiple-choice Test

This section contains 125 questions. In most testing situations, you would be expected to answer from 35-40 questions within 30 minutes. If you time yourself on the entire battery, take no more than 90 minutes.

Section III: Answer Key

Section I: Essay Prompts

Prompt A

Write an expository essay discussing effective teaching strategies for helping a heterogeneous class of ninth graders to appreciate literature. Select any appropriate piece(s) of world literature to use as examples in the discussion.

Prompt B

After reading the following passage from Alduous Huxley's *Brave New World,* discuss the types of reader responses possible with a group of eight graders.

> "He hated them all—all the men who came to visit Linda. One afternoon, when he had been playing with the other children—it was cold, he remembered, and there was snow on the mountains—he came back to the house and heard angry voices in the bedroom. They were women's voices, and they were words he didn't understand; but he knew they were dreadful words. Then suddenly, crash! something was upset; he heard people moving about quickly, and there was another crash and then a noise like hitting a mule, only not so bony; then Linda screamed. 'Oh, don't, don't, don't!' she said. He ran in. There were three women in dark blankets. Linda was on the bed. One of the women was holding her wrists. Another was lying across her legs, so she couldn't kick. The third was hitting her with a whip. Once, twice, three times; and each time Linda screamed."

Prompt C

Write a persuasive letter to the editor on any contemporary topic of special interest. Employ whatever forms of discourse, stylistic devices, and audience-appeal techniques that seem appropriate to the topic.

Section II: Writing and Language Skills

Part A

Directions: Each underlined portion of sentences 1-10 contains one or more errors in grammar, usage, mechanics, or sentence structure. Circle the choice which best corrects the error without changing the meaning of the original sentence.

Explanation of Rigor

Easy: The majority of test takers would get this question correct. It is a simple understanding of the facts and/or the subject matter is part of the basics of an education for teaching English.

Average Rigor: This question represents a test item that most people would pass. It requires a level of analysis or reasoning and/or the subject matter exceeds the basics of an education for teaching English.

Rigorous: The majority of test takers would have difficulty answering this question. It involves critical thinking skills such as a very high level of abstract thought, analysis or reasoning, and it would require a very deep and broad education for teaching English.

Part A

Each underlined portion of sentences 1-10 contains one or more errors in grammar, usage, mechanics, or sentence structure. Circle the choice which best corrects the error without changing the meaning of the original sentence.

1. Joe <u>didn't hardly know his cousin Fred</u> who'd had a rhinoplasty. (Skill 1.2, Easy)

   A. hardly did know his cousin Fred

   B. didn't know his cousin Fred hardly

   C. hardly knew his cousin Fred

   D. didn't know his cousin Fred

   E. didn't hardly know his cousin Fred

2. <u>Mixing the batter for cookies, the cat</u> licked the Crisco from the cookie sheet. (Skill 1.2, Average Rigor)

   A. While mixing the batter for cookies

   B. While the batter for cookies was mixing

   C. While I mixed the batter for cookies

   D. While I mixed the cookies

   E. Mixing the batter for cookies

3. Mr. Smith <u>respectfully submitted his resignation and had</u> a new job. (Skill 1.2, Average Rigor)

   A. respectfully submitted his resignation and has

   B. respectfully submitted his resignation before accepting

   C. respectfully submitted his resignation because of

   D. respectfully submitted his resignation and had

4. **Walt Whitman was famous for his composition, _Leaves of Grass_, serving as a nurse during the Civil War, and a devoted son.** (Skill 1.2, Rigorous)

   A. _Leaves of Grass_, his service as a nurse during the Civil War, and a devoted son.

   B. composing _Leaves of Grass_, serving as a nurse during the Civil War, and being a devoted son.

   C. his composition, _Leaves of Grass_, his nursing during the Civil War, and his devotion as a son.

   D. his composition _Leaves of Grass_, serving as a nurse during the Civil War and a devoted son.

   E. his composition _Leaves of Grass_, serving as a nurse during the Civil War. and a devoted son.

5. **There were _fewer pieces_ of evidence presented during the second trial.** (Skill 1.3, Easy)

   A. fewer peaces

   B. less peaces

   C. less pieces

   D. fewer pieces

6. **The teacher _implied_ from our angry words that there was conflict _between you and me._** (Skill 1.3, Average Rigor)

   A. Implied… between you and I

   B. Inferred… between you and I

   C. Inferred… between you and me

   D. Implied… between you and me

7. **A teacher _must know not only her subject matter but also the strategies of content teaching_.** (Skill 1.3, Rigorous)

   A. must not only know her subject matter but also the strategies of content teaching

   B. not only must know her subject matter but also the strategies of content teaching

   C. must not know only her subject matter but also the strategies of content teaching

   D. must know not only her subject matter but also the strategies of content teaching

8. Wally groaned, "Why do I have to do an oral interpretation of "The Raven." (Skill 7.3, Average Rigor)

   A. groaned "Why… of 'The Raven'?"

   B. groaned "Why… of "The Raven"?

   C. groaned ", Why… of "The Raven?"

   D. groaned, "Why… of "The Raven."

9. The coach offered her assistance but the athletes wanted to practice on their own. (Skill 7.3, Rigorous)

   A. The coach offered her assistance, however, the athletes wanted to practice on their own.

   B. The coach offered her assistance: furthermore, the athletes wanted to practice on their own.

   C. Having offered her assistance, the athletes wanted to practice on their own.

   D. The coach offered her assistance; however, the athletes wanted to practice on their own.

   E. The coach offered her assistance, and the athletes wanted to practice on their own.

10. <u>The Taj Mahal has been designated one of the Seven Wonders of the World, and people know it for its unique architecture</u>. (Skill 7.4, Rigorous)

A. The Taj Mahal has been designated one of the Seven Wonders of the World, and it is known for its unique architecture.

B. People know the Taj Mahal for its unique architecture, and it has been designated one of the Seven Wonders of the World.

C. People have known the Taj Mahal for its unique architecture, and it has been designated of the Seven Wonders of the World.

D. The Taj Mahal has designated itself one of the Seven Wonders of the World.

Part B

Directions: Select the best answer in each group of multiple choices.

11. To understand the origins of a word, one must study the (Skill 1.1, Easy)

    A. synonyms

    B. inflections

    C. phonetics

    D. etymology

12. The Elizabethans wrote in (Skill 1.1, Easy)

    A. Celtic

    B. Old English

    C. Middle English

    D. Modern English

13. Latin words that entered the English language during the Elizabethan age include (Skill 1.1, Average Rigor)

    A. allusion, education, and esteem

    B. vogue and mustache

    C. canoe and cannibal

    D. alligator, cocoa, and armadillo

14. Which event triggered the beginning of Modern English? (Skill 1.1, Average Rigor)

    A. Conquest of England by the Normans in 1066

    B. Introduction of the printing press to the British Isles

    C. Publication of Samuel Johnson's lexicon.

    D. American Revolution

15. Which of the following is *not* true about the English language? (Skill 1.1, Average Rigor)

    A. English is the easiest language to learn.

    B. English is the least inflected language.

    C. English has the most extensive vocabulary of any language.

    D. English originated as a Germanic tongue.

16. **What was responsible for the standardizing of dialects across America in the 20th century? (Skill 1.1, Rigorous)**

    A. With the immigrant influx, American became a melting pot of languages and cultures.

    B. Trains enabled people to meet other people of different languages and cultures.

    C. Radio, and later, television, used actors and announcers who spoke without pronounced dialects.

    D. Newspapers and libraries developed programs to teach people to speak English with an agreed-upon common dialect.

17. **If a student has a poor vocabulary, the teacher should recommend first that (Skill 1.2, Average Rigor)**

    A. the student read newspapers, magazines and books on a regular basis.

    B. the student enroll in a Latin class.

    C. the student write the words repetitively after looking them up in the dictionary.

    D. the student use a thesaurus to locate synonyms and incorporate them into his/her vocabulary

18. The synonyms *gyro, hero*, and *submarine* reflect which influence on language usage? (Skill 1.2, Average Rigor)

   A. Social

   B. Geographical

   C. Historical

   D. Personal

19. Which aspect of language is innate? (Skill 1.2, Rigorous)

   A. Biological capability to articulate sounds understood by other humans

   B. Cognitive ability to create syntactical structures

   C. Capacity for using semantics to convey meaning in a social environment

   D. Ability to vary inflections and accents

20. The arrangement and relationship of words in sentences or sentence structures best describes (Skill 1.2, Rigorous)

   A. style.

   B. discourse.

   C. thesis.

   D. syntax.

21. Which of the following sentences contains a subject-verb agreement error? (Skill 1.3, Average Rigor)

   A. Both mother and her two sisters were married in a triple ceremony.

   B. Neither the hen nor the rooster is likely to be served for dinner.

   C. My boss, as well as the company's two personnel directors, have been to Spain.

   D. Amanda and the twins are late again.

22. Which of the following is a formal reading-level assessment? (Skill 1.5, Average Rigor)

   A. A standardized reading test

   B. A teacher-made reading test

   C. An interview

   D. A reading diary

23. Which of the following is most true of expository writing? (Skill 1.6, Easy)

A. It is mutually exclusive of other forms of discourse.

B. It can incorporate other forms of discourse in the process of providing supporting details.

B. It should never employ informal expression.

D. It should only be scored with a summative evaluation.

24. In a class of non-native speakers of English, which type of activity will help students the most? (Skill 1.6, Rigorous)

A. Have students make oral presentations so that they can develop a phonological awareness of sounds.

B. Provide students more writing opportunities to develop their written communication skills.

C. Encourage students to listen to the new language on television and radio.

D. Provide a variety of methods to develop speaking, writing, and reading skills.

25. The new teaching intern is developing a unit on creative writing and is trying to encourage her freshman high school students to write poetry. Which of the following would *not* be an effective technique? (Skill 2.1, Average Rigor)

A. In groups, students will draw pictures to illustrate "The Love Song of J. Alfred Prufrock" by T.S. Eliot.

B. Either individually or in groups, students will compose a song, writing lyrics that try to use poetic devices.

C. Students will bring to class the lyrics of a popular song and discuss the imagery and figurative language.

D. Students will read aloud their favorite poems and share their opinions of and responses to the poems.

26. Explanatory or informative discourse is (Skill 2.2, Easy)

A. exposition.

B. narration.

C. persuasion.

D. description.

27. **What is the main form of discourse in this passage? (Skill 2.2, Average Rigor)**

It would have been hard to find a passer-by more wretched in appearance. He was a man of middle height, stout and hardy, in the strength of maturity; he might have been forty-six or seven. A slouched leather cap hid half his face, bronzed by the sun and wind, and dripping with sweat.

A. Description

B. Narration

C. Exposition

D. Persuasion

28. **Which of the following is *not* a technique of prewriting? (Skill 2.2, Easy)**

A. Clustering

B. Listing

C. Brainstorming

D. Proofreading

29. **In this paragraph from a student essay, identify the sentence that provides a detail. (Skill 2.2 Rigorous)**

(1) The poem concerns two different personality types and the human relation between them. (2) Their approach to life is totally different. (3) The neighbor is a very conservative person who follows routines. (4) He follows the traditional wisdom of his father and his father's father. (5) The purpose in fixing the wall and keeping their relationship separate is only because it is all he knows.

A. Sentence 1

B. Sentence 3

C. Sentence 4

D. Sentence 5

30. **Writing ideas quickly without interruption of the flow of thoughts or attention to conventions is called (Skill 2.3, Easy)**

A. brainstorming.

B. mapping.

C. listing.

D. free writing.

31. In general, the most serious drawback of using a computer in writing is that (Skill 2.3, Average Rigor)

    A. the copy looks so good that students tend to overlook major mistakes.

    B. the spell check and grammar programs discourage students from learning proper spelling and mechanics.

    C. the speed with which corrections can be made detracts from the exploration and contemplation of composing.

    D. the writer loses focus by concentrating on the final product rather than the details.

32. Which of the following is the least effective procedure for promoting consciousness of audience? (Skill 2.4, Average Rigor)

    A. Pairing students during the writing process

    B. Reading all rough drafts before the students write the final copies

    C. Having students compose stories or articles for publication in school literary magazines or newspapers

    D. Writing letters to friends or relatives

33. Reading a piece of student writing to assess the overall impression of the product is (Skill 2.5, Easy)

    A. holistic evaluation.

    B. portfolio assessment.

    C. analytical evaluation.

    D. using a performance system.

34. In preparing a speech for a contest, your student has encountered problems with gender specific language. Not wishing to offend either women or men, he seeks your guidance. Which of the following is *not* an effective strategy? (Skill 2.5, Rigorous)

    A. Use the generic "he" and explain that people will understand and accept the male pronoun as all-inclusive.

    B. Switch to plural nouns and use "they" as the gender-neutral pronoun.

    C. Use passive voice so that the subject is not required.

    D. Use male pronouns for one part of the speech and then use female pronouns for the other part of the speech.

35. A formative evaluation of student writing (Skill 2.5, Rigorous)

A. requires thorough markings of mechanical errors with a pencil or pen.

B. making comments on the appropriateness of the student's interpretation of the prompt and the degree to which the objective was met.

C. should require that the student hand in all the materials produced during the process of writing.

D. several careful readings of the text for content, mechanics, spelling, and usage.

36. In preparing a report about William Shakespeare, students are asked to develop a set of interpretive questions to guide their research. Which of the following would *not* be classified as an interpretive question? (Skill 3.1, Rigorous)

A. What would be different today if Shakespeare had not written his plays?

B. How will the plays of Shakespeare affect future generations?

C. How does the Shakespeare view nature in *A Midsummer's Night Dream* and *Much Ado About Nothing*?

D. During the Elizabethan age, what roles did young boys take in dramatizing Shakespeare's plays?

37. Which word in the following sentence is a bound morpheme: The quick brown fox jumped over the lazy dog"? (Skill 3.2, Rigorous)

A. The

B. fox

C. lazy

D. jumped

38. In writing a report, Hector has to explain where acid rain comes from and what it has done to the environment. What is the most likely form of organizational structure? (Skill 3.1, Easy)

   A. Cause and effect

   B. Problem and solution

   C. Exposition

   D. Definition

39. For their research paper on the effects of the Civil War on American literature, students have brainstormed a list of potential online sources and are seeking your authorization. Which of these represent the strongest source? (Skill 3.3, Rigorous)

   A. http://www.wikipedia.org/

   B. http://www.google.com

   C. http://www.nytimes.com

   D. http://docsouth. unc.edu/southlit/civilwar.html

40. The students in Mrs. Cline's seventh grade language arts class were invited to attend a performance of *Romeo and Juliet* presented by the drama class at the high school. To best prepare, they should (Skill 3.4, Average Rigor)

   A. read the play as a homework exercise.

   B. read a synopsis of the plot and a biographical sketch of the author.

   C. examine a few main selections from the play to become familiar with the language and style of the author.

   D. read a condensed version of the story and practice attentive listening skills.

41. The English department is developing strategies to encourage all students to become a community of readers. From the list of suggestions below, which would be the least effective way for teachers to foster independent reading? (Skill 3.4, Average Rigor)

A. Each teacher will set aside a weekly 30-minute in-class reading session during which the teacher and students read a magazine or book for enjoyment.

B. Teacher and students develop a list of favorite books to share with each other.

C. The teacher assigns at least one book report each grading period to ensure that students are reading from the established class list.

D. The students gather books for a classroom library so that books may be shared with each other.

42. Which of the following responses to literature typically give middle school students the most problems? (Skill 3.4, Average Rigor)

A. Interpretive

B. Evaluative

C. Critical

D. Emotional

43. Based on the excerpt below from Kate Chopin's short story "The Story of an Hour," what can students infer about the main character? (Skill 3.4, Rigorous)

She did not stop to ask if it were or were not a monstrous joy that held her. A clear and exalted perception enabled her to dismiss the suggestion as trivial. She knew that she would weep again when she saw the kind, tender hands folded in death; the face that had never looked save with love upon her, fixed and gray and dead. But she saw beyond that bitter moment a long procession of years to come that would belong to her absolutely. And she opened and spread her arms out to them in welcome.

A. She dreaded her life as a widow.

B. Although she loved her husband, she was glad that he was dead for he had never loved her.

C. She worried that she was too indifferent to her husband's death.

D. Although they had both loved each other, she was beginning to appreciate that opportunities had opened because of his death.

44. Recognizing empathy in literature is mostly a/an (Skill 3.4, Rigorous)

A. emotional response.

B. interpretive response.

C. critical response.

D. evaluative response.

45. The substitution of *went to his rest* for *died* is an example of a/an (Skill 4.1, Easy)

A. bowdlerism.

B. jargon.

C. euphemism.

D. malapropism.

46. In the following quotation, addressing the dead body of Caesar as though he were still a living being is to employ an (Skill 4.1, Average Rigor)

O, pardon me, though
Bleeding piece of earth
That I am meek and gentle with
These butchers.

-Marc Antony
from *Julius Caesar*

A. apostrophe

B. allusion

C. antithesis

D. anachronism

47. The literary device of personification is used in which example below? (Skill 4.1, Average Rigor)

   A. "Beg me no beggary by soul or parents, whining dog!"

   B. "Happiness sped through the halls cajoling as it went."

   C. "O wind thy horn, thou proud fellow."

   D. "And that one talent which is death to hide."

48. An extended metaphor comparing two very dissimilar things (one lofty one lowly) is a definition of a/an (Skill 4.1, Average Rigor)

   A. antithesis.

   B. aphorism.

   C. apostrophe.

   D. conceit.

49. Which of the following is a characteristic of blank verse? (Skill 4.1, Average Rigor)

   A. Meter in iambic pentameter

   B. Clearly specified rhyme scheme

   C. Lack of figurative language

   D. Unspecified rhythm

50. Which is the best definition of free verse, or vers libre? (Skill 4.1, Average Rigor)

   A. Poetry, which consists of an unaccented syllable followed by an unaccented sound.

   B. Short lyrical poetry written to entertain but with an instructive purpose.

   C. Poetry, which does not have a uniform pattern of rhythm.

   D. A poem which tells the story and has a plot

51. What is the salient literary feature of this excerpt from an epic? (Skill 4.1, Rigorous)

   Hither the heroes and the nymphs resorts,
   To taste awhile the pleasures of a court;
   In various talk th'instructive hours they passed,
   Who gave the ball, or paid the visit last;
   One speaks the glory of the English Queen,
   And another describes a charming Indian screen;
   A third interprets motion, looks, and eyes;
   At every word a reputation dies.

   A. Sprung rhythm

   B. Onomatopoeia

   C. Heroic couplets

   D. Motif

52. **What syntactic device is most evident from Abraham Lincoln's "Gettysburg Address"? (Skill 4.1, Rigorous)**

It is rather for us to be here dedicated to the great task remaining before us -- that from these honored dead we take increased devotion to that cause for which they gave the last full measure of devotion -- that we here highly resolve that these dead shall not have died in vain -- that this nation, under God, shall have a new birth of freedom -- and that government of the people, by the people, for the people, shall not perish from the earth.

A. Affective connotation

B. Informative denotations

C. Allusion

D. Parallelism

53. **Which poem is typified as a villanelle? (Skill 4.1, Rigorous)**

A. "Do not go gentle into that good night"

B. "Dover Beach"

C. *Sir Gawain and the Green Knight*

D. *Pilgrim's Progress*

54. **Which term best describes the form of the following poetic excerpt? (Skill 4.1, Rigorous)**

And more to lulle him in his slumber soft,
A trickling streake from high rock tumbling downe,
And ever-drizzling raine upon the loft.
Mixt with a murmuring winde, much like a swowne
No other noyse, nor peoples troubles cryes.
As still we wont t'annoy the walle'd towne,
Might there be heard: but careless Quiet lyes,
Wrapt in eternall silence farre from enemyes.

A. Ballad

B. Elegy

D. Spenserian stanza

D. Octava rima

55. **In the phrase "The Cabinet conferred with the President," Cabinet is an example of a/an (Skill 4.1, Rigorous)**

A. metonym

B. synecdoche

C. metaphor

D. allusion

56. In the following poem, what literary movement is reflected? (Skill 4.2, Rigorous)

"My Heart Leaps Up"
by William Wordsworth

My heart leaps up when I behold
   A rainbow in the sky:
So was it when my life began;
So is it now I am a man;
So be it when I shall grow old,
   Or let me die!
The Child is father of the Man;
And I could wish my days to be
Bound each to each by natural piety

A. Neo-classicism

B. Victorian literature

C. Romanticism

D. Naturalism

57. Which choice below best defines naturalism? (Skill 4.2, Rigorous)

A. A belief that the writer or artist should apply scientific objectivity in his/her observation and treatment of life without imposing value judgments.

B. The doctrine that teaches that the existing world is the best to be hoped for.

C. The doctrine that teaches that God is not a personality, but that all laws, forces and manifestations of the universe are God-related.

D. A philosophical doctrine that professes that the truth of all knowledge must always be in question.

58. A traditional, anonymous story, ostensibly having a historical basis, usually explaining some phenomenon of nature or aspect of creation, defines a (Skill 4.3, Easy)

A. proverb.

B. idyll.

C. myth.

D. epic.

59. Which of the following is *not* a characteristic of a fable? (Skill 4.3, Easy)

    A. Animals that feel and talk like humans.

    B. Happy solutions to human dilemmas.

    C. Teaches a moral or standard for behavior.

    D. Illustrates specific people or groups without directly naming them.

60. Which of the following would be the most significant factor in teaching Homer's *Iliad* and *Odyssey* to any particular group of students? (Skill 4.3, Average Rigor)

    A. Identifying a translation on the appropriate reading level

    B. Determining the students' interest level

    C. Selecting an appropriate evaluative technique

    D. Determining the scope and delivery methods of background study

61. Which of the following definitions best describes a parable? (Skill 4.3, Average Rigor)

    A. A short entertaining account of some happening, usually using talking animals as characters.

    B. A slow, sad song or poem, or prose work expressing lamentation.

    C. An extensive narrative work expressing universal truths concerning domestic life.

    D. A short, simple story of an occurrence of a familiar kind, from which a moral or religious lesson may be drawn.

62. How will literature help students in a science class understand the following passage? (Skill 4.3, Rigorous)

Just as was the case more than three decades ago, we are still sailing between the Scylla of deferring surgery for too long and risking irreversible left ventricular damage and sudden death, and the Charibdas of operating too early and subjecting the patient to the early risks of operation and the later risks resulting from prosthetic valves.
--E. Braunwald, *European Heart Journal*, July 2000

A. They will recognize the allusion to Scylla and Charibdas from Greek mythology and understand that the medical community has to select one of two unfavorable choices.

B. They will recognize the allusion to sailing and understand its analogy to doctors as sailors navigating unknown waters.

C. They will recognize that the allusion to Scylla and Charibdas refers to the two islands in Norse mythology where sailors would find themselves shipwrecked and understand how the doctors feel isolated by their choices.

D. They will recognize the metaphor of the heart and relate it to Eros, the character in Greek mythology who represents love. Eros was the love child of Scylla and Charibdas.

63. Which is *not* a Biblical allusion? (Skill 4.3, Rigorous)

A. The patience of Job

B. Thirty pieces of silver

C. "Man proposes; God disposes"

D. "Suffer not yourself to be betrayed by a kiss"

64. In classic tragedy, a protagonist's defeat is brought about by a tragic flaw which is called (Skill 4.3, Rigorous)

A. hubris

B. hamartia

C. catharsis

D. the skene

65. The tendency to emphasize and value the qualities and peculiarities of life in a particular geographic area exemplifies (Skill 4.4, Easy)

    A. pragmatism.

    B. regionalism.

    C. pantheism.

    D. abstractionism.

66. Which of the following is *not* a theme of Native American writing? (Skill 4.4, Average Rigor)

    A. Emphasis on the hardiness of the human body and soul

    B. The strength of multi-cultural assimilation

    C. Contrition for the genocide of native peoples

    D. Remorse for the love of the Indian way of life

67. Charles Dickens, Robert Browning, and Robert Louis Stevenson were (Skill 4.5, Easy)

    A. Victorians.

    B. Medievalists.

    C. Elizabethans.

    D. Absurdists.

68. Which of the following titles is known for its scathingly condemning tone? (Skill 4.5, Average Rigor)

    A. Boris Pasternak's *Dr Zhivago*

    B. Albert Camus' *The Stranger*

    C. Henry David Thoreau's "On the Duty of Civil Disobedience"

    D. Benjamin Franklin's "Rules by Which a Great Empire May Be Reduced to a Small One"

69. American colonial writers were primarily (Skill 4.5, Average Rigor)

    A. Romanticists.

    B. Naturalists.

    C. Realists.

    D. Neo-classicists.

70. Arthur Miller wrote *The Crucible* as a parallel to what twentieth century event? (Skill 4.5, Average Rigor)

    A. Sen. McCarthy's House un-American Activities Committee Hearing

    B. The Cold War

    C. The fall of the Berlin wall

    D. The Persian Gulf War

71. **Which of the writers below is a renowned Black poet? (Skill 4.5, Average Rigor)**

    A. Maya Angelou

    B. Sandra Cisneros

    C. Richard Wilbur

    D. Richard Wright

72. **The following lines from Robert Browning's poem "My Last Duchess" come from an example of what form of dramatic literature? (Skill 4.5, Rigorous)**

    That's my last Duchess painted on the wall,
    Looking as if she were alive. I call
    That piece a wonder
    now: Frà Pandolf's hands
    Worked busily a day
    and there she stands.
    Will 't please you sit and look at her?

    A. Tragedy

    B. Comic opera

    C. Dramatis personae

    D. Dramatic monologue

73. **"Every one must pass through Vanity Fair to get to the celestial city" is an allusion from a (Skill 4.5, Rigorous)**

    A. Chinese folk tale.

    B. Norse saga.

    C. British allegory.

    D. German fairy tale.

74. **Which author did *not* write satire? (Skill 4.5, Rigorous)**

    A. Joseph Addison

    B. Richard Steele

    C. Alexander Pope

    D. John Bunyan

75. **What were two major characteristics of the first American literature? (Skill 4.5, Rigorous)**

    A. Vengefulness and arrogance

    B. Bellicosity and derision

    C. Oral delivery and reverence for the land

    D. Maudlin and self-pitying egocentricism

76. Which sonnet form describes the following? (Skill 4.5, Rigorous)

My galley charg'd with
  forgetfulness,
Through sharp seas, in
  winter night doth pass
'Tween rock and rock; and
  eke mine enemy, alas,
That is my lord steereth with,
  cruelness.
And every oar a thought with
  readiness,
As though that death were
  light in such a case.
An endless wind doth tear
  the sail apace
Or forc'ed sighs and trusty
  fearfulness.
A rain of tears, a cloud of dark
  disdain,
Hath done the wearied
  cords great hinderance,
Wreathed with error and eke
  with ignorance.
The stars be hid that led me
  to this pain
Drowned is reason that
  should me consort,
And I remain despairing
  of the poet

A. Petrarchan or Italian sonnet

B. Shakespearian or
    Elizabethan sonnet

C. Romantic sonnet

D. Spenserian sonnet

77. Considered one of the first feminist plays, this Ibsen drama ends with a door slamming symbolizing the lead character's emancipation from traditional societal norms. (Skill 4.6, Easy)

A. *The Wild Duck*

B. *Hedda Gabler*

C. *Ghosts*

D. *The Doll's House*

78. Which of the following writers did *not* win a Nobel Prize for literature? (Skill 4.6, Average Rigor)

A. Gabriel Garcia-Marquez of Colombia

B. Nadine Gordimer of South Africa

C. Pablo Neruda of Chile

D. Alice Walker of the United States

79. The writing of Russian naturalists is (Skill 4.6, Average Rigor)

A. optimistic.

B. pessimistic.

C. satirical.

D. whimsical.

80. **Which of the following is the best definition of existentialism? (Skill 4.6, Rigorous)**

    A. The philosophical doctrine that matter is the only reality and that everything in the world, including thought, will and feeling, can be explained only in terms of matter.

    B. Philosophy that views things as they should be or as one would wish them to be.

    C. A philosophical and literary movement, variously religious and atheistic, stemming from Kierkegaard and represented by Sartre.

    D. The belief that all events are determined by fate and are hence inevitable.

81. **Which teaching method would best engage underachievers in the required senior English class? (Skill 4.7, Average Rigor)**

    A. Assign use of glossary work and extensively footnoted excerpts of great works.

    B. Have students take turns reading aloud the anthology selection

    C. Let students choose which readings they'll study and write about.

    D. Use a chronologically arranged, traditional text, but assigning group work, panel presentations, and portfolio management

82. Hoping to take advantage of the popularity of the Harry Potter series, a teacher develops a unit on mythology comparing the story and characters of Greek and Roman myths with the story and characters of the Harry Potter books. Which of these is a commonality that would link classical literature to popular fiction? (Skill 4.7, Rigorous)

A. The characters are gods in human form with human-like characteristics.

B. The settings are realistic places in the world where the characters interact as humans would.

C. The themes center on the universal truths of love and hate and fear.

D. The heroes in the stories are young males and only they can overcome the opposing forces.

83. Among junior-high school students of low-to-average readability levels, which work would most likely stir reading interest? (Skill 4.8, Easy)

A. *Elmer Gantry*, Sinclair Lewis

B. *Smiley's People*, John Le Carre

C. *The Outsiders*, S.E. Hinton

D. *And Then There Were None*, Agatha Christie.

84. What is the best course of action when a child refuses to complete a reading/ literature assignment on the grounds that it is morally objectionable? (Skill 4.8, Average Rigor)

A. Speak with the parents and explain the necessity of studying this work

B. Encourage the child to sample some of the text before making a judgment

C. Place the child in another teacher's class where they are studying an acceptable work

D. Provide the student with alternative selections that cover the same performance standards that the rest of the class is learning.

85. Most children's literature prior to the development of popular literature was intended to be didactic. Which of the following would *not* be considered didactic? (Skill 4.8, Average Rigor)

    A. "A Visit from St. Nicholas" by Clement Moore

    B. McGuffy's Reader

    C. Any version of Cinderella

    D. Parables from the Bible

86. Written on the sixth grade reading level, most of S. E. Hinton's novels (for instance, *The Outsiders*) have the greatest reader appeal with (Skill 4.8, Average Rigor)

    A. sixth graders.

    B. ninth graders.

    C. twelfth graders.

    D. adults.

87. Children's literature became established in the (Skill 4.8, Average Rigor)

    A. seventeenth century

    B. eighteenth century

    C. nineteenth century

    D. twentieth century

88. After watching a movie of a train derailment, a child exclaims, "Wow, look how many cars fell off the tracks. There's junk everywhere. The engineer must have really been asleep." Using the facts that the child is impressed by the wreckage and assigns blame to the engineer, a follower of Piaget's theories would estimate the child to be about (Skill 4.8, Rigorous)

    A. ten years old.

    B. twelve years old.

    C. fourteen years old.

    D. sixteen years old.

89. **The most significant drawback to applying learning theory research to classroom practice is that (Skill 4.8, Rigorous)**

    A. today's students do not acquire reading skills with the same alacrity as when greater emphasis was placed on reading classical literature.

    B. development rates are complicated by geographical and cultural In analyzing literature and in looking for ways to bring a work to life for an audience, the use of comparable themes and ideas from other pieces of literature and from one's own life experiences, including from reading the daily newspaper, is very important and useful.

    C. homogeneous grouping has contributed to faster development of some age groups.

    D. social and environmental conditions have contributed to an escalated maturity level than research done twenty of more years ago would seem to indicate.

90. **To explore the relationship of literature to modern life, which of these activities would *not* enable students to explore comparable themes? (Skill 4.9, Average Rigor)**

    A. After studying various world events, such as the Palestinian-Israeli conflict, students write an updated version of *Romeo and Juliet* using modern characters and settings.

    B. Before studying *Romeo and Juliet*, students watch *West Side Story*.

    C. Students research the major themes of *Romeo and Juliet* by studying news stories and finding modern counterparts for the story.

    D. Students would explore compare the romantic themes of *Romeo and Juliet* and *The Taming of the Shrew*.

91. In preparing students for their oral presentations, the instructor provided all of these guidelines, except one. Which is *not* an effective guideline? (Skill 5.1, Average Rigor)

   A. Even if you are using a lectern, feel free to move about. This will connect you to the audience.

   B. Your posture should be natural, not stiff. Keep your shoulders toward the audience.

   C. Gestures can help communicate as long as you don't overuse them or make them distracting.

   D. You can avoid eye contact if you focus on your notes. This will make you appear more knowledgeable.

92. In literature, evoking feelings of pity or compassion is to create (Skill 5.3, Average Rigor)

   A. colloquy.

   B. irony.

   C. pathos.

   D. paradox

93. What type of reasoning does Henry David Thoreau use in the following excerpt from "Civil Disobedience"? (Skill 5.3, Rigorous)

Unjust laws exist; shall we be content to obey them, or shall we endeavor to amend them, and obey them until we have succeeded, or shall we transgress them at once? Men generally, under such a government as this, think that they ought to wait until they have persuaded the majority to alter them. They think that, if they should resist, the remedy would be worse than the evil. But it is the fault of the government itself that the remedy is worse than the evil. ... Why does it always crucify Christ, and excommunicate Copernicus and Luther, and pronounce Washington and Franklin rebels?
"Civil Disobedience"
by Henry David Thoreau

   A. Ethical reasoning

   B. Inductive reasoning

   C. Deductive reasoning

   D. Intellectual reasoning

94. **Which of the following is *not* a fallacy in logic? (Skill 5.3 Rigorous)**

    A. All students in Ms. Suarez's fourth period class are bilingual.
    Beth is in Ms. Suarez's fourth period.
    Beth is bilingual.

    B. All bilingual students are in Ms. Suarez's class.
    Beth is in Ms. Suarez's fourth period.
    Beth is bilingual.

    C. Beth is bilingual.
    Beth is in Ms. Suarez's fourth period.
    All students in Ms. Suarez's fourth period are bilingual.

    D. If Beth is bilingual, then she speaks Spanish.
    Beth speaks French.
    Beth is not bilingual.

95. **Identify the type of appeal used by Molly Ivins's in this excerpt from her essay "Get a Knife, Get a Dog, But Get Rid of Guns." (Skill 5.3, Rigorous)**

    As a civil libertarian, I, of course, support the Second Amendment. And I believe it means exactly what it says:
    *A well regulated militia being necessary to the security of a free state, the right of the people to keep and bear arms shall not be infringe*d.

    A. Ethical

    B. Emotional

    C. Rational

    D. Literary

96. **What is the common advertising technique used by these advertising slogans? (Skill 5.3, Rigorous)**

    "It's everywhere you want to be." - Visa
    "Have it your way." - Burger King
    "When you care enough to send the very best" - Hallmark
    "Be all you can be" – U.S. Army

    A. Peer Approval

    B. Rebel

    C. Individuality

    D. Escape

97. In presenting a report to peers about the effects of Hurricane Katrina on New Orleans, the students wanted to use various media in their argument to persuade their peers that more needed to be done. Which of these would be the most effective? (Skill 5.4 Rigorous)

A   A PowerPoint presentation showing the blueprints of the levees before the flood and redesigned now for current construction..

B. A collection of music clips made by the street performers in the French Quarter before and after the flood.

C. A recent video showing the areas devastated by the floods and the current state of rebuilding.

D. A collection of recordings of interviews made by the various government officials and local citizens affected by the flooding.

98. Which of the following is *not* correct? (Skill 5.5, Easy)

A. Because most students have wide access to media, teachers should refrain from using it in their classrooms to diminish the overload.

B. Students can use CD-ROMs to explore information using a virtual reality experience.

C. Teacher can make their instruction more powerful by using educational media.

D. The Internet enables students to connect with people across cultures and to share interests.

99. Which of the following statements indicates an instructional goal for using multimedia in the classroom? (Skill 5.5, Average Rigor)

A. Audio messages invite the listener to form mental images consistent with the topic of the audio.

B. Print messages appeal almost exclusively to the mind and push students to read with more thought.

C. Listening to an audio message is more passive than reading a print message.

D. Teachers who develop activities to foster a critical perspective on audiovisual presentation will decrease passivity.

100. Which of the following type of question will *not* stimulate higher-level critical thinking? (Skill 5.6, Rigorous)

A. A hypothetical question

B. An open-ended question

C. A close-ended question

D. A judgment question

101. Which of the following would *not* be a major concern in an oral presentation? (Skill 5.7, Average Rigor)

A. Establishing the purpose of the presentation

B. Evaluating the audience's demographics and psychographics.

C. Creating a PowerPoint slide for each point.

D. Developing the content to fit the occasion.

102. Mr. Ledbetter has instructed his students to prepare a slide presentation that illustrates an event in history. Students are to include pictures, graphics, media clips and links to resources. What competencies will students exhibit at the completion of this project? (Skill 5.7, Rigorous)

A. Analyze the impact of society on media.

B. Recognize the media's strategies to inform and persuade.

C. Demonstrate strategies and creative techniques to prepare presentations using a variety of media.

D. Identify the aesthetic effects of a media presentation.

103 **If a student uses slang and expletives, what is the best course of action to take in order to improve the student's formal communication skills? (Skill 6.1, Average Rigor)**

A. Ask the student to paraphrase their writing, that is, translate it into language appropriate for the school principal to read.

B. Refuse to read the student's papers until he conforms to a more literate style.

C. Ask the student to read his work aloud to the class for peer evaluation.

D. Rewrite the flagrant passages to show the student the right form of expression.

104. **Modeling is a practice that requires students to (Skill 6.1, Average Rigor)**

A. create a style unique to their own language capabilities.

B. emulate the writing of professionals.

C. paraphrase passages from good literature.

D. peer evaluate the writings of other students.

105. **Mr. Phillips is creating a unit to study *To Kill a Mockingbird* and wants to familiarize his high school freshmen with the attitudes and issues of the historical period. Which activity would familiarize students with the attitudes and issues of the Depression-era South? (Skill 6.1, Rigorous)**

A. Create a detailed timeline of 15-20 social, cultural, and political events that focus on race relations in the 1930s.

B. Research and report on the life of its author Harper Lee. Compare her background with the events in the book.

C. Watch the movie version and note language and dress.

D. Write a research report on the stock market crash of 1929 and its effects.

106. What is *not* one of the advantages of collaborative or cooperative learning? (Skill 6.2, Easy)

   A. Students that work together in groups or teams develop their skills in organizing, leadership, research, communication, and problem solving.

   B. Working in teams can help students overcome anxiety in distance learning courses and contribute a sense of community and belonging for the students.

   C. Students tend to learn more material being taught and retain the information longer than when the same information is taught using different methods.

   D. Teachers reduce their workload and the time spent on individuals the assignments, and grading.

107. Overcrowded classes prevent the individual attention needed to facilitate language development. This drawback can be best overcome by (Skill 6.2, Average Rigor)

   A. dividing the class into independent study groups.

   B. assigning more study time at home.

   C. using more drill practice in class.

   D. team teaching.

108. For students to prepare for a their roles in a dramatic performance, (Skill 6.2, Rigorous)

   A. they should analyze their characters to develop a deeper understanding of the character's attitudes and motivations.

   B. they should attend local plays to study settings and stage design.

   C. they should read articles and books on acting methodology.

   D. they should practice the way other actors have performed in these roles.

109. **Students returning from a field trip to the local newspaper want to thank their hosts for the guided tour. As their teacher, what form of communication should you encourage them to use? (Skill 6.3, Average Rigor)**

    A. Each student will send an email expressing his or her appreciation.

    B. As a class, students will create a blog, and each student will write about what they learned.

    C. Each student will write a thank you letter that the teacher will fax to the newspaper.

    D. Each student will write a thank you note that the teacher will mail to the newspaper.

110. **Middle and high school students are more receptive to studying grammar and syntax (Skill 6.4, Average Rigor)**

    A. through worksheets and end of lessons practices in textbooks.

    B. through independent, homework assignment.

    C. through analytical examination of the writings of famous authors.

    D. through application to their own writing.

111. **Which definition is the best for defining diction? (Skill 7.2, Easy)**

    A. The specific word choices of an author to create a particular mood or feeling in the reader.

    B. Writing which explains something thoroughly.

    C. The background, or exposition, for a short story or drama.

    D. Word choices that help teach a truth or moral.

112. **Which of the following should *not* be included in the opening paragraph of an informative essay? (Skill 7.2, Easy)**

    A. Thesis sentence

    B. Details and examples supporting the main idea

    C. Broad general introduction to the topic

    D. A style and tone that grabs the reader's attention

113. **In the paragraph below, which sentence does *not* contribute to the overall task of supporting the main idea? (Skill 7.2 Easy)**

    1) The Springfield City Council met Friday to discuss new zoning restrictions for the land to be developed south of the city. 2) Residents who opposed the new restrictions were granted 15 minutes to present their case. 3) Their argument focused on the dangers that increased traffic would bring to the area. 4) It seemed to me that the Mayor Simpson listened intently. 5) The council agreed to table the new zoning until studies would be performed.

    A. Sentence 2

    B. Sentence 3

    C. Sentence 4

    D. Sentence 5

114. **In an "inverted triangle" introductory paragraphs, the thesis sentence occurs (Skill 7.3, Easy)**

    A. at the beginning of the paragraph.

    B. in the middle of the paragraph.

    C. at the end of the paragraph.

    D. in the second paragraph.

115. Which of the following sentences contains a capitalization error? (Skill 7.3, Average Rigor)

A. The commander of the English navy was Admiral Nelson

B. Napoleon was the president of the French First Republic

C. Queen Elizabeth II is the Monarch of the British Empire

D. William the Conqueror led the Normans to victory over the British

116. In preparing your high school freshmen to write a research paper about a social problem, what recommendation can you make so they can determine the credibility of their information? (Skill 7.4, Easy)

A. Assure them that information on the Internet has been peer-reviewed and verified for accuracy.

B. Find one solid source and use that exclusively.

C. Use only primary sources.

D. Cross check your information with another credible source.

117. Which of the following are secondary research materials? (Skill 7.4, Average Rigor)

A. The conclusions and inferences of other historians.

B. Literature and nonverbal materials, novels, stories, poetry and essays from the period, as well as coins, archaeological artifacts, and art produced during the period.

C. Interviews and surveys conducted by the researcher.

D. Statistics gathered as the result of the research's experiments.

118. **Which of the following is an example of the post hoc fallacy? (Skill 7.4, Rigorous)**

   A. When the new principal was hired, student-reading scores improved; therefore, the principal caused the increase in scores.

   B. Why are we spending money on the space program when our students don't have current textbooks?

   C. You can't give your class a 10-minute break. Once you do that, we'll all have to give our students a 10-minute break.

   D. You can never believe anything he says because he's not from the same country as we are.

119. **To determine the credibility of information, researchers should do all of the following except (Skill 7.4, Rigorous)**

   A. establish the authority of the document.

   B. disregard documents with bias.

   C. evaluate the currency and reputation of the source.

   D. use a variety of research sources and methods.

120. **Which of the following situations is *not* an ethical violation of intellectual property? (Skill 7.4, Rigorous)**

   A. A student visits ten different websites and writes a report to compare the costs of downloading music. He uses the names of the websites without their permission.

   B. A student copies and pastes a chart verbatim from the Internet but does not document it because it is available on a public site.

   C. From an online article found in a subscription database, a student paraphrases a section on the problems of music piracy. She includes the source in her Works Cited but does not provide an in-text citation.

   D. A student uses a comment from M. Night Shyamalan without attribution claiming the information is common knowledge.

121. **Students have been asked to write a research paper on automobiles and have brainstormed a number of questions they will answer based on their research findings. Which of the following is *not* an interpretive question to guide research? (Skill 7.4, Rigorous)**

   A. Who were the first ten automotive manufacturers in the United States?

   B. What types of vehicles will be used fifty years from now?

   C. How do automobiles manufactured in the United States compare and contrast with each other?

   D. What do you think is the best solution for the fuel shortage?

122. **Which of the following should students use to improve coherence of ideas within an argument? (Skill 7.5, Easy)**

   A. Transitional words or phrases to show relationship of ideas.

   B. Conjunctions like "and" to join ideas together.

   C. Use direct quotes extensively to improve credibility.

   D. Adjectives and adverbs to provide stronger detail.

123. **Which transition word would show contrast between these two ideas? (Skill 7.5, Average Rigor)**

   We are confident in our skills to teach English. We welcome new ideas on this subject.

   A. We are confident in our skills to teach English, and we welcome new ideas on this subject.

   B. Because we are confident in our skills to teach English, we welcome new ideas on the subject.

   C. When we are confident in our skills to teach English, we welcome new ideas on the subject.

   D. We are confident in our skills to teach English; however, we welcome new ideas on the subject.

124. **Which sentence below best minimizes the impact of bad news?** (Skill 7.5, Rigorous)

    A. We have denied you permission to attend the event.

    B. Although permission to attend the event cannot be given, you are encouraged to buy the video.

    C. Although you cannot attend the event, we encourage you to buy the video.

    D. Although attending the event is not possible, watching the video is an option.

125. **Which part of a classical argument is illustrated in this excerpt from the essay "What Should Be Done About Rock Lyrics?"** (Skill 7.5, Rigorous)

    But violence against women is greeted by silence. It shouldn't be.
    This does not mean censorship, or book (or record) burning. In a society that protects free expression, we understand a lot of stuff will float up out of the sewer. Usually, we recognize the ugly stuff that advocates violence against any group as the garbage it is, and we consider its purveyors as moral lepers. We hold our nose and tolerate it, but we speak out against the values it proffers.
    --"What Should Be Done About Rock Lyrics?" Caryl Rivers

    A. Narration

    B. Confirmation

    C. Refutation and concession

    D. Summation

1	C	26	A	51	C	76	A	101	C
2	C	27	A	52	D	77	D	102	B
3	C	28	D	53	A	78	D	103	A
4	B	29	C	54	D	79	B	104	B
5	D	30	D	55	B	80	C	105	A
6	C	31	C	56	C	81	C	106	D
7	D	32	B	57	A	82	C	107	A
8	A	33	A	58	C	83	C	108	A
9	D	34	A	59	D	84	D	109	D
10	A	35	B	60	A	85	A	110	D
11	D	36	D	61	D	86	B	111	A
12	D	37	D	62	A	87	A	112	B
13	A	38	A	63	C	88	A	113	C
14	B	39	D	64	B	89	D	114	C
15	A	40	D	65	B	90	D	115	C
16	C	41	C	66	B	91	D	116	D
17	A	42	B	67	A	92	C	117	A
18	B	43	D	68	D	93	C	118	A
19	A	44	C	69	D	94	A	119	B
20	D	45	C	70	A	95	A	120	A
21	B	46	A	71	A	96	C	121	A
22	A	47	B	72	D	97	C	122	B
23	B	48	D	73	C	98	A	123	D
24	A	49	A	74	D	99	D	124	B
25	A	50	C	75	D	100	C	125	C

Rigor Table

	Easy 20%	Average Rigor 40%	Rigorous 40%
Question #	1, 5, 11, 12, 23, 26, 28, 30, 33, 38, 45, 58, 59, 65, 67, 77, 83, 98, 106, 111, 112, 113, 114, 116, 122,	2, 3, 6, 8, 13, 14, 15, 17, 18, 21, 22, 25, 27, 31, 32, 40, 41, 42, 46, 47, 48, 49, 50, 60, 61, 66, 68, 69, 70, 71, 78, 79, 81, 84, 85, 86, 87, 90, 91, 92, 99, 101, 103, 104, 107, 109, 110, 115, 117, 123,	4, 7, 9, 10, 16, 19, 20, 24, 29, 34, 35, 36, 37, 39, 43, 44, 51, 52, 53, 54, 55, 56, 57, 62, 63, 64, 72, 73, 74, 75, 76, 80, 82, 88, 89, 93, 94, 95, 96, 97, 100, 102, 105, 108, 118, 119, 120, 121, 124, 125

RATIONALES

Part A

Each underlined portion of sentences 1-10 contains one or more errors in grammar, usage, mechanics, or sentence structure. Circle the choice which best corrects the error without changing the meaning of the original sentence.

1. Joe <u>didn't hardly know his cousin Fred</u> who'd had a rhinoplasty. (Skill 1.2, Easy)

    A. hardly did know his cousin Fred

    B. didn't know his cousin Fred hardly

    C. hardly knew his cousin Fred

    D. didn't know his cousin Fred

    E. didn't hardly know his cousin Fred

The answer is C. Using the adverb "hardly" to modify the verb creates a negative, and adding "not" creates the dreaded double negative.

2. <u>Mixing the batter for cookies, the cat</u> licked the Crisco from the cookie sheet. (Skill 1.2, Average Rigor)

    A. While mixing the batter for cookies

    B. While the batter for cookies was mixing

    C. While I mixed the batter for cookies

    D. While I mixed the cookies

    E. Mixing the batter for cookies

The answer is C. Choices A and E give the impression that the cat was mixing the batter (it is a dangling modifier.), Choice B that the batter was mixing itself, and Choice D lacks precision: it is the batter that was being mixed, not the cookies themselves.

3.   **Mr. Smith <u>respectfully submitted his resignation and had</u> a new job.** **(Skill 1.2, Average Rigor)**

A. respectfully submitted his resignation and has

B. respectfully submitted his resignation before accepting

C. respectfully submitted his resignation because of

D. respectfully submitted his resignation and had

The answer is C. Choice A eliminates any relationship of causality between submitting the resignation and having the new job. Choice B just changes the sentence and does not indicate the fact that Mr. Smith had a new job before submitting his resignation. Choice D means that Mr. Smith first submitted his resignation, and then got a new job.

4.   **Walt Whitman was famous for his composition, <u>*Leaves* of Grass, serving as a nurse during the Civil War, and a devoted son</u>. (Skill 1.2, Rigorous)**

A. *Leaves of Grass*, his service as a nurse during the Civil War, and a devoted son

B. composing *Leaves of Grass*, serving as a nurse during the Civil War, and being a devoted son

C. his composition, *Leaves of Grass*, his nursing during the Civil War, and his devotion as a son

D. his composition *Leaves of Grass,* serving as a nurse during the Civil War and a devoted son

E. his composition *Leaves of Grass*, serving as a nurse during the Civil War. and a devoted son

The answer is B: In order to be parallel, the sentence needs three gerunds. The other sentences use both gerunds and nouns, which is a lack of parallelism.

5. There were <u>fewer pieces</u> of evidence presented during the second trial. (Skill 1.3, Easy)

   A. fewer peaces

   B. less peaces

   C. less pieces

   D. fewer pieces

The answer is D. Use "fewer" for countable items; use "less" for amounts and quantities, such as fewer minutes but less time "Peace" is the opposite of war, not a "piece" of evidence.

6. The teacher <u>implied</u> from our angry words that there was conflict <u>between you and me</u>. (Skill 1.3, Average Rigor)

   A.   Implied… between you and I

   B.   Inferred… between you and I

   C.   Inferred… between you and me

   D.   Implied… between you and me

The answer is C. The difference between the verb "to imply" and the verb "to infer" is that implying is directing an interpretation toward other people; to infer is to deduce an interpretation from someone else's discourse. Moreover, "between you and I" is grammatically incorrect: after the preposition "between," the object (or 'disjunctive' with this particular preposition) pronoun form, "me," is needed.

7. **A teacher <u>must know not only her subject matter but also the strategies of content teaching</u>. (Skill 1.3, Rigorous)**

    A. must not only know her subject matter but also the strategies of content teaching

    B. not only must know her subject matter but also the strategies of content teaching

    C. must not know only her subject matter but also the strategies of content teaching

    D. must know not only her subject matter but also the strategies of content teaching

The answer is D. "Not only" must come directly after "know" because the intent is to create the clearest meaning link with the "but also" predicate section later in the sentence.

8. **8. Wally <u>groaned</u>, "Why do I have to do an oral interpretation <u>of "The Raven."</u> (Skill 7.3, Average Rigor)**

    A. groaned "Why... of 'The Raven'?"

    B. groaned "Why... of "The Raven"?

    C. groaned ", Why... of "The Raven?"

    D. groaned, "Why... of "The Raven."

The answer is A. The question mark in a quotation that is an interrogation should be within the quotation marks. Also, when quoting a work of literature within another quotation, one should use single quotation marks ('...') for the title of this work, and they should close before the final quotation mark.

9.   The coach <u>offered her assistance but the athletes wanted to practice on their own</u>. (Skill 7.3, Rigorous)

   A.   The coach offered her assistance, however, the athletes wanted to practice on their own.

   B.   The coach offered her assistance: furthermore, the athletes wanted to practice on their own.

   C.   Having offered her assistance, the athletes wanted to practice on their own.

   D.   The coach offered her assistance; however, the athletes wanted to practice on their own.

   E.   The coach offered her assistance, and the athletes wanted to practice on their own.

The answer is D. A semicolon precedes a transitional adverb that introduces an independent clause. Choice A is a comma splice. In Choice B, the colon is used incorrectly since the second clause does not explain the first. In Choice C, the opening clause confuses the meaning of the sentence. In Choice E, the conjunction "and" is weak since the two ideas show contrast rather than an additional thought.

10. **The Taj Mahal has been designated one of the Seven Wonders of the World, and people know it for its unique architecture.** (Skill 7.4, Rigorous)

   A. The Taj Mahal has been designated one of the Seven Wonders of the World, and it is known for its unique architecture.

   B. People know the Taj Mahal for its unique architecture, and it has been designated one of the Seven Wonders of the World.

   C. People have known the Taj Mahal for its unique architecture, and it has been designated of the Seven Wonders of the World.

   D. The Taj Mahal has designated itself one of the Seven Wonders of the World.

The answer is A because both clauses are passive voice. In the original sentence, the first clause is passive voice and the second clause is active voice, causing a voice shift. Choice B merely switches the clauses but does not correct the voice shift. In Choice C, only the verb tense in the first clause has been changed but it still active voice. Choice D changes the meaning.

Part B

Directions: Select the best answer in each group of multiple choices.

11. **To understand the origins of a word, one must study the (Skill 1.1, Easy)**

   A. synonyms

   B. inflections

   C. phonetics

   D. etymology

The answer is D. Etymology is the study of word origins. A synonym is an equivalent of another word and can substitute for it in certain contexts. Inflection is a modification of words according to their grammatical functions, usually by employing variant word-endings to indicate such qualities as tense, gender, case, and number. Phonetics is the science devoted to the physical analysis of the sounds of human speech, including their production, transmission, and perception.

12. **The Elizabethans wrote in (Skill 1.1, Easy)**

   A. Celtic

   B. Old English

   C. Middle English

   D. Modern English

The answer is D. There is no document written in Celtic in England, and a work such as *Beowulf* is representative of Old English in the eighth century. It is also the earliest Teutonic written document. Before the fourteenth century, little literature is known to have appeared in Middle English, which had absorbed many words from the Norman French spoken by the ruling class, but at the end of the fourteenth century there appeared the works of Chaucer, John Gower, and the novel *Sir Gawain and the Green Knight*. The Elizabethans wrote in modern English and their legacy is very important: they imported the Petrarchan, or Italian, sonnet, which Sir Thomas Wyatt and Sir Philip Sydney illustrated in their works. Sir Edmund Spencer invented his own version of the Italian sonnet and wrote *The Faerie Queene*. Other literature of the time includes the hugely important works of Shakespeare and Marlowe.

13. **Latin words that entered the English language during the Elizabethan age include (Skill 1.1, Average Rigor)**

    A. allusion, education, and esteem

    B. vogue and mustache

    C. canoe and cannibal

    D. alligator, cocoa, and armadillo

The answer is A. These words reflect the Renaissance interest in the classical world and the study of ideas. The words in Choice B are French derivation, and the words in Choices C and D are more modern with younger etymologies.

14. **Which event triggered the beginning of Modern English? (Skill 1.1, Average Rigor)**

    A. Conquest of England by the Normans in 1066

    B. Introduction of the printing press to the British Isles

    C. Publication of Samuel Johnson's lexicon.

    D. American Revolution

The answer is B. With the arrival of the written word, reading matter became mass-produced, so the public tended to adopt the speech and writing habits printed in books and the language became more stable.

15. Which of the following is *not* true about the English language? (Skill 1.1, Average Rigor)

    A. English is the easiest language to learn.

    B. English is the least inflected language.

    C. English has the most extensive vocabulary of any language.

    D. English originated as a Germanic tongue.

The answer is A. Just like any other language, English has inherent difficulties which make it difficult to learn, even though English has no declensions such as those found in Latin, Greek, or contemporary Russian, or a tonal system such Chinese.

16. What was responsible for the standardizing of dialects across America in the 20th century? (Skill 1.1, Rigorous)

    A. With the immigrant influx, American became a melting pot of languages and cultures.

    B. Trains enabled people to meet other people of different languages and cultures.

    C. Radio, and later, television, used actors and announcers who spoke without pronounced dialects.

    D. Newspapers and libraries developed programs to teach people to speak English with an agreed-upon common dialect.

The answer is C. The growth of immigration in the early part of the 20th century created pockets of language throughout the country. Coupled with regional differences already in place, the number of dialects grew. Transportation enabled people to move to different regions where languages and dialects continued to merge. With the growth of radio and television, however, people were introduced to a standardized dialect through actors and announcers who spoke so that anyone across American could understand them. Newspapers and libraries never developed programs to standardize spoken English.

17. **If a student has a poor vocabulary, the teacher should recommend first that (Skill 1.2, Average Rigor)**

    A. the student read newspapers, magazines and books on a regular basis.

    B. the student enroll in a Latin class.

    C. the student write the words repetitively after looking them up in the dictionary.

    D. the student use a thesaurus to locate synonyms and incorporate them into his/her vocabulary

The answer is A. It is up to the teacher to help the student choose reading material, but the student must be able to choose where to search for the reading pleasure indispensable for enriching vocabulary.

18. **The synonyms *gyro, hero,* and *submarine* reflect which influence on language usage? (Skill 1.2, Average Rigor)**

    A. Social

    B. Geographical

    C. Historical

    D. Personal

The answer is B. They are interchangeable but their use depends on the region of the United States, not on the social class of the speaker. Nor is there any historical context around any of them. The usage can be personal but will most often vary with the region.

19. **Which aspect of language is innate?** (Skill 1.2, Rigorous)

    A. Biological capability to articulate sounds understood by other humans

    B. Cognitive ability to create syntactical structures

    C. Capacity for using semantics to convey meaning in a social environment

    D. Ability to vary inflections and accents

The answer is A. Language ability is innate and the biological capability to produce sounds lets children learn semantics and syntactical structures through trial and error. Linguists agree that language is first a vocal system of word symbols that enable a human to communicate his/her feelings, thoughts, and desires to other human beings.

20. **The arrangement and relationship of words in sentences or sentence structures best describes** (Skill 1.2, Rigorous)

    A. style.

    B. discourse.

    C. thesis.

    D. syntax.

The answer is D. Syntax is the grammatical structure of sentences. Style is the manner of expression of writing or speaking. Discourse is an extended expression of thought through either oral or written communication. A thesis is the unifying main idea that can be either explicit or implicit.

21. **Which of the following sentences contains a subject-verb agreement error? (Skill 1.3, Average Rigor)**

    A. Both mother and her two sisters were married in a triple ceremony.

    B. Neither the hen nor the rooster is likely to be served for dinner.

    C. My boss, as well as the company's two personnel directors, have been to Spain.

    D. Amanda and the twins are late again.

The answer is B. The reason for this is that the true subject of the verb is "My boss," not "two personnel directors."

22. **Which of the following is a formal reading-level assessment? (Skill 1.5, Average Rigor)**

    A. A standardized reading test

    B. A teacher-made reading test

    C. An interview

    D. A reading diary

The answer is A. If assessment is standardized, it has to be objective whereas Choices B, C and D are all subjective assessments.

23. **Which of the following is most true of expository writing? (Skill 1.6, Easy)**

    A. It is mutually exclusive of other forms of discourse.

    B. It can incorporate other forms of discourse in the process of providing supporting details.

    B. It should never employ informal expression.

    D. It should only be scored with a summative evaluation.

The answer is B. Expository writing sets forth an explanation or an argument about any subject and can use distinct or combined forms of discourse, a sign of academic literacy. This directly contradicts Choice A. Writing can use formal and informal language and can be evaluated in many subjective and objective ways.

24. **In a class of non-native speakers of English, which type of activity will help students the most? (Skill 1.6, Rigorous)**

    A. Have students make oral presentations so that they can develop a phonological awareness of sounds.

    B. Provide students more writing opportunities to develop their written communication skills.

    C. Encourage students to listen to the new language on television and radio.

    D. Provide a variety of methods to develop speaking, writing, and reading skills.

The answer is A. Research indicates that non-native speakers of English develop stronger second language skills by understanding the phonological differences in spoken words.

25. **The new teaching intern is developing a unit on creative writing and is trying to encourage her freshman high school students to write poetry. Which of the following would *not* be an effective technique? (Skill 2.1, Average Rigor)**

   A. In groups, students will draw pictures to illustrate "The Love Song of J. Alfred Prufrock" by T.S. Eliot.

   B. Either individually or in groups, students will compose a song, writing lyrics that try to use poetic devices.

   C. Students will bring to class the lyrics of a popular song and discuss the imagery and figurative language.

   D. Students will read aloud their favorite poems and share their opinions of and responses to the poems.

The answer is A. While drawing is creative, it will not accomplish as much as the other activities to encourage students to write their own poetry. Furthermore, "The Love Song of J. Alfred Prufrock" is not a freshman-level poem. The other activities involve students in music and their own favorites, which will be more appealing.

26. **Explanatory or informative discourse is (Skill 2.2, Easy)**

   A.   exposition.

   B.   narration.

   C.   persuasion.

   D.   description.

The answer is A. Exposition sets forth a systematic explanation of any subject. It can also introduce the characters of a literary work, and their situations in the story. Narration relates a sequence of events (the story) told through a process of narration (discourse), in which events are recounted in a certain order (the plot). Persuasion strives to convince either a character in the story or the reader.

27. **What is the main form of discourse in this passage? (Skill 2.2, Average Rigor)**

    It would have been hard to find a passer-by more wretched in appearance. He was a man of middle height, stout and hardy, in the strength of maturity; he might have been forty-six or seven. A slouched leather cap hid half his face, bronzed by the sun and wind, and dripping with sweat.

    A. Description

    B. Narration

    C. Exposition

    D. Persuasion

The answer is A. A description presents a thing or a person in detail, and tells the reader about the appearance of whatever it is presenting. Narration relates a sequence of events (the story) told through a process of narration (discourse), in which events are recounted in a certain order (the plot). Exposition is an explanation or an argument within the narration. It can also be the introduction to a play or a story. Persuasion strives to convince either a character in the story or the reader.

28. **Which of the following is *not* a technique of prewriting? (Skill 2.2, Easy)**

    A. Clustering

    B. Listing

    C. Brainstorming

    D. Proofreading

The answer is D. Proofreading cannot be a method of prewriting, since it is done on already written texts only. Clustering, listing, and brainstorming are all prewriting strategies.

29. **In this paragraph from a student essay, identify the sentence that provides a detail. (Skill 2.2 Rigorous)**

(1) The poem concerns two different personality types and the human relation between them. (2) Their approach to life is totally different. (3) The neighbor is a very conservative person who follows routines. (4) He follows the traditional wisdom of his father and his father's father. (5) The purpose in fixing the wall and keeping their relationship separate is only because it is all he knows.

A. Sentence 1

B. Sentence 3

C. Sentence 4

D. Sentence 5

The answer is C. Sentence 4 provides a detail to sentence 3 by explaining how the neighbor follows routine. Sentence 1 is the thesis sentence, which is the main idea of the paragraph. Sentence 3 provides an example to develop that thesis. Sentence 4 is a reason that explains why.

30. **Writing ideas quickly without interruption of the flow of thoughts or attention to conventions is called (Skill 2.3, Easy)**

A. brainstorming.

B. mapping.

C. listing.

D. free writing.

The answer is D. Free writing for ten or fifteen minutes allows students to write out their thoughts about a subject. This technique allows the students to develop ideas that they are conscious of, but it also helps them to develop ideas that are lurking in the subconscious. It is important to let the flow of ideas run through the hand. If the students get stuck, they can write the last sentence over again until inspiration returns.

31. In general, the most serious drawback of using a computer in writing is that (Skill 2.3, Average Rigor)

    A. the copy looks so good that students tend to overlook major mistakes.

    B. the spell check and grammar programs discourage students from learning proper spelling and mechanics.

    C. the speed with which corrections can be made detracts from the exploration and contemplation of composing.

    D. the writer loses focus by concentrating on the final product rather than the details.

The answer is C. Because the process of revising is very quick with the computer, it can discourage contemplation, exploring, and examination, which are very important in the writing process.

32. Which of the following is the least effective procedure for promoting consciousness of audience? (Skill 2.4, Average Rigor)

    A. Pairing students during the writing process

    B. Reading all rough drafts before the students write the final copies

    C. Having students compose stories or articles for publication in school literary magazines or newspapers

    D. Writing letters to friends or relatives

The answer is B. Reading all rough drafts will not encourage the students to take control of their text and might even inhibit their creativity. On the contrary, pairing students will foster their sense of responsibility, and having them compose stories for literary magazines will boost their self-esteem as well as their organization skills.

33. **Reading a piece of student writing to assess the overall impression of the product is (Skill 2.5, Easy)**

    A. holistic evaluation.

    B. portfolio assessment.

    C. analytical evaluation.

    D. using a performance system.

The answer is A. Holistic scoring assesses a piece of writing as a whole. Usually a paper is read quickly through once to get a general impression. The writing is graded according to the impression of the whole work rather than the sum of its parts. Often holistic scoring uses a rubric that establishes the overall criteria for a certain score to evaluate each paper.

34. **In preparing a speech for a contest, your student has encountered problems with gender specific language. Not wishing to offend either women or men, he seeks your guidance. Which of the following is *not* an effective strategy? (Skill 2.5, Rigorous)**

    A. Use the generic "he" and explain that people will understand and accept the male pronoun as all-inclusive.

    B. Switch to plural nouns and use "they" as the gender-neutral pronoun.

    C. Use passive voice so that the subject is not required.

    D. Use male pronouns for one part of the speech and then use female pronouns for the other part of the speech.

The answer is A. No longer is the male pronoun considered the universal pronoun. Speakers and writers should choose gender-neutral words and avoid nouns and pronouns that inaccurately exclude one gender or another.

35. **A formative evaluation of student writing (Skill 2.5, Rigorous)**

    A. requires thorough markings of mechanical errors with a pencil or pen.

    B. making comments on the appropriateness of the student's interpretation of the prompt and the degree to which the objective was met.

    C. should require that the student hand in all the materials produced during the process of writing.

    D. several careful readings of the text for content, mechanics, spelling, and usage.

The answer is B. It is important to give students numerous experiences with formative evaluation (evaluation as the student writes the piece). Formative evaluation will assign points to every step of the writing process, even though it is not graded. The criteria for the writing task should be very clear, and the teacher should read each step twice. Responses should be non critical and supportive, and the teacher should involve students in the process of defining criteria, and make it clear that formative and summative evaluations are two distinct processes.

36. **In preparing a report about William Shakespeare, students are asked to develop a set of interpretive questions to guide their research. Which of the following would *not* be classified as an interpretive question? (Skill 3.1, Rigorous)**

    A. What would be different today if Shakespeare had not written his plays?

    B. How will the plays of Shakespeare affect future generations?

    C. How does the Shakespeare view nature in *A Midsummer's Night Dream* and *Much Ado About Nothing*?

    D. During the Elizabethan age, what roles did young boys take in dramatizing Shakespeare's plays?

The answer is D. This question requires research into the historical facts; Shakespeare in Love notwithstanding, women did not act In Shakespeare's plays, and their parts were taken by young boys. Choices A and B are hypothetical questions requiring students to provide original thinking and interpretation. Choice C requires comparison and contrast, which are interpretive skills.

37. **Which word in the following sentence is a bound morpheme: "The quick brown fox jumped over the lazy dog"? (Skill 3.2, Rigorous)**

    A. The

    B. fox

    C. lazy

    D. jumped

The answer is D. The suffix "–ed" is an affix that cannot stand alone as a unit of meaning. Thus it is bound to the free morpheme "jump." "The" is always an unbound morpheme since no suffix or prefix can alter its meaning. As written, "fox" and "lazy" are unbound but their meaning is changed with affixes, such as "foxes" or "laziness."

38. **In writing a report, Hector has to explain where acid rain comes from and what it has done to the environment. What is the most likely form of organizational structure? (Skill 3.1, Easy)**

    A. Cause and effect

    B. Problem and solution

    C. Exposition

    D. Definition

The answer is A. This report would discuss what has caused acid rain and what effects acid rain has had on the environment. Although it could offer a solution, the report questions do not focus on that. Most report writing is expository because it provided information and an explanation. While a definition might be an important detail, it would not be the major organizational structure.

39. For their research paper on the effects of the Civil War on American literature, students have brainstormed a list of potential online sources and are seeking your authorization. Which of these represent the strongest source? (Skill 3.3, Rigorous)

    A. http://www.wikipedia.org/

    B. http://www.google.com

    C. http://www.nytimes.com

    D. http://docsouth.unc.edu/southlit/civilwar.html

The answer is D. Sites with an "edu" domain are associated with educational institutions and tend to be more trustworthy for research information. Wikipedia has an "org" domain, which means it is a nonprofit. While Wikipedia may be appropriate for background reading, its credibility as a research site is questionable. Both Google and the New York Times are "com" sites, which are for profit. Even though this does not discredit their information, each site is problematic for researchers. With Google, students will get overwhelmed with hits and may not choose the most reputable sites for their information. As a newspaper, the New York Times would not be a strong source for historical information.

40. The students in Mrs. Cline's seventh grade language arts class were invited to attend a performance of *Romeo and Juliet* presented by the drama class at the high school. To best prepare, they should (Skill 3.4, Average Rigor)

    A. read the play as a homework exercise.

    B. read a synopsis of the plot and a biographical sketch of the author.

    C. examine a few main selections from the play to become familiar with the language and style of the author.

    D. read a condensed version of the story and practice attentive listening skills.

The answer is D. By reading a condensed version of the story, students will know the plot and therefore be able to follow the play on stage. It is also important for them to practice listening techniques such as one one-to-one tutoring and peer-assisted reading.

41. The English department is developing strategies to encourage all students to become a community of readers. From the list of suggestions below, which would be the least effective way for teachers to foster independent reading? (Skill 3.4, Average Rigor)

A. Each teacher will set aside a weekly 30-minute in-class reading session during which the teacher and students read a magazine or book for enjoyment.

B. Teacher and students develop a list of favorite books to share with each other.

C. The teacher assigns at least one book report each grading period to ensure that students are reading from the established class list.

D. The students gather books for a classroom library so that books may be shared with each other.

The answer is C. Teacher-directed assignments such as book reports appear routine and unexciting. Students will be more excited about reading when they can actively participate. In Choice A, the teacher is modeling reading behavior and providing students with a dedicated time during which time they can read independently and still be surrounded by a community of readers. In Choices B and D, students share and make available their reading choices.

42. **Which of the following responses to literature typically give middle school students the most problems? (Skill 3.4, Average Rigor)**

    A. Interpretive

    B. Evaluative

    C. Critical

    D. Emotional

The answer is B. Middle school readers will exhibit both emotional and interpretive responses. In middle/junior high school, organized study models enable students to identify main ideas and supporting details, to recognize sequential order, to distinguish fact from opinion, and to determine cause/effect relationships. Also, a child's being able to say why a particular book was boring or why a particular poem made him/her sad evidences critical reactions on a fundamental level. It is a bit early for evaluative responses, however. These depend on the reader's consideration of how the piece represents its genre, how well it reflects the social/ethical mores of a given society, and how well the author has approached the subject for freshness and slant. Evaluative responses are made only by a few advanced high school students.

43. **Based on the excerpt below from Kate Chopin's short story "The Story of an Hour," what can students infer about the main character? (Skill 3.4, Rigorous)**

She did not stop to ask if it were or were not a monstrous joy that held her. A clear and exalted perception enabled her to dismiss the suggestion as trivial. She knew that she would weep again when she saw the kind, tender hands folded in death; the face that had never looked save with love upon her, fixed and gray and dead. But she saw beyond that bitter moment a long procession of years to come that would belong to her absolutely. And she opened and spread her arms out to them in welcome.

  A. She dreaded her life as a widow.

  B. Although she loved her husband, she was glad that he was dead for he had never loved her.

  C. She worried that she was too indifferent to her husband's death.

  D. Although they had both loved each other, she was beginning to appreciate that opportunities had opened because of his death.

The answer is D. Dismissing her feeling of "monstrous joy" as insignificant, the young woman realizes that she will mourn her husband who had been good to her and had loved her. But that "long procession of years" does not frighten her; instead she recognizes that this new life belongs to her alone and she welcomes it with open arms.

44. **Recognizing empathy in literature is mostly a/an (Skill 3.4, Rigorous)**

  A. emotional response.

  B. interpretive response.

  C. critical response.

  D. evaluative response.

The answer is C. In critical responses, students make value judgments about the quality and atmosphere of a text. Through class discussion and written assignments, students react to and assimilate a writer's style and language.

45. The substitution of *went to his rest* for *died* is an example of a/an (Skill 4.1, Easy)

    A. bowdlerism.

    B. jargon.

    C. euphemism.

    D. malapropism.

The answer is C. A euphemism replaces an unpleasant or offensive word or expression by a more agreeable one. It also alludes to distasteful things in a pleasant manner, and it can even paraphrase offensive texts. Bowdlerism is named after Thomas Bowdler who excised from Shakespeare what he considered vulgar and offensive. Jargon is a specialized language used by a particular group. What was "groovy" to one generation has become "awesome" to another. Named after Mrs. Malaprop, a character in a play by Richard Sheridan, a malapropism is a misuse of words, often to comical effect. Mrs. Malaprop once said "...she's as headstrong as an allegory on the banks of Nile" misusing allegory for alligator.

46.   In the following quotation, addressing the dead body of Caesar as though he were still a living being is to employ an (Skill 4.1, Average Rigor)

O, pardon me, though
Bleeding piece of earth
That I am meek and gentle with
These butchers.
        -Marc Antony from *Julius Caesar*

A. apostrophe

B. allusion

C. antithesis

D. anachronism

The answer is A. This rhetorical figure addresses personified things, absent people or gods. An allusion, on the other hand, is a quick reference to a character or event known to the public. An antithesis is a contrast between two opposing viewpoints, ideas, or presentation of characters. An anachronism is the placing of an object or person out of its time with the time of the text. The best-known example is the clock in Shakespeare's *Julius Caesar*.

47.   The literary device of personification is used in which example below? (Skill 4.1, Average Rigor)

A. "Beg me no beggary by soul or parents, whining dog!"

B. "Happiness sped through the halls cajoling as it went."

C. "O wind thy horn, thou proud fellow."

D. "And that one talent which is death to hide."

The answer is B. "Happiness," an abstract concept, is described as if it were a person with the words "sped" and "cajoling."

48. **An extended metaphor comparing two very dissimilar things (one lofty one lowly) is a definition of a/an (Skill 4.1, Average Rigor)**

    A. antithesis.

    B. aphorism.

    C. apostrophe.

    D. conceit.

The answer is D. A conceit is an unusually far-fetched metaphor in which an object, person or situation is presented in a parallel and simpler analogue between two apparently very different things or feelings, one very sophisticated and one very ordinary, usually taken either from nature or a well known every day concept, familiar to both reader and author alike. The conceit was first developed by Petrarch and spread to England in the sixteenth century.

49. **Which of the following is a characteristic of blank verse? (Skill 4.1, Average Rigor)**

    A. Meter in iambic pentameter

    B. Clearly specified rhyme scheme

    C. Lack of figurative language

    D. Unspecified rhythm

The answer is A. An iamb is a metrical unit of verse having one unstressed syllable followed by one stressed syllable. This is the most commonly used metrical verse in English and American poetry. An iambic pentameter is a ten-syllable verse made of five of these metrical units, either rhymed as in sonnets, or unrhymed as in free, or blank, verse.

50. **Which is the best definition of free verse, or *vers libre*? (Skill 4.1, Average Rigor)**

    A. Poetry, which consists of an unaccented syllable followed by an unaccented sound.

    B. Short lyrical poetry written to entertain but with an instructive purpose.

    C. Poetry, which does not have a uniform pattern of rhythm.

    D. A poem which tells the story and has a plot

    The answer is C. Free verse has lines of irregular length (but it does not run on like prose).

51. **What is the salient literary feature of this excerpt from an epic? (Skill 4.1, Rigorous)**

    > Hither the heroes and the nymphs resorts,
    > To taste awhile the pleasures of a court;
    > In various talk th'instructive hours they passed,
    > Who gave the ball, or paid the visit last;
    > One speaks the glory of the English Queen,
    > And another describes a charming Indian screen;
    > A third interprets motion, looks, and eyes;
    > At every word a reputation dies.

    A. Sprung rhythm

    B. Onomatopoeia

    C. Heroic couplets

    D. Motif

    The answer is C. A couplet is a pair of rhyming verse lines, usually of the same length. It is one of the most widely used verse-forms in European poetry. Chaucer established the use of couplets in English, notably in the *Canterbury Tales,* using rhymed iambic pentameters (a metrical unit of verse having one unstressed syllable followed by one stressed syllable) later known as heroic couplets. Other authors who used heroic couplets include Ben Jonson, Dryden, and especially Alexander Pope, who became the master of them.

52. **What syntactic device is most evident from Abraham Lincoln's "Gettysburg Address"? (Skill 4.1, Rigorous)**

It is rather for us to be here dedicated to the great task remaining before us -- that from these honored dead we take increased devotion to that cause for which they gave the last full measure of devotion -- that we here highly resolve that these dead shall not have died in vain -- that this nation, under God, shall have a new birth of freedom -- and that government of the people, by the people, for the people, shall not perish from the earth.

A. Affective connotation

B. Informative denotations

C. Allusion

D. Parallelism

The answer is D. Parallelism is the repetition of grammatical structure. In speeches such as this as well as speeches of Martin Luther King, Jr., parallel structure creates a rhythm and balance of related ideas. Lincoln's repetition of clauses beginning with "that" ties four examples back "to the great task." Connotation is the emotional attachment of words; denotation is the literal meaning of words. Allusion is a reference to a historic event, person, or place.

53. **Which poem is typified as a villanelle? (Skill 4.1, Rigorous)**

A. "Do not go gentle into that good night"

B. "Dover Beach"

C. *Sir Gawain and the Green Knight*

D. *Pilgrim's Progress*

The answer is A. This poem by Dylan Thomas typifies the villanelle because it was written as such. A villanelle is a form that was invented in France in the sixteenth century, and used mostly for pastoral songs. It has an uneven number (usually five) of tercets rhyming aba, with a final quatrain rhyming abaa. This poem is the most famous villanelle written in English. "Dover Beach" by Matthew Arnold is not a villanelle, while *Sir Gawain and the Green Knight* was written in alliterative verse by an unknown author usually referred to as The Pearl Poet around 1370. *Pilgrim's Progress* is a prose allegory by John Bunyan.

54. **Which term best describes the form of the following poetic excerpt? (Skill 4.1, Rigorous)**

And more to lulle him in his
slumber soft,
A trickling streake from high rock
tumbling downe,
And ever-drizzling raine upon
the loft.
Mixt with a murmuring winde,
much like a swowne
No other noyse, nor peoples
troubles cryes.
As still we wont t'annoy the
walle'd towne,
Might there be heard: but
careless Quiet lyes,
Wrapt in eternall silence farre
from enemyes.

A. Ballad

B. Elegy

D. Spenserian stanza

D. *Octava rima*

The answer is D. The *octava rima* is a specific eight-line stanza whose rhyme scheme is abababcc. A ballad is a narrative poem. An elegy is a form of lyric poetry typically used to mourn someone who has died. A form of the English sonnet created by Edmond Spenser combines the English form and the Italian. The Spenserian sonnet follows the English quatrain and couplet pattern but resembles the Italian in its rhyme scheme, which is linked: abab bcbc cdcd ee.

55. **In the phrase "The Cabinet conferred with the President," Cabinet is an example of a/an (Skill 4.1, Rigorous)**

    A. metonym.

    B. synecdoche.

    C. metaphor.

    D. allusion.

The answer is B. In a synecdoche, a whole is referred to by naming a part of it. Also, a synecdoche can stand for a whole of which it is a part: for example, the Cabinet for the Government. Metonymy is the substitution of a word for a related word. For example, "hit the books" means "to study." A metaphor is a comparison such as "a cat burglar." An allusion is a reference to someone or something in history. To say that 'she met her Waterloo and was fired" alludes to Napoleon's defeat.

56. **In the following poem, what literary movement is reflected? (Skill 4.2, Rigorous)**

"My Heart Leaps Up" by William Wordsworth

My heart leaps up when I behold
  A rainbow in the sky:
So was it when my life began;
So is it now I am a man;
So be it when I shall grow old,
  Or let me die!
The Child is father of the Man;
And I could wish my days to be
Bound each to each by natural piety

A. Neo-classicism

B. Victorian literature

C. Romanticism

D. Naturalism

The answer is C. The Romantic period of the 19th century is known for its emphasis on feelings, emotions, and passions. William Wordsworth and William Blake were two notable poets from this period. In the neoclassicism of the previous period, the literature echoed the classical ideals of proportion, common sense, and reason over raw emotion and imagination, and the purpose was more didactic than celebratory. The Victorian period of the late 19th century exerted more restraint on emotions and feelings. In naturalistic writing, authors depict the world more harshly and more objectively.

57. **Which choice below best defines naturalism? (Skill 4.2, Rigorous)**

   A. A belief that the writer or artist should apply scientific objectivity in his/her observation and treatment of life without imposing value judgments.

   B. The doctrine that teaches that the existing world is the best to be hoped for.

   C. The doctrine that teaches that God is not a personality, but that all laws, forces and manifestations of the universe are God-related.

   D. A philosophical doctrine that professes that the truth of all knowledge must always be in question.

The answer is A. Naturalism is a movement that was started by French writers Jules and Edmond de Goncourt with their novel *Germinie Lacerteux* (1865), but its real leader is Emile Zola, who wanted to bring "a slice of life" to his readers. His saga, *Les Rougon Macquart,* consists in twenty-two novels depicting various aspects of social life. English writing authors representative of this movement include George Moore and George Gissing in England, but the most important naturalist novel in English is Theodore Dreiser's *Sister Carrie.*

58. **A traditional, anonymous story, ostensibly having a historical basis, usually explaining some phenomenon of nature or aspect of creation, defines a (Skill 4.3, Easy)**

   A. proverb.

   B. idyll.

   C. myth.

   D. epic.

The answer is C. A myth is usually traditional and anonymous and explains natural and supernatural phenomena. Myths are usually about creation, divinity, the significance of life and death, and natural phenomena. A proverb is a saying or adage. An idyll is a short, pastoral poem. In its simplest form, an epic is a narrative poem.

59. **Which of the following is *not* a characteristic of a fable? (Skill 4.3, Easy)**

    A. Animals that feel and talk like humans.

    B. Happy solutions to human dilemmas.

    C. Teaches a moral or standard for behavior.

    D. Illustrates specific people or groups without directly naming them.

The answer is D. A fable is a short tale with animals, humans, gods, or even inanimate objects as characters. Fables often conclude with a moral, delivered in the form of an epigram (a short, witty, and ingenious statement in verse). Fables are among the oldest forms of writing in human history: it appears in Egyptian papyri of c 1500 BC. The most famous fables are those of Aesop, a Greek slave living in about 600 BC. In India, the *Pantchatantra* appeared in the third century. The most famous modern fables are those of seventeenth century French poet Jean de La Fontaine.

60. **Which of the following would be the most significant factor in teaching Homer's *Iliad* and *Odyssey* to any particular group of students? (Skill 4.3, Average Rigor)**

    A. Identifying a translation on the appropriate reading level

    B. Determining the students' interest level

    C. Selecting an appropriate evaluative technique

    D. Determining the scope and delivery methods of background study

The answer is A. Students will learn the importance of these two works if the translation reflects both the vocabulary that they know and their reading level. Greece will always be foremost in literary assessments due to Homer's works. Homer is the most often cited author, next to Shakespeare. Greece is the cradle of both democracy and literature. This is why it is so crucial that Homer be included in the works assigned.

61. **Which of the following definitions best describes a parable? (Skill 4.3, Average Rigor)**

   A. A short entertaining account of some happening, usually using talking animals as characters.

   B. A slow, sad song or poem, or prose work expressing lamentation.

   C. An extensive narrative work expressing universal truths concerning domestic life.

   D. A short, simple story of an occurrence of a familiar kind, from which a moral or religious lesson may be drawn.

The answer is D. A parable is usually brief, and should be interpreted as an allegory teaching a moral lesson. Jesus' forty parables are the model of the genre, but modern, secular examples exist such as Wilfred Owen's "The Parable of The Young Man" and "The Young" (1920), or John Steinbeck's prose work *The Pearl* (1948).

62. **How will literature help students in a science class able understand the following passage? (Skill 4.3, Rigorous)**

Just as was the case more than three decades ago, we are still sailing between the Scylla of deferring surgery for too long and risking irreversible left ventricular damage and sudden death, and the Charibdas of operating too early and subjecting the patient to the early risks of operation and the later risks resulting from prosthetic valves.
--E. Braunwald, *European Heart Journal,* July 2000

   A. They will recognize the allusion to Scylla and Charibdas from Greek mythology and understand that the medical community has to select one of two unfavorable choices.

   B. They will recognize the allusion to sailing and understand its analogy to doctors as sailors navigating unknown waters.

   C. They will recognize that the allusion to Scylla and Charibdas refers to the two islands in Norse mythology where sailors would find themselves shipwrecked and understand how the doctors feel isolated by their choices.

   D. They will recognize the metaphor of the heart and relate it to Eros, the character in Greek mythology who represents love. Eros was the love child of Scylla and Charibdas.

The answer is A. Scylla and Charibdas were two sea monsters guarding a narrow channel of water. Sailors trying to elude one side would face danger by sailing too close to the other side. The allusion indicates two equally undesirable choices.

63. Which is *not* a Biblical allusion? (Skill 4.3, Rigorous)

    A. The patience of Job

    B. Thirty pieces of silver

    C. "Man proposes; God disposes"

    D. "Suffer not yourself to be betrayed by a kiss"

The answer is C. This saying is attributed to Thomas à Kempis (1379-1471) in his *Imitation of Christ,* Book 1, chapter 19. Anyone who exhibits the patience of Job is being compared to the Old Testament biblical figure who retained his faith despite being beset by a series of misfortunes. "Thirty pieces of silver" refers to the amount of money paid to Judas to identify Jesus. Used by Patrick Henry, the quote in Choice D is a biblical reference to Judas' betrayal of Judas by a kiss.

64. In classic tragedy, a protagonist's defeat is brought about by a tragic flaw which is called (Skill 4.3, Rigorous)

    A. hubris.

    B. hamartia.

    C. catharsis.

    D. the skene.

The answer is B. Hubris is excessive pride, a type of tragic flaw. Catharsis is an emotional purging the character feels. *Skene* is the Greek word for scene. All of these terms come from Greek drama.

65. **The tendency to emphasize and value the qualities and peculiarities of life in a particular geographic area exemplifies (Skill 4.4, Easy)**

   A. pragmatism.

   B. regionalism.

   C. pantheism.

   D. abstractionism.

The answer is B. Pragmatism is a philosophical doctrine according to which there is no absolute truth. All truths change their trueness as their practical utility increases or decreases. The main representative of this movement is William James who in 1907 published *Pragmatism: A New Way for Some Old Ways of Thinking*. Pantheism is a philosophy according to which God is omnipresent in the world, everything is God and God is everything. The great representative of this sensibility is Spinoza. Also, the works of writers such as Wordsworth, Shelly and Emerson illustrate this doctrine. Abstract Expressionism is one of the most important movements in American art. It began in the 1940's with artists such as Willem de Kooning, Mark Rothko and Arshile Gorky. The paintings are usually large and non-representational.

66. **Which of the following is *not* a theme of Native American writing? (Skill 4.4, Average Rigor)**

   A. Emphasis on the hardiness of the human body and soul

   B. The strength of multi-cultural assimilation

   C. Contrition for the genocide of native peoples

   D. Remorse for the love of the Indian way of life

The answer is B. Native American literature was first a vast body of oral traditions from as early as before the fifteenth century. The characteristics include reverence for and awe of nature and the interconnectedness of the elements in the life cycle. The themes often reflect the hardiness of body and soul, remorse for the destruction of the Native American way of life, and the genocide of many tribes by the encroaching settlements of European Americans. These themes are still present in today's contemporary Native American literature, such as in the works of Duane Niatum, Gunn Allen, Louise Erdrich and N. Scott Momaday.

67. **Charles Dickens, Robert Browning, and Robert Louis Stevenson were (Skill 4.5, Easy)**

    A. Victorians.

    B. Medievalists.

    C. Elizabethans.

    D. Absurdists.

The answer is A. The Victorian Period is remarkable for the diversity and quality of its literature. Robert Browning wrote chilling monologues such as "My Last Duchess," and long poetic narratives such as *The Pied Piper of Hamlin*. Robert Louis Stevenson wrote his works partly for young adults, whose imaginations were quite taken by his *Treasure Island* and *The Case of Dr. Jekyll and Mr. Hyde*. Charles Dickens tells of the misery of the time and the complexities of Victorian society in novels such as *Oliver Twist* or *Great Expectations*.

68. **Which of the following titles is known for its scathingly condemning tone? (Skill 4.5, Average Rigor)**

    A. Boris Pasternak's *Dr Zhivago*

    B. Albert Camus' *The Stranger*

    C. Henry David Thoreau's "On the Duty of Civil Disobedience"

    D. Benjamin Franklin's "Rules by Which a Great Empire May Be Reduced to a Small One"

The answer is D. In this work, Benjamin Franklin adopts a scathingly ironic tone to warn the British about the probable outcome in their colonies if they persist with their policies. These are discussed one by one in the text, and the absurdity of each is condemned.

69. **American colonial writers were primarily (Skill 4.5, Average Rigor)**

    A. Romanticists.

    B. Naturalists.

    C. Realists.

    D. Neo-classicists.

The answer is D. The early colonists had been schooled in England, and even though their writing became quite American in content, their emphasis on clarity and balance in their language remained British. This literature reflects the lives of the early colonists, such as William Bradford's excerpts from "The Mayflower Compact," Anne Bradstreet's poetry and William Byrd's journal, *A History of the Dividing Line*.

70. **Arthur Miller wrote *The Crucible* as a parallel to what twentieth century event? (Skill 4.5, Average Rigor)**

    A. Sen. McCarthy's House un-American Activities Committee Hearing

    B. The Cold War

    C. The fall of the Berlin wall

    D. The Persian Gulf War

The answer is A. The episode of the seventeenth century witch-hunt in Salem, Mass., gave Miller a storyline that was very comparable to what was happening to persons suspected of communist beliefs in the 1950s.

71. **Which of the writers below is a renowned Black poet? (Skill 4.5, Average Rigor)**

    A. Maya Angelou

    B. Sandra Cisneros

    C. Richard Wilbur

    D. Richard Wright

The answer is A. Among her most famous work are *I Know Why the Caged Bird Sings* (1970), *And Still I Rise* (1978), and *All God's Children Need Traveling Shoes* (1986). Richard Wilbur is a poet and a translator of French dramatists Racine and Moliere, but he is not African American. Richard Wright is a very important African American author of novels such as *Native Son* and *Black Boy*. However, he was not a poet. Sandra Cisneros is a Latina author who is very important in developing Latina Women's literature.

72. **The following lines from Robert Browning's poem "My Last Duchess" come from an example of what form of dramatic literature? (Skill 4.5, Rigorous)**

    That's my last Duchess painted on the wall,
    Looking as if she were alive. I call
    That piece a wonder
    now: Frà Pandolf's hands
    Worked busily a day
    and there she stands.
    Will 't please you sit and look at her?

    A. Tragedy

    B. Comic opera

    C. Dramatis personae

    D. Dramatic monologue

The answer is D. A dramatic monologue is a speech given by a character or narrator that reveals characteristics of the character or narrator. This form was first made popular by Robert Browning, a Victorian poet. Tragedy is a form of literature in which the protagonist is overwhelmed by opposing forces. Comic opera is a form of sung music based on a light or happy plot. Dramatis personae is the Latin phrase for the cast of a play.

73. **"Every one must pass through Vanity Fair to get to the celestial city" is an allusion from a (Skill 4.5, Rigorous)**

    A.   Chinese folk tale.

    B.   Norse saga.

    C.   British allegory.

    D.   German fairy tale.

The answer is C. This is a reference to John Bunyan's *Pilgrim's Progress* from *This World to That Which Is to Come* (Part I, 1678; Part II, 1684), in which the hero, Christian, flees the City of Destruction and must undergo different trials and tests to get to the Celestial City.

74. **Which author did *not* write satire? (Skill 4.5, Rigorous)**

    A. Joseph Addison

    B. Richard Steele

    C. Alexander Pope

    D. John Bunyan

The answer is D. John Bunyan was a religious writer, known for his autobiography, *Grace Abounding to the Chief of Sinners,* as well as other books, all religious in their inspiration, such as *The Holy City, or the New Jerusalem* (1665), *A Confession of My Faith,* and *A Reason of My Practice* (1672), or *The Holy War* (1682).

75. **What were two major characteristics of the first American literature? (Skill 4.5, Rigorous)**

A. Vengefulness and arrogance

B. Bellicosity and derision

C. Oral delivery and reverence for the land

D. Maudlin and self-pitying egocentricism

The answer is D. This characteristic can be seen in Captain John Smith's work, as well as William Bradford's and Michael Wigglesworth's works.

76. **Which sonnet form describes the following? (Skill 4.5, Rigorous)**

My galley charg'd with
  forgetfulness,
Through sharp seas, in
  winter night doth pass
'Tween rock and rock; and
  eke mine enemy, alas,
That is my lord steereth with,
  cruelness.
And every oar a thought with
  readiness,
As though that death were
  light in such a case.
An endless wind doth tear
  the sail apace
Or forc'ed sighs and trusty
  fearfulness.
A rain of tears, a cloud of dark
  disdain,
 Hath done the wearied
  cords great hinderance,
Wreathed with error and eke
  with ignorance.
The stars be hid that led me
  to this pain
Drowned is reason that
  should me consort,
And I remain despairing
  of the poet

A. Petrarchan or Italian sonnet

B. Shakespearian or
    Elizabethan sonnet

C. Romantic sonnet

D. Spenserian sonnet

The answer is A. The Petrarchan sonnet, also known as Italian sonnet, is named after the Italian poet Petrarch (1304-74). It is divided into an octave rhyming abbaabba and a sestet normally rhyming cdecde.

77. **Considered one of the first feminist plays, this Ibsen drama ends with a door slamming symbolizing the lead character's emancipation from traditional societal norms. (Skill 4.6, Easy)**

   A. *The Wild Duck*

   B. *Hedda Gabler*

   C. *Ghosts*

   D. *The Doll's House*

The answer is D. Nora in *The Doll's House* leaves her husband and her children when she realizes her husband is not the man she thought he was. Hedda Gabler, another feminist icon, shoots herself. *The Wild Duck* deals with the conflict between idealism and family secrets. *Ghosts,* considered one of Ibsen's most controversial plays, deals with many social ills, some of which include alcoholism, incest, and religious hypocrisy.

78. **Which of the following writers did *not* win a Nobel Prize for literature? (Skill 4.6, Average Rigor)**

   A. Gabriel Garcia-Marquez of Colombia

   B. Nadine Gordimer of South Africa

   C. Pablo Neruda of Chile

   D. Alice Walker of the United States

The answer is D. Even though Alice Walker received the Pulitzer Price and the American Book Award for her best-known novel, *The Color Purple*, and is the author of six novels and three collections of short stories that have received wide critical acclaim, she has not yet received the Nobel Prize.

79. **The writing of Russian naturalists is (Skill 4.6, Average Rigor)**

A. optimistic.

B. pessimistic.

C. satirical.

D. whimsical.

The answer is B. Although the movement, which originated with the critic Vissarion Belinsky, was particularly strong in the 1840's, it can be said that the works of Dostoevsky, Tolstoy, Chekov, Turgenev and Pushkin owe much to it. These authors' works are among the best in international literature, yet are shrouded in stark pessimism. Tolstoy's *Anna Karenina* or Dostoevsky's *Crime and Punishment* are good examples of this dark outlook.

80. **Which of the following is the best definition of existentialism? (Skill 4.6, Rigorous)**

A. The philosophical doctrine that matter is the only reality and that everything in the world, including thought, will and feeling, can be explained only in terms of matter.

B. Philosophy that views things as they should be or as one would wish them to be.

C. A philosophical and literary movement, variously religious and atheistic, stemming from Kierkegaard and represented by Sartre.

D. The belief that all events are determined by fate and are hence inevitable.

The answer is C. Even though there are other very important thinkers in the movement known as Existentialism, such as Camus and Merleau-Ponty, Sartre remains the main figure in this movement.

81. **Which teaching method would best engage underachievers in the required senior English class? (Skill 4.7, Average Rigor)**

    A. Assign use of glossary work and extensively footnoted excerpts of great works.

    B. Have students take turns reading aloud the anthology selection

    C. Let students choose which readings they'll study and write about.

    D. Use a chronologically arranged, traditional text, but assigning group work, panel presentations, and portfolio management

The answer is C. It will encourage students to react honestly to literature. Students should take notes on what they're reading so they will be able to discuss the material. They should not only react to literature, but also experience it. Small-group work is a good way to encourage them. The other answers are not fit for junior-high or high school students. They should be encouraged, however, to read critics of works in order to understand criteria work.

82. **Hoping to take advantage of the popularity of the Harry Potter series, a teacher develops a unit on mythology comparing the story and characters of Greek and Roman myths with the story and characters of the Harry Potter books. Which of these is a commonality that would link classical literature to popular fiction? (Skill 4.7, Rigorous)**

    A. The characters are gods in human form with human-like characteristics.

    B. The settings are realistic places in the world where the characters interact as humans would.

    C. The themes center on the universal truths of love and hate and fear.

    D. The heroes in the stories are young males and only they can overcome the opposing forces.

The answer is C. Although the gods in Greek and Roman myths take human form, they are immortal as gods must be. The characters in Harry Potter may be wizards, but they are not immortal. Although the settings in these stories have familiar associations, their worlds are vastly different from those inhabited by mortals and Muggles. While male heroes may dominate the action, the females (Hera, Dianna, Hermione) are powerful as well.

83. **Among junior-high school students of low-to-average readability levels, which work would most likely stir reading interest? (Skill 4.8, Easy)**

    A. *Elmer Gantry,* Sinclair Lewis

    B. *Smiley's People,* John Le Carre

    C. *The Outsiders,* S.E. Hinton

    D. *And Then There Were None*, Agatha Christie.

The answer is C. The students can easily identify with the characters, the social issues, the vocabulary, and the themes in the book. The book deals with teenage concerns such as fitting-in, cliques, and appearance in ways that have proven very engaging for young readers. S.E. Hinton has actually said about this book: "*The Outsiders* is definitely my best-selling book; but what I like most about it is how it has taught a lot of kids to enjoy reading."

84. **What is the best course of action when a child refuses to complete a reading/ literature assignment on the grounds that it is morally objectionable? (Skill 4.8, Average Rigor)**

    A. Speak with the parents and explain the necessity of studying this work

    B. Encourage the child to sample some of the text before making a judgment

    C. Place the child in another teacher's class where they are studying an acceptable work

    D. Provide the student with alternative selections that cover the same performance standards that the rest of the class is learning.

The answer is D. In the case of a student finding a reading offensive, it is the responsibility of the teacher to assign another title. As a general rule, it is always advisable to notify parents if a particularly sensitive piece is to be studied.

85. **Most children's literature prior to the development of popular literature was intended to be didactic. Which of the following would *not* be considered didactic? (Skill 4.8, Average Rigor)**

    A. "A Visit from St. Nicholas" by Clement Moore

    B. *McGuffy's Reader*

    C. Any version of Cinderella

    D. Parables from the Bible

    The answer is A. "A Visit from St. Nicholas" is a cheery, non-threatening child's view of "The Night before Christmas." Didactic means intended to teach some lesson.

86. **Written on the sixth grade reading level, most of S. E. Hinton's novels (for instance, *The Outsiders*) have the greatest reader appeal with (Skill 4.8, Average Rigor)**

    A. sixth graders.

    B. ninth graders.

    C. twelfth graders.

    D. adults.

    The answer is B. Adolescents are concerned with their changing bodies, their relationships with each other and adults, and their place in society. Reading *The Outsiders* makes them confront different problems that they are only now beginning to experience as teenagers, such as gangs and social identity. The book is universal in its appeal to adolescents.

87. **Children's literature became established in the (Skill 4.8, Average Rigor)**

    A. seventeenth century.

    B. eighteenth century.

    C. nineteenth century.

    D. twentieth century.

The answer is A. In the seventeenth Century, authors such as Jean de La Fontaine and his fables, Pierre Perreault's tales, Mme d'Aulnoye's novels based on old folktales and Mme de Beaumont's *Beauty and the Beast* all created a children's literature genre. In England, Perreault was translated and a work allegedly written by Oliver Smith, *The Renowned History of Little Goody Two Shoes,* also helped to establish children's literature in England.

88. **After watching a movie of a train derailment, a child exclaims, "Wow, look how many cars fell off the tracks. There's junk everywhere. The engineer must have really been asleep." Using the facts that the child is impressed by the wreckage and assigns blame to the engineer, a follower of Piaget's theories would estimate the child to be about (Skill 4.8, Rigorous)**

    A. ten years old.

    B. twelve years old.

    C. fourteen years old.

    D. sixteen years old.

The answer is A. According to Piaget's theory, children seven-to-eleven years old begin to apply logic to concrete things and experiences. They can combine performance and reasoning to solve problems. They have internalized moral values and are willing to confront rules and adult authority.

89. **The most significant drawback to applying learning theory research to classroom practice is that (Skill 4.8, Rigorous)**

   A. today's students do not acquire reading skills with the same alacrity as when greater emphasis was placed on reading classical literature.

   B. development rates are complicated by geographical and cultural In analyzing literature and in looking for ways to bring a work to life for an audience, the use of comparable themes and ideas from other pieces of literature and from one's own life experiences, including from reading the daily newspaper, is very important and useful.

   C. homogeneous grouping has contributed to faster development of some age groups.

   D. social and environmental conditions have contributed to an escalated maturity level than research done twenty of more years ago would seem to indicate.

The answer is D. Because of the rapid social changes, topics that were not interesting to younger readers are now topics of books for even younger readers. Many books dealing with difficult topics, and it is difficult for the teacher to steer students toward books that they are ready for and to try to keep them away from books whose content, although well written, are not yet appropriate for their level of cognitive and social development. There is a fine line between this and censorship.

90. **To explore the relationship of literature to modern life, which of these activities would *not* enable students to explore comparable themes? (Skill 4.9, Average Rigor)**

    A. After studying various world events, such as the Palestinian-Israeli conflict, students write an updated version of *Romeo and Juliet* using modern characters and settings.

    B. Before studying *Romeo and Juliet,* students watch *West Side Story*.

    C. Students research the major themes of *Romeo and Juliet* by studying news stories and finding modern counterparts for the story.

    D. Students would explore compare the romantic themes of *Romeo and Juliet* and *The Taming of the Shrew*.

The answer is D. By comparing the two plays by Shakespeare, students will be focusing on the culture of the period in which the plays were written. In Choice A, students should be able to recognize modern parallels with current culture clashes. By comparing the *Romeo and Juliet* to the 1950's update of *West Side Story,* students can study how themes are similar in two completely different historical periods. In Choice C, students can study local, national, and international news for comparable stories and themes.

91. **In preparing students for their oral presentations, the instructor provided all of these guidelines, except one. Which is *not* an effective guideline? (Skill 5.1, Average Rigor)**

    A. Even if you are using a lectern, feel free to move about. This will connect you to the audience.

    B. Your posture should be natural, not stiff. Keep your shoulders toward the audience.

    C. Gestures can help communicate as long as you don't overuse them or make them distracting.

    D. You can avoid eye contact if you focus on your notes. This will make you appear more knowledgeable.

The answer is D. Although many people are nervous about making eye contact, they should focus on two or three people at a time. Body language, such as movement, posture, and gestures, helps the speaker connect to the audience.

92. **In literature, evoking feelings of pity or compassion is to create (Skill 5.3, Average Rigor)**

    A. colloquy.

    B. irony.

    C. pathos.

    D. paradox

The answer is C. A very well known example of pathos is Desdemona's death in *Othello*, but there are many other examples of pathos. In *King Lear*, Cordelia accepts defeat with this line: "We are not the first / Who with best meaning have incurred the worst."

93. **What type of reasoning does Henry David Thoreau use in the following excerpt from "Civil Disobedience"? (Skill 5.3, Rigorous)**

    Unjust laws exist; shall we be content to obey them, or shall we endeavor to amend them, and obey them until we have succeeded, or shall we transgress them at once? Men generally, under such a government as this, think that they ought to wait until they have persuaded the majority to alter them. They think that, if they should resist, the remedy would be worse than the evil. But it is the fault of the government itself that the remedy *is* worse than the evil. ... Why does it always crucify Christ, and excommunicate Copernicus and Luther, and pronounce Washington and Franklin rebels?

    --"Civil Disobedience" by Henry David Thoreau

    A. Ethical reasoning

    B. Inductive reasoning

    C. Deductive reasoning

    D. Intellectual reasoning

The answer is C. Deductive reasoning begins with a general statement that leads to the particulars. In this essay, Thoreau begins with the general question about what should be done about unjust laws. His argument leads to the government's role in suppressing dissent.

94.   **Which of the following is *not* a fallacy in logic? (Skill 5.3 Rigorous)**

   A. All students in Ms. Suarez's fourth period class are bilingual.
       Beth is in Ms. Suarez's fourth period.
       Beth is bilingual.

   B. All bilingual students are in Ms. Suarez's class.
       Beth is in Ms. Suarez's fourth period.
       Beth is bilingual.

   C. Beth is bilingual.
       Beth is in Ms. Suarez's fourth period.
       All students in Ms. Suarez's fourth period are bilingual.

   D. If Beth is bilingual, then she speaks Spanish.
       Beth speaks French.
       Beth is not bilingual.

The correct answer is A. The second statement, or premise, is tested against the first premise. Both premises are valid and the conclusion is logical. In Choice B, the conclusion is invalid because the first premise does not exclude other students. In Choice C, the conclusion cannot be logically drawn from the preceding premises—you cannot conclude that all students are bilingual based on one example. In Choice D, the conclusion is invalid because the first premise is faulty.

95. **Identify the type of appeal used by Molly Ivins's in this excerpt from her essay "Get a Knife, Get a Dog, But Get Rid of Guns." (Skill 5.3, Rigorous)**

As a civil libertarian, I, of course, support the Second Amendment. And I believe it means exactly what it says:
A well regulated militia being necessary to the security of a free state, the right of the people to keep and bear arms shall not be infringed.

A. Ethical

B. Emotional

C. Rational

D. Literary

The answer is A. An ethical appeal is using the credentials of a reliable and trustworthy authority. In this case, Ivins cites the Constitution. Pathos is an emotional appeal and logos is an rational appeal. Literature might appeal to you but it's not a rhetorical appeal.

96. **What is the common advertising technique used by these advertising slogans? (Skill 5.3, Rigorous)**

"It's everywhere you want to be." - Visa
"Have it your way." - Burger King
"When you care enough to send the very best" - Hallmark
"Be all you can be" – U.S. Army

A. Peer Approval

B. Rebel

C. Individuality

D. Escape

The answer is C. All of these ads associate products with people who can think and act for themselves. Products are linked to individual decision making. With peer approval, the ads would associate their products with friends and acceptance. For rebelling, the ads would associates products with behaviors or lifestyles that oppose society's norms. Escape would suggest the appeal of getting away from it all.

97. **In presenting a report to peers about the effects of Hurricane Katrina on New Orleans, the students wanted to use various media in their argument to persuade their peers that more needed to be done. Which of these would be the most effective? (Skill 5.4 Rigorous)**

   A   A PowerPoint presentation showing the blueprints of the levees before the flood and redesigned now for current construction..

   B. A collection of music clips made by the street performers in the French Quarter before and after the flood.

   C. A recent video showing the areas devastated by the floods and the current state of rebuilding.

   D. A collection of recordings of interviews made by the various government officials and local citizens affected by the flooding.

The answer is C. For maximum impact, a video would offer dramatic scenes of the devastated areas. A video by its very nature is more dynamic than a static PowerPoint presentation. Further, the condition of the levees would not provide as much impetus for change as seeing the devastated areas. Oral messages such as music clips and interviews provide another way of supplementing the message but, again, they are not as dynamic as video.

98. **Which of the following is *not* correct? (Skill 5.5, Easy)**

   A. Because most students have wide access to media, teachers should refrain from using it in their classrooms to diminish the overload.

   B. Students can use CD-ROMs to explore information using a virtual reality experience.

   C. Teacher can make their instruction more powerful by using educational media.

   D. The Internet enables students to connect with people across cultures and to share interests.

The answer is A. Teachers can use media in productive ways to enrich instruction. Rather than ignoring it, educators should use a wide assortment of media for the benefit of their students.

99. **Which of the following statements indicates an instructional goal for using multimedia in the classroom? (Skill 5.5, Average Rigor)**

   A. Audio messages invite the listener to form mental images consistent with the topic of the audio.

   B. Print messages appeal almost exclusively to the mind and push students to read with more thought.

   C. Listening to an audio message is more passive than reading a print message.

   D. Teachers who develop activities to foster a critical perspective on audiovisual presentation will decrease passivity.

The answer is D. Each of the statements is true but only the last one establishes a goal for using multimedia in the classroom.

100. **Which of the following type of question will *not* stimulate higher-level critical thinking? (Skill 5.6, Rigorous)**

   A. A hypothetical question

   B. An open-ended question

   C. A close-ended question

   D. A judgment question

The answer is C. A close-ended question requires a simple answer, like a "yes" or "no." An open-ended question can generate an extended response that would require critical thinking. Both a hypothetical question and a judgment question require deeper thinking skills.

101. **Which of the following would *not* be a major concern in an oral presentation? (Skill 5.7, Average Rigor)**

    A. Establishing the purpose of the presentation

    B. Evaluating the audience's demographics and psychographics.

    C. Creating a PowerPoint slide for each point.

    D. Developing the content to fit the occasion.

The answer is C. PowerPoint slides should be kept to a minimum of one slide per minute and should not overwhelm the presentation. The slides should be a supplement so that the speaker can accomplish the purpose. To reach that goal, the speaker should understand the makeup of the audience: demographics, such as age, education level or other quantifiable characteristic; and, psychographics, such as attitudes or values. Knowing the purpose and the audience will enable the speaker to develop the content to fit the occasion.

102. **Mr. Ledbetter has instructed his students to prepare a slide presentation that illustrates an event in history. Students are to include pictures, graphics, media clips and links to resources. What competencies will students exhibit at the completion of this project? (Skill 5.7, Rigorous)**

    A. Analyze the impact of society on media.

    B. Recognize the media's strategies to inform and persuade.

    C. Demonstrate strategies and creative techniques to prepare presentations using a variety of media.

    D. Identify the aesthetic effects of a media presentation.

The answer is B. Students will have learned how to use various media to convey a unified message.

103. **If a student uses slang and expletives, what is the best course of action to take in order to improve the student's formal communication skills? (Skill 6.1, Average Rigor)**

   A. Ask the student to paraphrase their writing, that is, translate it into language appropriate for the school principal to read.

   B. Refuse to read the student's papers until he conforms to a more literate style.

   C. Ask the student to read his work aloud to the class for peer evaluation.

   D. Rewrite the flagrant passages to show the student the right form of expression.

The answer is A. Asking the student to write for a specific audience will help him become more involved in his writing. If he continues writing to the same audience—the teacher—he will continue seeing writing as just another assignment, and he will not apply grammar, vocabulary and syntax the way they should be. By rephrasing his own writing, the student will learn to write for a different public.

104. **Modeling is a practice that requires students to (Skill 6.1, Average Rigor)**

   A. create a style unique to their own language capabilities.

   B. emulate the writing of professionals.

   C. paraphrase passages from good literature.

   D. peer evaluate the writings of other students.

The answer is B. Modeling has students analyze the writing of a professional writer and try to reach the same level of syntactical, grammatical and stylistic mastery as the author whom they are studying.

105. **Mr. Phillips is creating a unit to study *To Kill a Mockingbird* and wants to familiarize his high school freshmen with the attitudes and issues of the historical period. Which activity would familiarize students with the attitudes and issues of the Depression-era South? (Skill 6.1, Rigorous)**

A. Create a detailed timeline of 15-20 social, cultural, and political events that focus on race relations in the 1930s.

B. Research and report on the life of its author Harper Lee. Compare her background with the events in the book.

C. Watch the movie version and note language and dress.

D. Write a research report on the stock market crash of 1929 and its effects.

The answer is A. By identifying the social, cultural, and political events of the 1930s, students will better understand the attitudes and values of America during the time of the novel. While researching the author's life could add depth to their understanding of the novel, it is unnecessary to the appreciation of the novel by itself. The movie version is an accurate depiction of the novel's setting but it focuses on the events in the novel, not the external factors that fostered the conflict. The stock market crash and the subsequent Great Depression would be important to note on the timeline but students would be distracted from themes of the book by narrowing their focus to only these two events.

106. **What is *not* one of the advantages of collaborative or cooperative learning? (Skill 6.2, Easy)**

A. Students that work together in groups or teams develop their skills in organizing, leadership, research, communication, and problem solving.

B. Working in teams can help students overcome anxiety in distance learning courses and contribute a sense of community and belonging for the students.

C. Students tend to learn more material being taught and retain the information longer than when the same information is taught using different methods.

D. Teachers reduce their workload and the time spent on individuals the assignments, and grading.

The answer is D. Teacher continue to expend time in planning, monitoring and evaluating the students, their groups, and their activities.

107. **Overcrowded classes prevent the individual attention needed to facilitate language development. This drawback can be best overcome by (Skill 6.2, Average Rigor)**

    A. dividing the class into independent study groups.

    B. assigning more study time at home.

    C. using more drill practice in class.

    D. team teaching.

The answer is A. Dividing a class into small groups fosters peer enthusiasm and evaluation, and sets an atmosphere of warmth and enthusiasm. It is preferable to divide the class into smaller study groups than to lecture, which will bore students and fail to facilitate curricular goals. This is preferred rather than engaging the whole class in a general teacher-led discussion because teacher-led discussions favor the loquacious and inhibit the shy.

108. **For students to prepare for a their roles in a dramatic performance, (Skill 6.2, Rigorous)**

    A. they should analyze their characters to develop a deeper understanding of the character's attitudes and motivations.

    B. they should attend local plays to study settings and stage design.

    C. they should read articles and books on acting methodology.

    D. they should practice the way other actors have performed in these roles.

The answer is A. By examining how their characters feel and think the students will understand the characters' attitudes and motivation.

109. **Students returning from a field trip to the local newspaper want to thank their hosts for the guided tour. As their teacher, what form of communication should you encourage them to use? (Skill 6.3, Average Rigor)**

   A. Each student will send an email expressing his or her appreciation.

   B. As a class, students will create a blog, and each student will write about what they learned.

   C. Each student will write a thank you letter that the teacher will fax to the newspaper.

   D. Each student will write a thank you note that the teacher will mail to the newspaper.

   The answer is D. Courtesy requires a hand-written message that is brief and specific. While using technology such as emails, blogs, and faxes are quicker, they are less personal.

110. **Middle and high school students are more receptive to studying grammar and syntax (Skill 6.4, Average Rigor)**

   A. through worksheets and end of lessons practices in textbooks.

   B. through independent, homework assignment.

   C. through analytical examination of the writings of famous authors.

   D. through application to their own writing.

   The answer is D. At this age, students learn grammatical concepts best through practical application in their own writing.

111. **Which definition is the best for defining diction?** (Skill 7.2, Easy)

    A. The specific word choices of an author to create a particular mood or feeling in the reader.

    B. Writing which explains something thoroughly.

    C. The background, or exposition, for a short story or drama.

    D. Word choices that help teach a truth or moral.

    The answer is A. Diction refers to an author's choice of words, expressions and style to convey his/her meaning.

112. **Which of the following should *not* be included in the opening paragraph of an informative essay?** (Skill 7.2, Easy)

    A. Thesis sentence

    B. Details and examples supporting the main idea

    C. Broad general introduction to the topic

    D. A style and tone that grabs the reader's attention

    The answer is B. The introductory paragraph should introduce the topic, capture the reader's interest, state the thesis and prepare the reader for the main points in the essay. Details and examples, however, should be given in the second part of the essay, so as to help develop the thesis presented at the end of the introductory paragraph, following the inverted triangle method consisting of a broad general statement followed by some information, and then the thesis at the end of the paragraph.

113. **In the paragraph below, which sentence does *not* contribute to the overall task of supporting the main idea? (Skill 7.2 Easy)**

1) The Springfield City Council met Friday to discuss new zoning restrictions for the land to be developed south of the city. 2) Residents who opposed the new restrictions were granted 15 minutes to present their case. 3) Their argument focused on the dangers that increased traffic would bring to the area. 4) It seemed to me that the Mayor Simpson listened intently. 5) The council agreed to table the new zoning until studies would be performed.

    A. Sentence 2

    B. Sentence 3

    C. Sentence 4

    D. Sentence 5

The answer is C. The other sentences provide detail to the main idea of the new zoning restrictions. Because sentence 4 provides no example or relevant detail, it should be omitted.

114. **In an "inverted triangle" introductory paragraphs, the thesis sentence occurs (Skill 7.3, Easy)**

    A. at the beginning of the paragraph.

    B. in the middle of the paragraph.

    C. at the end of the paragraph.

    D. in the second paragraph.

The answer is C. The introduction to an essay should begin with a broad general statement, followed by one or more sentences adding interest and information to the topic. The thesis should be written at the end of the introduction.

115. **Which of the following sentences contains a capitalization error? (Skill 7.3, Average Rigor)**

    A. The commander of the English navy was Admiral Nelson

    B. Napoleon was the president of the French First Republic

    C. Queen Elizabeth II is the Monarch of the British Empire

    D. William the Conqueror led the Normans to victory over the British

The answer is C. Words that represent titles and offices are not capitalized unless used with a proper name. This is not the case here.

116. **In preparing your high school freshmen to write a research paper about a social problem, what recommendation can you make so they can determine the credibility of their information? (Skill 7.4, Easy)**

    A. Assure them that information on the Internet has been peer-reviewed and verified for accuracy.

    B. Find one solid source and use that exclusively.

    C. Use only primary sources.

    D. Cross check your information with another credible source.

The answer is D. When researchers find the same information in multiple reputable sources, the information is considered credible. Using the Internet for research requires strong critical evaluation of the source. Nothing from the Internet should be taken without careful scrutiny of the source. To rely on only one source is dangerous and short-sighted. Most high school freshmen would have limited skills to conduct primary research for a paper about a social problem.

117. **Which of the following are secondary research materials? (Skill 7.4, Average Rigor)**

    A. The conclusions and inferences of other historians.

    B. Literature and nonverbal materials, novels, stories, poetry and essays from the period, as well as coins, archaeological artifacts, and art produced during the period.

    C. Interviews and surveys conducted by the researcher.

    D. Statistics gathered as the result of the research's experiments.

The answer is A. Secondary sources are works written significantly after the period being studied and based upon primary sources. In this case, historians have studied artifacts of the time and drawn their conclusion and inferences. Primary sources are the basic materials that provide raw data and information. Students or researchers may use literature and other data they have collected to draw their own conclusions or inferences.

118. **Which of the following is an example of the post hoc fallacy? (Skill 7.4, Rigorous)**

    A. When the new principal was hired, student-reading scores improved; therefore, the principal caused the increase in scores.

    B. Why are we spending money on the space program when our students don't have current textbooks?

    C. You can't give your class a 10-minute break. Once you do that, we'll all have to give our students a 10-minute break.

    D. You can never believe anything he says because he's not from the same country as we are.

The correct answer is A. A post hoc fallacy assumes that because one event preceded another, the first event caused the second event. In this case, student scores could have increased for other reasons. Choice B is a red herring fallacy in which one raises an irrelevant topic to side track from the first topic. In this case, the space budget and the textbook budget have little effect on each other. Choice C is an example of a slippery slope, in which one event is followed precipitously by another event. Choice D is an ad hominem ("to the man") fallacy in which a person is attacked rather than the concept or interpretation.

119. To determine the credibility of information, researchers should do all of the following except (Skill 7.4, Rigorous)

    A. establish the authority of the document.

    B. disregard documents with bias.

    C. evaluate the currency and reputation of the source.

    D. use a variety of research sources and methods.

The answer is B. Keep an open mind. Researchers should examine the assertions, facts and reliability of the information.

120. Which of the following situations is *not* an ethical violation of intellectual property? (Skill 7.4, Rigorous)

    A. A student visits ten different websites and writes a report to compare the costs of downloading music. He uses the names of the websites without their permission.

    B. A student copies and pastes a chart verbatim from the Internet but does not document it because it is available on a public site.

    C. From an online article found in a subscription database, a student paraphrases a section on the problems of music piracy. She includes the source in her Works Cited but does not provide an in-text citation.

    D. A student uses a comment from M. Night Shyamalan without attribution claiming the information is common knowledge.

The answer is A. In this scenario, the student is conducting primary research by gathering the data and using it for his own purposes. He is not violating any principle by using the names of the websites. In Choice B, students who copy and paste from the Internet without documenting the sources of their information are committing plagiarism, a serious violation of intellectual property. Even when a student puts information in her own words by paraphrasing or summarizing as in Choice C, the information is still secondary and must be documented. While dedicated movie buffs might consider anything that M. Night Shyamalan says to be common knowledge in Choice D, his comments are not necessarily known in numerous places or known by a lot of people.

121. **Students have been asked to write a research paper on automobiles and have brainstormed a number of questions they will answer based on their research findings. Which of the following is *not* an interpretive question to guide research? (Skill 7.4, Rigorous)**

    A. Who were the first ten automotive manufacturers in the United States?

    B. What types of vehicles will be used fifty years from now?

    C. How do automobiles manufactured in the United States compare and contrast with each other?

    D. What do you think is the best solution for the fuel shortage?

    The answer is A. The question asks for objective facts. Choice B is a prediction that asks how something will look or be in the future, based on the way it is now. Choice C asks for similarities and differences, which is a higher-level research activity that requires analysis. Choice D is a judgment question that requires informed opinion.

122. **Which of the following should students use to improve coherence of ideas within an argument? (Skill 7.5, Easy)**

    A. Transitional words or phrases to show relationship of ideas.

    B. Conjunctions like "and" to join ideas together.

    C. Use direct quotes extensively to improve credibility.

    D. Adjectives and adverbs to provide stronger detail.

    The answer is B. Transitional words and phrases are two-way indicators that connect the previous idea to the following idea. Sophisticated writers use transitional devices to clarify text (for example), to show contrast (despite), to show sequence (first, next), to show cause (because).

123. **Which transition word would show contrast between these two ideas?** (Skill 7.5, Average Rigor)

We are confident in our skills to teach English. We welcome new ideas on this subject.

A. We are confident in our skills to teach English, and we welcome new ideas on this subject.

B. Because we are confident in our skills to teach English, we welcome new ideas on the subject.

C. When we are confident in our skills to teach English, we welcome new ideas on the subject.

D. We are confident in our skills to teach English; however, we welcome new ideas on the subject.

The answer is D. Transitional words, phrases and sentences help clarify meanings. In Choice A, the transition word "and" introduces another equal idea. In Choice B, the transition word "because" indicates cause and effect. In Choice C, the transition word "when" indicates order or chronology. In Choice D, "however," shows that these two ideas contrast with each other.

124. **Which sentence below best minimizes the impact of bad news?** (Skill 7.5, Rigorous)

A. We have denied you permission to attend the event.

B. Although permission to attend the event cannot be given, you are encouraged to buy the video.

C. Although you cannot attend the event, we encourage you to buy the video.

D. Although attending the event is not possible, watching the video is an option.

The answer is B. Subordinating the bad news and using passive voice minimizes the impact of the bad news. In Choice A, the sentence is active voice and thus too direct. The word "denied" sets a negative tone. In Choice C, the bad news is subordinated but it is still active voice with negative wording. In Choice D, the sentence is too unclear.

125. **Which part of a classical argument is illustrated in this excerpt from the essay "What Should Be Done About Rock Lyrics?" (Skill 7.5, Rigorous)**

But violence against women is greeted by silence. It shouldn't be. This does not mean censorship, or book (or record) burning. In a society that protects free expression, we understand a lot of stuff will float up out of the sewer. Usually, we recognize the ugly stuff that advocates violence against any group as the garbage it is, and we consider its purveyors as moral lepers. We hold our nose and tolerate it, but we speak out against the values it proffers.

--"What Should Be Done About Rock Lyrics?" Caryl Rivers

A. Narration

B. Confirmation

C. Refutation and concession

D. Summation

The answer is C. The author acknowledges refutes the idea of censorship and concedes that society tolerates offensive lyrics as part of our freedom of speech. Narration provides background material to produce an argument. In confirmation, the author details the argument with claims that support the thesis. In summation, the author concludes the argument by offering the strongest solution.

CPSIA information can be obtained
at www.ICGtesting.com
Printed in the USA
BVOW07s1252210417
481909BV00004B/139/P